The Total Shiba

A gloriously red-colored Shiba bred in England. M. Clews.

The Total Shiba

Gretchen Haskett and Susan Houser

with Japanese translation by Yuko Salvadori
illustrated by Monica Flynn

Alpine
Blue Ribbon Books

Alpine Publications
Loveland, Colorado

The Total Shiba

ISBN: 1-57779-049-9

Library of Congress Cataloging in Publication Data

Haskett, Gretchen, 1959-
The Total Shiba / Gretchen Haskett and Susan Houser:
with Japanese translation by Yuko Salvadori; illustrated by Monica Flynn.
p.   cm.
Includes bibliographical references (p.) and index.
ISBN 0-931866-98-7
1. Shiba dogs. I. Houser, Susan, 1949- . II. Title.
SF429.S63H37 1997
636.72-dc21   96-39711
CIP

This book is available at special quantity discounts for breeders
and for club promotions, premiums, or educational use.
Write the publisher for details.

Second Edition
2 3 4 5 6 7 8 9 0

*Front Cover: Tetsuka No Gen of Sanuki Mizumotoso owned by Miyako Morimine of Japan.
Top sire of Nippo National Merit Award winners and multiple Nippo Honbusho winner.
Back Cover: (Top) Photo by J. Gilmore; (Bottom) Photo by P. Doescher.*

*Design by Dianne Nelson, Shadow Canyon Graphics, Golden, Colorado
Edited by: Erin McKay*

Printed in the United States of America

Contents

*Ch. Nikkou Go Ryuukyuu Uruma at one year of age. Nik was Best of Winners at the 2000 NSCA National Specialty.
Bred by Yuichi Tomimoto and owned by Leslie Ann Engen, Ann Lanterman, and Frank Sakayeda. © S. Evans.*

DEDICATION

*The authors dedicate this book to breed club volunteers everywhere,
without whom the sport of purebred dogs would not be possible.*

BISS, NIPPO/USA, Ch. Ogon No Narihime of Paladin. 2002 NSCA National Specialty Best of Breed and 2001 Shiba Classic Jun Saikosho (BOS). Bred by Mitzi Reid and owned by Rosie Van Laanen. © Tom DiGiacomo.

BISS, NIPPO/USA, AKC/INT Ch., U-CD, U-AG11 Hi-Jinx Black N Dekker CD, NA, CGC. Dekker is a three-time Shiba Classic competitor. Second Place Waka Inu I in 1997, First Place Soken in 1998, and winner of Saikosho (Best In Show) in 1999. Bred by Pat Doescher and owned by Jane Chapin.

Foreword

GRETCHEN HASKETT AND SUSAN HOUSER have given us a book about the Shiba that can be described with many adjectives. First, it is

concise. The fat has been deftly trimmed, leaving a lean, meaty morsel that will continue to satisfy even after much mastication. Indeed, you will greatly benefit from repeated readings. Second, it is

constructive. You may have chosen the word "instructive" (which this book certainly is), but I mean to also emphasize that the authors acknowledge the political climate at the American Kennel Club and other breed clubs while providing a very good picture of the breed as well as the dog-fancy society it finds itself in. Third, the information in this book is

accurate. Using the writings of the breed's Japanese architects and the observations of committed "dog people" (some of whom have observed the Shiba in its native land, and some of whom are Japanese or Japanese-Americans), the authors have meticulously exposed both the overall picture and the details, especially in their discussion of the "ideal Shiba." Finally, *The Total Shiba* is **comprehensive.** Without bowing to the convention of including chapters on all the subjects usually found in the multitude of beginners' breed books, this work provides everything you need to be properly introduced to the Shiba. This is a book for the person with a general knowledge of dogs who wants to get to know the Shiba.

One problem has been overlooked, which I feel compelled to mention. The tendency of kennel clubs to host a great number of shows creates pressure to approve more and more judges, most of whom will have read only a "skeleton standard." The importance of certain details of breed *type* will be (and now is being) overlooked, with structurally sound but relatively nondescript "generic" dogs replacing those with more correct and specific Shiba characteristics. I have exhibited and judged for many years (in several countries) and know that we can properly educate only a relatively small percentage of judges. Much greater weight must be given to wins at breed specialty shows and shows that invite judges who have pored over the breed literature and analytically observed a good number of Shibas. We must not play the numbers or ratings game if we are to preserve this breed; rather, we must understand and strive for quality in both judging and in the breed itself.

— *Fred Lanting*

BEST OF BREED
GIG HARBOR
KENNEL CLUB
Photography By
Steven Ross
FALL - 1999

BOB 2000 Westminster Kennel Club Ch. San Jo Satori My Oh My. Myah was #1 Bitch in 1999 with many Non-Sporting Group awards. She is a multiple NSCA National Specialty Award of Merit winner and the first Shiba bitch to go BOB at the prestigious Westminster Kennel Club show. She is also a producer of outstanding quality and consistent style. Bred by Engen and Sakayeda, owned by Leslie Ann Engen, Ann Lanterman, and Frank Sakayeda.
© Steven Ross.

Preface

THE LATE 1990's is an exciting time for Shiba fanciers. The breed is increasing rapidly in popularity both in the U.S. and throughout the world, and in 1993 the American Kennel Club (AKC) accepted the Shiba into its Non-sporting Group. The AKC has also recognized the Japan Kennel Club's registry, thereby guaranteeing a continuing source of imports from the breed's country of origin.

Recent translations about breed history and the current status of the Shiba in Japan have also become available. The efforts of the American Shiba Fanciers Club (Beikoku Shibainu Aikokai) and the first breed club, the Shiba Club of America (SCA) in bringing Japanese judges from the Nihon Ken Hozonkai (Nippo) to the United States has also contributed much to our understanding.

Given these factors, it is easy to see that the Shiba fancy is in a state of great flux and change. While this is an exciting time to be a "Shiba person," it is a difficult time to write a book on the breed because what we write is in danger of becoming outdated by the time it appears in print! However, we have attempted to provide a record of the important foundations of the Shiba in America, as well as provide some basic guidelines for breeders entering the fancy as well as those who simply want a specimen of this fascinating breed for a companion.

Susan Houser
Gretchen Haskett

NIPPO/USA Ch. Kori Bushi of Kitsunebiso ROM. Bred by co-author Gretchen Haskett of Foxfire Shibas/Kitsunebiso and owned by Pat Doescher, Kori was 1998 Shiba Classic Saikosho (BIS). © M. Ross.

Myah daughter, Ch. San Jo B. Dazzled was awarded Winners Bitch and an Award of Merit at the 2000 NSCA National Specialty at the tender age of six months and eleven days. Bred by Engen, Lanterman, and Sakayeda. Owned by Tia Bailey and Leslie Ann Engen. © Bill Meyer.

Another pretty Myah daughter, Ch. San Jo Scandalous, was Reserve Winners Bitch at the NSCA 2002 National Specialty and First Award of Merit at a NSCA Regional Specialty in 2002. Bred by Engen, Lanterman, and Sakayeda and owned by Susan Evans and Leslie Ann Engen. S. Evans

Acknowledgements

THE AUTHORS WOULD LIKE TO THANK a number of people for helping to make this book possible. Monica Flynn did the wonderful drawings that appear in "The Ideal Shiba" chapter. It's true that a picture is worth a thousand words. Yuko Salvadori spent many hours on the phone to Japan making sure the information from Nippo was translated accurately. Terukuni Uki, president of Nippo, deserves our undying gratitude for the pictures and information that he sent in two gigantic collections from the Nippo magazine. Many of the pictures of Japanese dogs that appear in this book, especially the historical pictures, are from Nippo. Several people have proven to be invaluable because of their experience with and knowledge of the Shiba. Kaiji and Toshiko Katsumoto have been working to promote the true Japanese Shiba for years and have been of great help to many Shiba owners. We want to thank them especially for their help with information about the early American history of the breed. Fred Lanting gave us extensive writings based on his experiences in Japan. Chris Ross, Laura Perkinson, and George Heath provided information on importing Shibas. Kathy Brown helped enormously with information on the bloodlines of American Shibas. Merry and Frank Atkinson, Maureen Reed, and Julia Cadwell provided pictures and much valuable information on the early days of the breed in America. Mitsuko Williams served as interpreter on coauthor Gretchen Haskett's trip to Japan to interview breeders and judges. The Morimine family, Shiba breeders from Okayama, served as hosts for their trip to the Nippo national show. In addition, many other people—too numerous to mention here—have supplied pictures and information for the book, and we are grateful to all.

Kori (left) and his son Runner, Ch. Hi-Jinx Pimiento ROM (right), share a similarity of type and success as stud dogs. Kori is the sire of twenty AKC Champions and Runner, bred and owned by Patricia Doescher, is the sire of another eleven. P. Doescher.

This young male was very interested in the construction of an addition to his house.
On several occasions he offered to help. P. Doescher.

Characteristics of the Shiba

WHERE DID YOU FIRST SEE A SHIBA? Maybe you saw this regal little dog pictured in a magazine or in competition at a dog show, or trotting merrily down the street on an evening's walk with his proud owner. No matter where or how you saw your first Shiba, you were probably captivated by his foxy little face and aristocratic bearing. Whether you have just gotten a Shiba or are thinking about acquiring one, this book will help you answer the question, "What kind of dog is the Shiba?"

The Shiba is a Japanese breed, with only a brief American history. There are three sizes of Japanese native dogs: large-sized (the Akita), medium-sized (this size range includes four breeds: Kai, Hokkaido, Kishu, and Shikoku), and small-sized (the Shiba). Shiba females stand 13.5 to 15.5 inches at the shoulder and males are 14.5 to 16.5 inches. The average weight for females is 19 to 22 pounds and for males is 22 to 25 pounds. Three colors are preferred: red, red sesame, and black-and-tan.

Some people have the idea that the Shiba is a little Akita. While there is a close resemblance between Shibas and *Japanese* Akitas, when novice Shiba fanciers tried to compare their Shibas to *American* Akitas, they saw that the Shiba was anything but a little American Akita. Their puzzlement was to be expected, as American Akitas do not resemble their Japanese counterparts. The American Akita is a powerful, heavy-boned dog that comes in a rainbow of colors. It should never serve as a model of type for the Shiba, which is a **small** dog with a **medium** build and has only **three** preferred coat colors.

The name Shiba means "brushwood" in Japanese. The brushwood is a small tree or bush, and there are a few theories on why the small dog was named after this bush. One is that the Shiba was originally used for hunting in the type of terrain where the brushwood occurs. Another theory is that the leaves of the brushwood, when they turn reddish-brown in the fall, resemble the coat of the Shiba. A third idea is that *shiba* once meant small in the Nagano dialect (for example, *shibaguri* means "small walnut"), but this theory is less accepted.

Shiba temperament is a mixture of spitz-, terrier-, and cat-like characteristics. Shibas are proud, loyal, stubborn, smart, clean, athletic, brave, and energetic. They are patient with children and generally will tolerate being hugged, dressed in doll clothes, and dragged around on a leash. The Japanese have a word, "kan-i", meaning spirited boldness, that captures the essence of the Shiba temperament—brave and outgoing, but not foolhardy or disobedient.

Shibas are incredibly beautiful, with foxy expressions and brush-like tails, and they are just the right size for a house or apartment. Although some Shibas are chatterboxes and will let you know their opinion about everything (employing a wide range of vocal styles to do so), Shibas as a rule do not bark aimlessly. They are excellent watchdogs, and a Shiba's bark usually means that a human or canine is approaching. They are easy to care for, requiring only an occasional bath and brushing to remove loose hair. Dirt seems to flake off their thick coats. They are nice to cuddle and pet, with their furry coats and sunny dispositions, yet they are tough and strong enough to keep up with the most active members of your family.

Shibas are natural show dogs, stepping around the ring like they were born to do it. They are smart enough to train in obedience and able to sniff their way through the toughest tracking course. They are athletic, agile, and have not lost the hunting instinct for which they were originally bred. (These little dogs were used primarily to hunt birds and small animals, although they have been used for wild boar and, occasionally, even for bear hunting.)

Shibas show no fear of larger dogs, which can sometimes lead to disaster. Not all dogs are as tolerant of Shiba antics as this Rottweiler. C. Kaufmann.

Despite all of these positives, there are a few drawbacks to owning a Shiba. Many Shibas (especially females) emit a bloodcurdling scream to warn their owners that someone is approaching the house, and this can be a bit much when you have friends over to a dinner party. All puppies love to chew, but some Shibas never outgrow the urge. As with any dog, your Shiba should be trained early to obey the commands "drop it" and "no chew." Shibas must be provided with a good supply of nylon bones and bouncy, hard rubber toys. Soft squeaky toys, stuffed animals, and rawhide strips are not safe for most Shibas. These items are just not rugged enough for your Shiba's strong jaws and sharp teeth, and could be dangerous to him if swallowed.

A Shiba should never be allowed to run off-lead unless trained to come on command. Once a Shiba is off and running, catching him is almost impossible! Before deciding to find out what you're yelling about, he could become the victim of a passing car. Shibas possess a strong hunting instinct, and their noses can lead them into trouble before they realize how far away from home they've followed a scent. A Shiba off-lead may well set off in a purposeful trot and keep going for miles.

The Shiba's digging and jumping talents require special attention. Many Shibas dig holes whenever and wherever possible, with great purpose and dedication. Rather than allow your Shiba to use your lawn for these important excavations, set aside a special area. A Shiba can scramble over six feet of chain link fence or tunnel underneath the same fence in a matter of minutes. So, if you are planning to keep your Shiba outdoors unsuper-

Although the Shiba is considered an exotic pet in the United States, it is the most popular companion dog in Japan. B. Scott.

vised for any length of time, you should take these abilities into consideration when planning a kennel. A backyard stockade fence with patio blocks around the perimeter is generally adequate to contain a Shiba that is a family pet and spends most of his time in the house, but runs with tops and cement floors are recommended for Shibas that spend long periods of time outside. Of course, not all Shibas are escape artists, but it is better to prepare a secure enclosure now than to regret it later.

Shibas are known for their loyalty, and become very attached to their human families. They are territorial, and many will not tolerate another dog of the same sex in the house. Some Shibas are so possessive that even the family cat or a dog of the opposite sex will be considered a rival. Fortunately, few are jealous to this degree. Most get along quite well with cats but should not be trusted with ferrets, gerbils, or hamsters!

A male-female pair of Shibas is a joy to own. They will spend hours entertaining themselves (and you) with their antics. Shibas love to bat a ball around with their paws in a cat-like manner, and a pair of Shibas playing this game look as graceful and athletic as soccer pros! Hide-and-seek is also a popular game with Shibas, but batten down the hatches and hold on to the china when they start a game of tag in the house! Fortunately, there are quiet moments too. Shiba pals are very affectionate toward one another, and they will take turns cleaning each other's ears and teeth before curling up together at bedtime.

The Shiba will defend his yard to the death against all strange dogs, and can cause quite a lot of damage with his long sharp teeth. He may not win a fight with a larger dog but will never "cry uncle." In fact, when Shibas first came to the United States several breeders let them run with their Akitas, and the results were, sadly, fatal to the Shibas. The Shiba's refusal to submit to a larger dog's dominance is his downfall.

Shibas can often coexist happily with the family cat. J. Vanderpool.

Shiba puppies are quicker and more agile than many more familiar breeds. C. Kaufmann.

The dominance hierarchy of the canine pack is very evident in the Shiba. Only a strong-willed individual experienced in dog ownership should own an alpha male Shiba. He is quite a handful and needs more discipline and obedience training than the usual dog. With the right owner, he will exhibit all the characteristics most admired in man's best friend. With the wrong owner, he will most likely end up back with the breeder if he is lucky, or simply abandoned if he is not so fortunate. At the other extreme, a Shiba that is at the bottom of the dominance hierarchy will exhibit extreme shyness, submissive behavior, and even fear biting. The correct owner, proper training, and—above all—socialization will prevent this Shiba from becoming a problem.

Human contact is important in the formation of Shiba personality. No puppy should be left with his littermates without human contact during his formative months (especially the time period from one to four months of age). This appears to be truer of the Shiba than of many breeds. Puppies should be allowed to interact with people of different sizes and ages throughout the first year. Shibas not well socialized as puppies are often wary and fearful of strangers, but those raised with much human contact are usually quite friendly with neighbors. Young Shibas seem too busy visiting places and

Shibas can be aggressive toward other dogs, but rigorous training, socialization, and supervision allow this bunch to live together in harmony. P. Doescher.

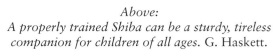

Above:
A properly trained Shiba can be a sturdy, tireless companion for children of all ages. G. Haskett.

Right, Middle:
MACH2 Kirinji Kashushibaso CD, ADCH, EAC, EGC, EJC, ADC, U-AG1 flies through an agility course for owner Ken Fairchild.

Right, Below:
Therapy dogs visit a senior center in England. M. Clews.

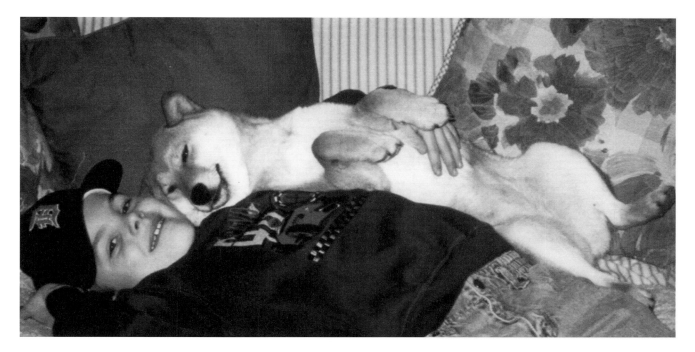

Japanese import Ryoko relaxing with her friend Bryce. L. Engen.

people to have time to do much cuddling, but a Shiba that lives with a family will gradually come to enjoy close physical contact as he grows older.

While only a few Americans have begun to use their Shibas for hunting, this is the purpose for which they were originally bred, and they still have the ability. Shibas love an outing in the woods or fields and are outstanding trackers. We have heard reports from Shiba owners that their dogs are able to leap several feet into the air to kill a bird, and they are quite capable of flushing and bringing down pheasants and other game birds on their own. They have been known to pounce catlike to capture rodents. Shiba puppies often play the same "hide and pounce" game kittens do to develop their hunting skills.

Shibas are naturally clean animals. They seldom require bathing and usually have no "doggy odor" or "dog breath." Because of their desire to keep themselves and their living areas clean, they are very easy to housebreak, and most learn to use their runs or their yard for elimination before they reach ten weeks of age. Several Shiba owners claim that although they are allergic to other breeds, they do not seem to suffer as severe a reaction with their Shibas. Shibas are a double-coated breed, and during their semiannual shedding, daily vacuuming

of the house may be required. Fortunately, the shedding process does not take long and can be hastened by bathing and combing.

A Shiba can quickly become the most popular dog in the neighborhood. Something about their diminutive size, bright "smile," little cat ears, and stuffed-animal looks makes children knock on your door and ask if your dog can come out and play! (Of course, no dog should be left unattended with young children, and the Shiba is no exception.) Perhaps the most striking thing about a Shiba is its tail. There are two basic wags—the "wind-up toy" wag, where the tail swiftly moves to one side and stops for an instant, then to the other (this wag is also seen when the Shiba is digging for moles), and the "fluttering fan" wag.

To sum up, Shibas are versatile dogs that can fit well into most homes, although they may fight for dominance in a multi-dog household. Almost all Shibas are enthusiastic, energetic, bright, tough, independent, and territorial. Some are very loving, some are dominant, and some are shy. Because of their escape-artist tendencies, they generally need more secure backyard fencing than most dogs, and it can be difficult to train a Shiba to be reliable off-lead. The Shiba's protective instinct makes him a useful watchdog, and his playful spirit and sense of fun will delight every member of the family.

Kurohime of Ryokushinso owned by Tsuyoshi Kumazawa. 84th Nippo National Seikensho.

Japanese History of the Shiba

ANCIENT HISTORY

JAPAN CONSISTS OF FOUR primary islands (the largest of which is Honshu, also known as the Main Island) and thousands of nearby smaller islands. About 75 percent of the land is mountainous, with most of the arable land located near the coasts. It is divided into forty-seven administrative divisions (or districts) known as prefectures.

Japan's original inhabitants immigrated to the country around 7,000 or 8,000 B.C. They are known as the *Jomonjin*, which means "rope-pattern people," a name derived from the pattern found on their earthenware. The Jomonjin are believed to have migrated to Japan from three different areas in Asia. Archeological excavations of the shell mounds left by people of this period show that they had small dogs, mostly in the size range of 14.5 to 19.5 inches. These may be the most remote ancestors of today's Shiba. Researchers have noted that the skull type of the smaller dogs from this era in Japan are distinctly different from those of dogs found in Europe during the same period. The origin of these ancient dogs is still being researched, but most scientists agree the dogs probably came from mainland China.

During the third century B.C., a new group of immigrants introduced agriculture and the use of metal implements, initiating what is called the *Yayoi* period (again named for the pattern found on pottery from this era). These new people also brought dogs, which interbred with those of the Jomonjin to produce offspring that had pointed, erect ears and curly or sickle tails.

Japanese recorded history began in the sixth century A.D., when Buddhist monks introduced the Chinese writing system to the country. The Yamato court gained power by conquering regional political leaders and promulgated a written constitution. This imperial court also established the "dog keeper's office," which helped cause native breeds to become an integral part of Japanese culture. Over the next several hundred years, military families gradually gained power, and the political climate of Japan came to resemble a feudal system. An emphasis on military skills and pursuits developed, leading to the gradual emergence of the samurai class.

In 1603, the Tokugawa Shogunate (one of the military families) established a centralized government at Edo (now Tokyo), and ruled over Japan until the mid-nineteenth century. During this time, the country was effectively closed to foreigners with the exception of some Dutch and Chinese visitors. In the absence of constant fighting, hunting became a very popular activity of the samurai. Deer and wild boar were especially sought after. The fifth Shogun, Tsunayoshi, has been called the "dog shogun" because of his extraordinary love for dogs. He was said to have built kennels to house more than one-hundred-thousand homeless dogs. Under his regime, the rights of dogs were more important than human rights.

Around the eighteenth century the profession of veterinary medicine came into being, and drugs to combat canine diseases were advertised and sold. Over the centuries, wealthy Japanese occasionally imported dogs for hunting and companion purposes. Large dogs such as Mastiffs, Greyhounds, and Spaniels arrived from Europe, while smaller toy-type dogs were purchased from China. The newcomers often interbred with native dogs in the towns and cities, while hunting dogs in the country remained relatively pure. The Dutch doctor, Siebold, who visited Japan in the early 1800s, sketched two types of Japanese dogs: the town dog with droopy ears, and the country hunting dog with pointed ears.

Commodore Perry and the U.S. Navy forced the reopening of Japan's ports to foreigners and their goods in 1853. In the mid-nineteenth century, Emperor Meiji reestablished the imperial court following his victory over the Tokugawa Shogunate. After more than 250 years of isolation, Japan was still a quasi-feudal society and began to see itself as lagging behind America and Europe in terms of economic development and growth. This led to a renewed interest in foreign things, including dogs. The native Japanese dog began to receive less consideration as new breeds of dogs were introduced from other countries. By the early twentieth century, what had once been known as the pure Japanese native dog had disappeared from all but the most remote and isolated areas of the country.

MODERN HISTORY

In the early years of the twentieth century, a growing number of Japanese became aware that some aspects of their heritage were in danger of being obliterated in the rush to modernize and westernize Japan. A movement to preserve Japanese culture emerged, with one of the concerns being the preservation of native dog breeds. Leading ethnologists and zoologists assisted in the effort. The work of Dr. Hiroyoshi Saito was very important in the early years of this movement as he traveled throughout Japan to search out and study the native dogs. Up until the time Dr. Saito began his studies, the native dogs generally did not have true breed names and were known simply as *inu* (dog), *ji-inu* (native dog), *inoshishi inu* (wild boar dog), or *shika inu* (deer dog). Because the dogs kept by hunters differed in size and color by each region, Dr. Saito named the main types of native dog after the areas in which they had developed: the Akita from Akita Prefecture, the Shikoku from Shikoku Island, and so on. The name for the Shiba differs, since it does not refer to a specific geographical area.

Some modern Shibas are descended in part from the Mikawa, a small spitz breed similar to the Shiba. The Mikawa had a restless and timid character with large round eyes and no white shading on the cheeks or underbody. The breed was faulted for a black mask that lingered into adulthood rather than fading at maturity. These characteristics were considered to be a sign of mixed breeding with western dogs. The Mikawa was known at one time as the "Sanshu." They were occasionally crossed with Shibas, and some were even sold as Shibas. Japanese breeders did not consider the Mikawa to be a pure example of the Japanese native dog and its popularity gradually declined. The Mikawa/Sanshu is no longer registerable in Japan.

Originally there were three strains of Shibas, named according to the area from which they originated. The Shinshu Shiba was from Nagano Prefecture, the central mountainous area of Honshu; the Mino Shiba came from Gifu Prefecture, near Nagano; and the Sanin Shiba came from Tottori and Shimane Prefectures along the southwest coast of Honshu. Because there were too few small dogs to categorize by region, Dr. Saito grouped them all together under the traditional catch-all term, *shiba.*

The Shinshu Shiba was small and mostly red in color, with a thick, bristly outer coat and a dense undercoat. A tendency for round eyes and a lingering black mask inherited from the Mikawa were considered weaknesses of the line. The Mino Shiba was known particularly for its fiery red coat, deep brown triangular eyes, and rather thick ears. It had the sickle (*sachi-o*) tail rather than the curled (*maki-o*) tail of the other Shiba types. The Sanin Shiba was derived from the ancient Sekishu and Imba breeds, and it was a little larger than Shibas are today. Most of the Sanin Shibas were black but without the crisp tan-and-white markings favored today. They were known for having a feisty, independent temperament.

SHIBA CLUBS IN JAPAN

Nihon Ken Hozonkai (Nippo)

Dr. Hiroyoshi Saito and a small group of friends founded a club in 1928 for the purpose of preserving the native dog. Dr. Saito was the first president. Three of the club's founders who were particularly credited for preserving the Shiba were Tatsuo Nakajo (who studied the Shinshu Shiba), Masayu Ishikawa (who studied the Mino/Gifu Shiba), and Masuzo Ozaki (who studied the Sanin Shiba). These men did exhaustive research in their particular areas, searching out and cataloging the few remaining pure Shiba specimens. In 1932, four years after the first meeting, the club was named *Nihon Ken Hozonkai*, which means Association for the Preservation of the Japanese Dog. This organization is known as Nippo, (pronounced "knee-poe"), for short. In the early 1930s the government was granting the status of "Natural Monument" to things that were felt to be important in Japanese cultural life and, therefore, in need of government support and recognition. The first native dog designated as a Natural Monument (with the help of Nippo) was the Akita in 1931. It was followed by the Shiba in December 1936. Recognition by the Japanese government in 1937 gave the fledgling Nippo organization a big boost.

The establishment of a standard for the Japanese native breeds was the earliest goal of the new club. A standards committee was formed to draft a standard based on the work of zoologists and breeders, ancient records, and the examination of existing animals. Dog standards in foreign countries were reviewed, and the future purpose of the dogs was discussed. The Nippo Standard covered all six of the native Japanese breeds, which are all very similar in type but vary in size and, to some extent, in color. After four draft standards, the final version was published in 1934, and copies were mailed introducing the native breeds to western dog fanciers (who showed little interest in them other than as a curiosity).

Nippo held its first national dog show in Tokyo on November 6, 1932. Forty Japanese native dogs competed for trophies donated by the Japanese government and Dr. Saito. Fifteen Shibas entered, but only Tako, the first Shiba to be registered, was rated *suisho ken* (recommended dog). Early Shibas were considered to be lacking in overall standardization and quality when compared to the larger varieties and seldom received Merit Awards. As Nippo's membership increased, regional clubs were formed and more shows were held. The national show of 1939 was a memorable one for Shiba fanciers. Aka, a 10-month-old male, was awarded one of the major Merit Awards and was very much admired by the judges. He and his offspring would survive World War II and become the foundation bloodline of the modern Shiba. In the years before the war (from 1928 through 1942) dogs from the medium-sized breeds won most of the highest awards—a reflection of their popularity and numbers at that time. The national show was held every year until 1942, when World War II put a halt to dog-related activities.

Tetsushu of Sagami Murasakiso owned by Kikuo Watanabe. 85th Nippo National Waka Inusho. 86th Nippo National Seikensho.

During the war, food supplies dwindled to such an extent that the Japanese government asked dog owners to give up their dogs in order to supply rations to the military. The local governor in Mr. Ozaki's area gave him a special allowance for the support of his Shibas, but most breeders were not so fortunate. The breed was dealt another blow when distemper ravaged in the immediate postwar years. The Mino and Sanin Shibas were virtually wiped out during the war and its aftermath, but the Shinshu strain fared a little better. In the postwar years, serious breeders brought Shibas from the countryside into the cities to establish breeding programs, and the survivors of the various lines were combined to produce the bloodlines from which modern Shibas descended.

Nippo's activities resumed in 1948 with a general meeting held in April and several regional shows held during the year. A national show was held the following year and proved to be a memorable one for Shiba fanciers when a Shiba named Naka won the highest honors, upsetting the famous odds-on favorite, an Akita named Kongo. Naka's ancestors came from Shikoku, Sanin, and Yamanashi, but he was born in Nagano Prefecture.

Nippo celebrated its sixtieth anniversary on September 4, 1988, in Tokyo. In 1992, the organization

Tetsuka no Gen of Sanuki Mizumotoso owned by Miyako Morimine. Multiple Nippo Honbusho winner. Sire of many National merit award winning Shibas.

passing hunting tests with dangerous wild boar as the game.

The Shiba enjoys the status of the most popular small dog in Japan today. Its compact size and clean habits make it ideally suited to modern Japan, where space is at a premium.

Japan Kennel Club (JKC)

Founded shortly after the end of World War II, the Japan Kennel Club is similar in many ways to the American Kennel Club (AKC) in the United States. It is a large all-breed organization that registers more than one hundred breeds, including the Shiba. JKC registers approximately 10,000 Shibas annually.

JKC shows are run much like AKC shows, with the native breeds included in the Spitz and primitive types group. In these shows, the Best of Breed winners compete against each other for the group win, and the group winner goes on to Best in Show competition. Championship points are awarded, and Shibas may earn the JKC title of Champion. Shiba competition in JKC shows is usually sparse due to the higher prestige of Nippo awards among Japanese breeders.

Ch. Kori Bushi of Kitsunebiso bred by Gretchen Haskett and owned by Pat Doescher bears a strong resemblance to close ancestors Tetsuka no Gen and Hamaou. P. Doescher

had approximately sixteen-thousand members, including many in the United States. Of the total annual registrations of about sixty thousand, Shibas account for about fifty thousand; the balance consists of medium-sized dogs (mostly Kishu and Shikoku), and only a handful of Akitas. Over one million Japanese dogs have been registered with Nippo since its beginning.

Nippo now holds one national show in the fall. In addition there are forty-two local and eight regional shows held each spring and fall. The regional shows are held in conjunction with the host club's local show and rotate sites from year to year. In 1989 the total entry for the spring series of shows was 8,422.

Nippo also currently offers hunting courses to preserve the original purpose of the Japanese native breeds. The agility and fighting spirit of the ancient dogs of Japan are alive today in the modern Japanese Shiba. Japanese show dogs are successfully

Shiba Inu Hozonkai

The Shiba Inu Hozonkai was established in 1959 by Tatsuo Nakajo, a Shiba breeder and judge during the early days of Nippo. His ideal Shiba differed somewhat from the Nippo/JKC dog. The Shibaho Shiba was bred to re-create the small dogs of earlier centuries featuring the narrow head, shallow stop, and rangy body of a primitive hunting companion. Although Dr. Saito and friends studied the same skulls as Mr. Nakajo, modern views of canine beauty had a stronger influence in the development of the Nippo Standard. The membership of Shibaho is very small in comparison to Nippo; however, the club holds shows and issues pedigrees. Shibaho dogs are rare, but are being preserved by dedicated breeders.

The Japanese Standards

The Nippo Standard is arranged in two sections: the Basic Standard, which is a simple general description of the Japanese native dog with the medium-size dog serving as the model, and the Judging Resolutions. Two facts about the Nippo Standard—that it covers six distinct breeds and is in two separate sections—have led to much confusion in translating the Japanese standard into an American format. So, let's look at the Nippo Standard in some detail.

The original Nippo Standard was drawn up in the early 1930s soon after Nippo was formed, and it was written in a style of compressed prose that is similar to poetry. This Standard was considered to be a literary document with an aesthetic value of its own, and because of this, Nippo has been reluctant to allow modifications to the Basic Standard. However, since the Basic Standard is relatively brief (only one page in Japanese) and doesn't cover a lot of the important points of type, it was necessary to provide additional information for judging. The solution was the addition of the Judging Resolutions as a long appendix to the Basic Standard. The Judging Resolutions (ten pages, with diagrams) contain a great deal of information, and attempting to judge the Shiba without referring to the Resolutions would be very difficult. These Judging Resolutions, which are adopted by vote of the Nippo judges, are revised periodically, with recent changes primarily focused on tightening up the requirements for teeth. Most of the Judging Resolutions, however, have been in place for some time and are not likely to be changed.

Hamaou of Fudogataki Kensha owned by Y.S. Chuang of Taiwan. 1st Place Waka Inusho 85th Nippo National. Multiple Nippo Honbusho winner.

In the mid to late 1980s there was considerable controversy in America over the correct standard to use for the Shiba. Most of this controversy centered on two areas: correct color and allowable number of missing teeth. JKC and the Fédération Cynologique Internationale (FCI) used the Nippo Basic Standard to write their official Shiba standard, without including the breed-specific information from the Judging Resolutions. This resulted in some conflicts of interpretation. Since the Basic Standard lists the colors for *all six* native breeds, the JKC Standard in effect at the time the first American Shiba club standards were written included colors (white) that are not allowed for the Shiba according to the Judging Resolutions and colors (brindle and light gray) that do not exist in the Shiba at all. Also, since the Judging Resolutions contain the requirements for missing teeth and the Basic Standard does not mention missing teeth, this was another area of confusion.

It should be made clear that although the old JKC and Nippo Standards differed somewhat, actual Shiba judging in JKC rings followed Nippo judging practice very closely, and this included the information contained in the Judging Resolutions. In JKC shows, only the Shibas that have the proper colors as specified in the Judging Resolutions (red, red sesame, and black and tan) are considered for awards, and those Shibas missing more teeth than specified in the Judging Resolutions do not win awards. In 1995, the Japan Kennel Club modified its standard for the Shiba to allow only red, sesame, and black and tan; the same colors allowed for the Shiba in the Nippo Judging Resolutions.

Fred Lanting, who has observed Shiba judging in Japan, wrote an article for the September/October 1989 issue of *The Shiba Journal*, in which he discussed judging in Japan:

The standard for the Shiba as used by the FCI or even JKC is really a standard for the Japanese dog in all its six representatives. . . . The standard is only an introduction . . . All

Katsura of Fujinomiya Kensha owned by Harumi Suzuki. Multiple merit award winner at Nationals.

judges who officiate in the Japan Breed Group must know the multitude of details and preferences. But this doesn't come from reading only Standards, or even the books. One must have spent considerable time speaking with (listening to) the more highly regarded breeders and senior judges. Then these experienced people watch and advise the new judge until they deem him qualified.

Here, we present the text of the Nippo Basic Standard and relevant excerpts from the Judging Resolutions (in parentheses), as translated by Susan Houser, Shigekaze Kuribayashi, and Mitsuko Williams. In "The Ideal Shiba" chapter, we take each numbered section of the Standard and present a detailed commentary.

THE NIPPO BASIC STANDARD AND JUDGING RESOLUTIONS FOR THE SHIBA

"Essence" And Its Expression: *The dog has a spirited boldness with a good nature and a feeling of artlessness. It is alert and able to move quickly with nimble, elastic steps.*

General Physical Characteristics: *Males and females are obviously distinct, with proportioned bodies. The frame is compact with well-developed muscles. Males have a height to length ratio of 10 to 11; females, slightly longer. The height for males is 39.5 cm [15.55 inches]; for females, 36.5 cm [14.37 inches]. A range of 1.5 cm [.61 inches] taller or shorter is allowed.* (Body height is measured a little behind the tip of the shoulder blade, pressing down the coat. As for body height the mean is the ideal. Body height that is not within the range given in the standard is a fault. The dog with one testicle will get less than a "good" evaluation. Both testicles missing is a disqualification. A confirmed polyp is a disqualification. However, if the dog is completely recovered, it is satisfactory.)

Ears: *Ears are the shape of a small triangle, leaning forward slightly and standing up firmly.* (Thin ear leather, ears that are narrow at the bottom, high ear-set, long ears, flapping of the ear tip, incorrect ear lines, and lack of forward slant are all strongly hereditary and are faults.)

Eyes: *Eyes are somewhat triangular and slant upward toward the outside corner of the eye. The* *color of the iris is very dark brown.* (Very dark brown is the ideal, but the iris should not be so dark as to appear black. The brown color should be dark enough that it does not contrast noticeably with the black pupil of the eye. Dogs with eyes that are a little lighter than ideal but are still dark brown can nevertheless receive an "excellent" evaluation. Very light eyes, with the iris looking like a bull's-eye pattern because of the contrast between the black pupil and the light brown or yellow color of the iris, are a fault. Light yellow or ash gray eye color is a major fault. A strong gaze should be encouraged.)

Muzzle: *The bridge of the nose is straight, the sides of the mouth firm, the nose hard, and the lips are tight.* (The firm muzzle projects out from the full cheeks. The muzzle is thick, full, and round. The stop is defined, neither shallow nor deep. A particularly shallow stop or an obvious bulge on the bridge of the nose is a fault. A weak lower jaw is not desirable. Dewlap is a fault. The pigment of the nose, lips, anus, and skin should be black. Tongue spots are undesirable, however, they are not faulted if they are very small.)

Teeth are strong with scissors bite. (Missing teeth have the following deductions: First premolars—one minus mark for each tooth. Second premolars—three minus marks for each tooth. Any missing teeth other than first or second premolars—five minus marks for each tooth. A Shiba may win an "excellent" rating with up to two minus marks. A "very good" rating may be won by a Shiba with up to four minus marks. A Shiba with more than four minus marks will not be ranked. Missing teeth are treated the same whether inborn or acquired. The deduction for broken teeth, poor quality teeth, small, weak teeth, or rotten teeth is up to the judge's discretion. A dog with level bite or an irregular line of incisors cannot get an "excellent" rating.)

Head: *The forehead is wide, the cheeks well-developed, and the neck sturdy.*

Forelegs: *The shoulder blade has moderate angulation and is well-developed. Forearms are straight with paws well knuckled-up.* (A dog with straight shoulder blades, incorrect joint angles, or out-turned elbows will be faulted, as will a dog whose toes are long or not well knuckled-up.)

Hind legs: *Hind legs are strong with a wide natural stance. The hock joint is strong and the paws well knuckled-up.* (Deformity or weakness of the hip joint demands attention, and is a fault.)

Chest: *The chest is deep, with ribs moderately sprung. The forechest is well-developed.* (A chest depth that is about half the body height is ideal. However, a shallow chest (less than 45 percent of body height) is a fault. Poor development of the forechest is a fault.)

Back and Loin: *The topline is straight, the loin well tucked-up.*

Tail: *The tail is thick and powerful. It can be either sickle or curled. In length (when straightened out) it reaches almost to the hock joint.*

Coat: *Outer coat is stiff and straight; undercoat is soft and thick. Tail hair is slightly longer and stands off. Coat color is sesame, red, black, brindle, or white. The quality and color of the hair should express the characteristics typical of the Japanese dog.*

(White coat color in the Shiba is not desirable and is a fault. Color should be clear and intense, without muddiness. Faded (dilute) color is undesirable. A "reverse mask" (a white mask completely covering the muzzle and both cheeks and extending to the area around the eyes) is not desirable and is a fault. The coat colors regarded as ideal for the Shiba are red, red sesame, and black and tan.

Marime of Kawanishi Kasumiso owned by Y.S. Chuang of Taiwan. Waka Inusho Kinki Regional show.

The proper sesame is one that has a reasonably even mixture of black, red, and white hairs all over the body. A strong predominance of black hair in any area is not desirable. The black color in black and tan dogs should not be a shiny jet-black, but have a hint of brown, like a hint of smudging or a smoked color. For the black-and-tan color all of the following things are undesirable and are faults: The reverse mask; spots above the eyes that are too large; too much tan on the head, neck, back, trunk, etc.; the fading of the black color to gray-black or an eggplant dark blue color upon maturity.

White markings or shadings appear on the following areas: The sides of the muzzle and the cheeks (but not so much that it becomes a reverse mask); the underside of the jaw, neck, chest, and stomach; the forechest (extending as far as the shoulder joint, but not extending onto the shoulder itself); the forelegs to the elbow joint; the rear legs to the knee joint; the tip of the tail. White markings are a distinctive feature of the Japanese dog, but white in areas where it is not supposed to appear is a fault. Freckling in the white fur on the legs is a fault.)

Beniryu of Yamanashi Andoso owned by Tooru Kimida. 82nd Nippo National Monbu Daijinsho.

Additional Comments from the Judging Resolutions

(An injury or disease that affects the expression of one of the traits considered to be characteristic of the Japanese dog is a fault. Lifting up the head in order to hide improper joint angles or to conceal turning out of the elbows is prohibited. The handler should always stand behind the dog. As for the pose in the ring, the dog should stand in a natural way. In the judging of the Japanese dog, the dog must be evaluated as to its character the whole time it is in the ring, not just during the individual judging. Ring attitude, sounds the dog makes, and so on, should all be noted. Irregular bite, missing teeth, tongue spots, etc., should have a large influence on the appraisal, and this examination should be conducted strictly. Dogs that resist the examination of their mouth, even though the handler is assisting, do not have the proper temperament characteristics of spirited boldness and good nature. This is a major fault, and is even more serious than bad bites, missing teeth, and tongue spots. During comparison judging (facing off) the dogs should be a fixed distance apart, and the judge evaluates the dogs on their natural stance. Comparison judging faults are the following: The dogs are brought closer together than necessary; a dog takes an aggressive posture; or a dog is forced to behave in a manner different from its natural inclination. Use of unfair practices such as lying about the age of the dog, or artificial alteration of coat color, missing teeth, bite, monochordism, tongue spots, etc., is not allowed. As for this, a prize won is rescinded when circumstances of alteration are found out later on.)

Faults
Developmental defects and nutritional deficiency
Disharmony between the color of the body and the nose; for example, a pink nose on a colored dog. Small, temporary pink spots due to injury are allowable
White spots in the colored areas of the coat
Short tail caused by genetic defect

Disqualifications
Lacking the quality of a Japanese dog
Overshot or undershot bite

Notice: Any deviation from the standard should be faulted.

The following is the FCI Standard which follows the Standard of the Japan Kennel Club. The FCI Standard is used in most European dog shows with the exception of Great Britain.

FÉDÉRATION CYNOLOGIQUE INTERNATIONALE SECRÉTARIAT GENERAL:
13, Place Albert I - B6530 THUIN (Belg.)

FCI-Standard No. 257/14.04.1995/GB

SHIBA

ORIGIN: Japan

UTILIZATION: Hunting dog for birds and small animals, Companion dog

FCI'S CLASSIFICATION: Group 5 (Spitz and primitive types), Section 5 (Asian Spitz and related breeds), Without working trial.

BRIEF HISTORICAL SUMMARY: The Shiba has been a native breed to Japan since the primitive ages. The word "Shiba" originally refers to something "small," a "small dog." The Shiba's habitat was in the mountainous area facing the Sea of Japan and was used as a hunting dog for small animals and birds. There were slight differences in the breeds according to the areas where they were raised. As dogs like English Setters and English Pointers were imported from England during the period of 1868-1912, hunting became a sport in Japan and cross breeding of the Shiba with those English dogs became prevalent and a pure Shiba became rare so that by 1912-1926 pure Shibas confined to these areas became exceedingly scarce. Hunters and other educated persons became concerned with the preservation of the pure Shibas from around 1928 and the preservation of the limited number of pure strains began seriously, and the breed standard was finally unified in 1934. In 1937 the Shiba was designated as a natural monument after which the breed was bred and improved to become the superior breed known today.

GENERAL APPEARANCE: Small-sized dog, well balanced, well boned with well developed muscles. Constitution strong. Action quick, free and beautiful.

IMPORTANT PROPORTIONS: The ratio of height at withers to length of body is 10:11.

BEHAVIOUR AND TEMPERAMENT: The temperament is faithful, with keenness in sense and high alertness.

HEAD: Forehead broad, cheeks well developed and stop defined with slight furrow. Nasal bridge straight and nose black in color desirable. Muzzle moderately thick and tapering. Lips tight, and teeth strong with scissor bite.

EYES: Relatively small, triangular and dark brown in color; the corners of the eyes are upturned.

EARS: Relatively small, triangular, slightly inclining forward and firmly pricked.

NECK: Thick, strong, and well balanced with the head and the body.

BODY: Back straight and strong; loin broad and muscular. Chest deep, ribs moderately sprung, belly well drawn up.

TAIL: Set on high, thick, carried vigorously curled or curved as a sickle, the tip nearly reaching hocks when let down.

FOREQUARTERS: Shoulders moderately sloping, elbows tight; seen from the front, forelegs straight.

HINDQUARTERS: Upper thighs long, lower thighs short, but well developed. Hocks thick and tough.

FEET: Digits tightly closed and well arched. Pads hard and elastic. Nails hard and dark in color desirable.

GAIT: Light and brisk.

COAT:
   Hair: Outer coat harsh and straight, undercoat soft and dense; hair on tail slightly long and standing off.
   Color: Red, black and tan, sesame, black sesame, red sesame.

   "Definition of the color sesame" =
   Sesame: Equal mixture of white and black hairs.

Black sesame: More black than white hairs.
Red sesame: Ground color of hair red, mixture with black hairs.

All of the above mentioned colors must have "Urajiro."
"Urajiro" = whitish coat on the sides of the muzzle and on the cheeks, on the underside of the jaw and neck, on the chest and stomach and the underside of the tail, and on the inside of the legs.

SIZE: Height at withers Dogs 40 cm [15.75"]
Bitches 37 cm [14.60"]
There is a tolerance of 1.5 cm smaller or taller. [Dogs 15.20" to 16.30" and Bitches 14.00" to 15.20"]

FAULTS: Any departure from the foregoing points should be considered as a fault and the seriousness with which the fault should be regarded should be in exact proportion to its degree.

1) Shyness.
2) Bitchy dogs, doggy bitches.
3) Malocclusion (overshot or undershot mouth).
4) Numerous teeth missing.

DISQUALIFYING FAULTS
1) Ears not pricked.
2) Hanging or short tail.

N.B.: Male animals should have two apparently normal testicles fully descended into the scrotum.

U-UD, U-ACH Yankii's Tenshi UD rehearses with obstacles higher than those required by AKC. C. Kendle.

16

The Foundation of the Modern Shiba

AFTER WORLD WAR II, the greatly reduced number of dogs presented some troublesome issues to Japanese breeders trying to reestablish the Shiba. They could either stick to the tiny number of fairly pure Shibas remaining, or they could cross these Shibas with related dogs such as the Mikawa to build up the breed population. On the whole, most breeders went with the first option, and under the guidance of Nippo chose breeding stock from the tiny pool of remaining pure Shibas.

So, postwar Shibas were very inbred, and a widespread variety of health problems began to surface, such as missing teeth and patellar luxation (slipped stifles). These problems are endemic in the Shiba, and many people believe they can in part be traced back to the popular studs of the late 1940s and early 1950s.

On the positive side, using relatively pure stock made developing a breed close to the original Japanese native dog easier for Shiba fanciers than for breeders of other native dogs such as the Akita. The popularity of crossbreeding Akitas with large western breeds to produce superior fighting dogs was such that pure specimens could not be found, and the reestablishment of the original type has been very difficult. Whether the trade-off between type versus health was worth it is a matter of opinion, but it is very important for Shiba breeders today to be aware of the situation.

In his book *Shiba Dog*, Mr. Ishikawa names ten Shibas he feels have been most influential in forming the present-day Shiba. These include Ishi, Koro, and Aka (prewar period) and Naka, Nakaichi, Matsumaru, Meiho, Kurata no Ishi, Hideyoshi, and Tenko (postwar period). Mr. Ishikawa arrived at these ten dogs by studying the pedigrees of Shibas who were winners of the Minister's Awards at national shows. Of these dogs, Aka and Naka are considered to be the most important. Naka is an inbred grandson of Aka, and his pedigree is presented here for you to refer to as you read the descriptions of the individual dogs (Akaishiso is the kennel name):

```
                                    Ishi
                         Aka
                                    Koro
              Akani
                                    unknown
                         Meigetsu
                                    unknown
Naka of Akaishiso
                                    Ishi
                         Aka
                                    Koro
              Beniko
                                    unknown
                         Hana
                                    unknown
```

Naka of Akaishiso

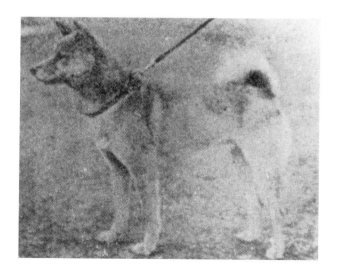

ISHI

Ishi was born on November 2, 1930. He was a red male who grew to be 39.5 cm (15.55 inches) tall. Ishi's sire was Hisahara, and his dam was Kochi. He was from the area of the Sanin Shibas, and his owner (who lived in Tokyo) was well known at the time as an authority on that variety. In 1936, Ishi won an award at the fifth Nippo national show. Ishi had too little rear angulation and was described as suffering from bad, almost popping hocks. (He may have had patellar luxation, but we can never know for sure.) Ishi also had slightly larger eyes than were desirable. His strong points were an excellent coat texture and overall style.

Koro.

Ishi.

KORO

Koro was born in September 1935. Her sire and dam are unknown. She was a black-and-tan from the Shinshu Shiba heritage who had been discovered in the Kochi mountain area in Shikoku. Hajime Watanabe judged her at a regional show in 1938 and observed the following in his critique: "Very typey Shiba, very well put together, extremely well-structured. This female possesses the ideal and admirable quality of the Shiba." Dr. Kinji Horiuchi purchased her, brought her to his home town of Kofu City, and bred her to Ishi. Subsequently, a litter of two puppies (Aka and Ishi Ichi) was born on January 6, 1939.

AKA OF FUGOKU

As his name implies, Aka was a red dog. When Aka was ten months old, he was shown at the eighth Nippo national show in Tokyo, in which only fifteen Shibas were entered. The Shiba judge, Mr. Ozaki, found that Aka was "a most successful case of complementing the parents' strengths and weaknesses." The judge described future prospects as follows:

As a young dog, he is extremely well-behaved and has a mature and classy attitude maintaining alertness and good spirit . . . This small dog seems to be gifted with insurmountable inner spirit, and by breeding him to an equally superior bitch, the quality that is currently lacking in small-sized Japanese dogs will be substantially upgraded. This future expectation is the reason behind selecting him as one of the three major winners for this show. I would like the owner to strive hard to maintain this excellent specimen for the best of the breed's future.

After Aka's win of an important award at this event, requests for stud service came flooding in, and Aka was ultimately bred to approximately 200 bitches. He was especially known for good bone structure, coat, angulation, and temperament.

Aka of Fugoku.

Aka's best-known first-generation offspring was Beniko, the daughter of a female named Hana who was reported to be lame. He also produced a male named Akani from a bitch named Meigetsu. Akani was important as the father of Naka.

NAKA OF AKAISHISO

Because Beniko had many of Aka's qualities, she was bred to Aka's son Akani in order to preserve these qualities. Of the six puppies from this breeding, by far the most important was the red male, Naka. He was the first Shiba to win the Nippo Honbusho (Nippo's highest award) by defeating the Best of Breed winners from the Akita and middle-size breeds at the twelfth national show on April 17, 1949.

Naka was lucky to have survived long enough to win this show. After being transferred to a new owner at age four months, he contracted distemper, and his new owners had to provide round-the-clock care for the next three months to save his life. When he was a year old, he was attacked by a large neighborhood dog on his own territory, and in the fight that followed, both dogs were badly injured. The attacker was vanquished and ran away, but Naka needed a month to recover from his wounds.

Although Naka was born in Kofu City, he lived most of his life in Nagano Prefecture. He produced five winners of important awards at national shows, and his offspring were scattered throughout Japan. He is known as the father of the restoration

of the Shiba, and because of him, the Nagano Prefecture was the dominant area for Shibas for many years. He lived to the age of fifteen years and eight months. It was said of him that such a dog comes along only once every 50 to 100 years.

NAKAICHI OF AKAISHISO

In an effort to further preserve the influence of Aka, his daughter Beniko was bred to her son Naka, who was himself inbred on Aka. The litter of five puppies born in 1955 contained a male named Nakaichi, who became very influential and produced many prize-winning offspring. Nakaichi was light red in color and a little over 38 cm (15 inches). His ear set was unique in that the center ear line was almost straight, and the outer ear line was slightly curved, making it look like a pouch. His forehead was very wide, and his eyes were described as being brilliantly alert. He had a

Nakaishi of Akaishiso.

19

broad, strong muzzle, with a slight dip. Although body structure was well-balanced, his tail was too tightly curled. Nakaichi's leg was hurt in a fight with one of his littermates, which caused him problems in the show ring. However, he did receive a first-place award from judge Watanabe at a regional show.

In the same litter that produced Nakaichi was a bitch named Nakakoro, who was also extremely typey and described as having a very alert look. She is also an important foundation Shiba and is found in many pedigrees.

These five Shibas—Ishi, Koro, Aka, Naka, and Nakaichi—form the basis of the Shiba breed as we know it today, and they can be found in the background of virtually all Shiba pedigrees. In an effort to stabilize Shiba type, the offspring of Naka and Nakaichi were very heavily inbred. An example of a rather extreme case of this is a dog named Koronaka, a black-and-tan male born on November 13, 1957, who is well known in his own right.

Koronaka.

```
                        Nakaichi
              Koroichi
                        Nakakoro
       Koro
                        Naka
              Nakakitome
                        Nakakisanme
Koronaka
                        Nakaichi
              Benimaru
                        Ichimari
                        (a Nakaichi daughter)
       Kurohana
                        Nakaichi
              Nakaichihachi
                        Hachi
```

Influential Producers of the 1960s and 1970s

In addition to the five foundation Shibas discussed above, six more Shibas were very influential. These Shibas are noteworthy because a number of their descendants have done outstandingly well at the Nippo shows.

TENKO OF JONENSO

```
                              Akani
                     Naka
                              Beniko
            Senko
                              Naka
                     Nachihime
                              Chisato
Tenko
                              Korokoma
                     Korooh
                              Mari
            Tamahime
                              Ichitaro
                     Ichishinme
                              Ishihime
```

As can be seen from his pedigree, Tenko's sire Senko was linebred on Naka. He also traces back to Naka on the dam's side. Tenko was the sire of two Minister's Award winners, and he is found in the pedigree of eleven very important Shibas. His own show career was not as illustrious as some of his offspring because he had a few missing teeth, although he did win at regional shows six times and placed three times at national shows. His coat color was described as being a red like the brilliant red sun and was very much admired for its similarity to the original color of the classic Shiba.

Tenko of Jonenso.

Matsumaru of Shinshu Nakajimaso.

MATSUMARU OF SHINSHU NAKAJIMASO

```
                        Benimaru (Nakaichi son)
            Beniryu
                        Benishiro
                        (Nakaichi daughter)
    Benisachi
                        Nakayu
            Sachihime
                        Komamidori
Matsumaru
                        Ichi
            Dai
                        Ichihime
    Aka Fusame
                        Korosaku
            Miyakkohime
                        Tsurumidori
```

A large number of the top-winning dogs shown at recent Nippo national shows have Matsumaru in their pedigrees. Matsumaru is unique in that both he and his daughter have won a Minister's Award at national shows. On November 15, 1970, his daughter Maruhime took the top award, and one-and-one-half years later, he himself won. Matsumaru was a red dog, and he died of old age in 1979 after siring many litters.

MEIHO OF SHIMAMURA

```
                        Koroichi
            Koro
                        Nakakitome
    Koronaka
                        Benimaru
            Kurohana
                        Nakaichihachi
Meiho
                        Nakaichi
            Nakaichibumi
                        Fumihime
    Eienme
                        Pochi
            Haruhime
                        Fukihime
```

Meiho was a red male who is found in the pedigree of nearly as many of the top-winning Shibas as is Matsumaru, and he is known for siring a son who won a Minister's Award. Meiho is heavily inbred on Naka and Nakaichi, and he is a (younger) full brother of the famous Fujinishiki. Meiho was well known for having perfect dentition. According to *The Shiba Dog*, by Mr. Ishikawa, Genzo Satoda, a top authority on Japanese dogs, described Meiho thus:

> This dog manifests the superior Shiba quality transmitted by the well-known Koronaka line. His eyes are exceptionally good. That his brother Fujinishiki was a winner also proves that this lineage is as good as the one of Korooh and Fumioh. Strong and powerful expression together with an excellent shape of muzzle, good angulation, white on the back of the tail, and well composed ring manner are all credited to the breeder's effort.

Kurata No Ishi.

KURATA NO ISHI OF KURATASO

```
                        Naka
                Nakaichi
                        Beniko
        Ichiroku
                        Nakaichi
                Ichimaru
                        Kobi
Kurata no Ishi
                        Nakaichi
                Nakaichibun
                        Fumihime
        Korohime
                        Korooh
                Koroichime
                        Fumikocho
```

Fujio Kurata, who firmly believed that Nakaichi was the best Shiba in the history of the breed, inbred heavily on Nakaichi to produce Kurata no Ishi, a red male. Kurata no Ishi had a good winning record in regional shows, and he also received the Minister of Agriculture award at the 45th national show. He was bred to a number of high-quality bitches and has many winning offspring.

HIDEYOSHI OF SHINSHU KIRINSO

```
                        Benimaru
                Beniryu
                        Benishiro
        Benisachi
                        Nakayu
                Sachihime
                        Komamidori
Hideyoshi
                        Nakamidori
                Ichiroku
                        Suzuroku
        Umehime
                        Korooh
                Korohime
                        Fujiwakame
```

Hideyoshi was a red male who was born in the early 1960s. He became the first Shiba from the Kyushu area to receive a Minister's Award. According to *The Shiba Dog*, Judge Watanabe said of Hideyoshi at the 44th National show:

> This dog is gifted with mature dignity, probably due to his long career in the show rings. Very masculine head, wide forehead, good cheek, tight muzzle, and wonderful outline of face. Expression very nice and natural with well-balanced structure. Good stance, good waterproof coat texture, and ideal color. He

Hideyoshi of Shinshu Kirinso.

was in top condition in this show, and this could be the result of loving care and management by his owner.

TAKETOYO OF HOKOSO

<pre>
                          Meiho
                  Meiho Kurojishi
                          Tomiyo
             Meiho Benikoma no Tetsu
                          Fujinishiki
                  Nazakurahime
                          Sakuranishiki
Taketoyo
                          Koronaka
                  Fumioh
                          Fumi Yakko
        Kuro Yakko
                          Senko
                  Mami
                          Teru
</pre>

Taketoyo, a red male winner of the Prime Minister's award, was born in 1968. He lived to be nineteen years and was the pride and joy of his owner, Akio Aoki. Taketoyo was heavily inbred on Naka through Koronaka. He is the close ancestor of many of the original imports to the United States in the early 1980s and sired a number of Nippo national Merit Award winners in Japan. *The Shiba Dog* quotes Judge Yoshimi Isobe's evaluation of Taketoyo:

> His ring attitude is dignified with strong kan-i and manliness. His condition is excellent. His forehead is well-developed, his cheeks are full, showing male characteristics. His legs have good bone construction, curly tail has strong expression, total appearance is impressive. I admire the owner's efforts for everyday management up to today.

By studying these pedigrees, you can see that the foundation stock for the breed was very inbred. Before American breeders decide to follow the Japanese example, they should understand that the Japanese breeders practiced inbreeding to the extent they did out of necessity. In contrast, today's top Japanese breeders have a wide choice of good Shibas to choose from, and inbreeding has fallen out of favor because of the health problems associated with it. In most five-generation pedigrees of today's top-winning Japanese Shibas, you will not find even one name repeated.

Mr. Watanabe commented on inbreeding and recommended against it in his book *Nihon Ken Hyakka*. He notes that the Japanese government

Taketoyo of Hokoso.

23

recommends that humans more closely related than the third degree (presumably meaning the equivalent of first cousins) should not marry and have children, and he suggests that dog breeders follow the same rule in planning their litters. Inbreeding and linebreeding are controversial subjects (see the Genetics for Breeders chapter for a discussion). But it is fairly obvious that the degree of inbreeding used to form the foundation of the Shiba in Japan was excessive and has led to at least some of the health problems that we see in the breed today.

The Nippo National draws large crowds every November. G. Haskett.

The Shiba in America

AMERICAN SHIBA CLUBS

Shiba Club of America, 1980 to 1990—On July 19, 1980, Merry and Frank Atkinson, Julia Cadwell, Audie Bach, Eugene Kravitz, and Anita Regehr met at the Wind Cave restaurant in Santa Rosa, California, and officially established the Shiba Club of America (SCA). The club began a studbook, and this was the first time Shibas were registered by a U.S. organization.

The first show in which Shibas were known to have participated was the California Rare Breed Dog Association show held on October 26, 1980, at Palomares Park in Pomona. Julia Cadwell's Rusty was Best of Breed and the Atkinson's Benitakehime of Dairy Farm (Termite) was Best of Opposite Sex at this show, with Shiba breeder and importer Kaiji Katsumoto judging. There were a few shows here and there over the next year. Shiba fanciers became frustrated because many judges were not knowledgeable about the Nippo Standard, and so in 1981 the members of the fledgling SCA and Mr. Katsumoto joined forces to put on the first SCA National Specialty. Keiche Jige, a JKC judge from Japan, was invited to officiate at this historic show that took place in October. Best of Breed was the Atkinson's Kuroyuki of Nanko Suzuki Kensha (Kaze), and Best of Opposite Sex was Termite. Best of Winners was Kayame of Chigasaki Morobashi.

While Mr. Jige was in the United States, he presented a seminar at which he examined and critiqued two Shibas and answered questions on the breed. Mr. Jige commented on the two health problems widespread in the breed—dislocating kneecaps and missing teeth—which he stated became prevalent as a result of inbreeding within the small population in Japan after World War II.

In his opinion, no Shiba—male or female—should be bred before the age of one-and-one-half years. Bitches should not be bred more than once a year, and their first heat should always be skipped. He also stated that after the age of about six months, when a Shiba has reached its full size, it is almost impossible to give it too much exercise.

In 1982, the SCA held its second National Specialty, with Dick Beauchamp judging. This show had a higher attendance than the first, reflecting the rapidly growing number of Shiba fanciers.

Japan Kennel Club judge Mr. Keiche Jige with Rusty at the first Shiba seminar in 1981. M. Atkinson

Organizational meeting of the Shiba Club of America (1980). M. Atkinson.

the club Secretary and wrote the SCA newsletter, which was a valuable source of information on the Nippo Standard.

National Shiba Club of America—On the East Coast, Maureen Reed, now Maureen Lacey (Deer Lace kennel), and some of her Shiba-loving friends founded a second breed club, the National Shiba Club of America (NSCA), in 1983. This club was formed with the idea of getting the Shiba accepted by the AKC as soon as possible. The NSCA encouraged showing at rare breed shows and matches and started its own stud book, whose standard caused some controversy when it appeared. The SCA had been using the Nippo Standard, but the NSCA

First United States National Specialty for the breed, held by the Shiba Club of America (1981). Japan Kennel Club judge Mr. Keiche Jige selected Kaze, handled by Merry Atkinson, as BOB. M. Atkinson.

Kaze was Best of Breed once again, with the Katsumoto's Shishi of Kenwaso (Bell) the Winners Dog. As in the previous year, the 1983 SCA National had an increase in attendance. Judge Jack Shafer did the honors for well over a dozen Shibas, with the Best of Breed winner being Frank and Alice Sakayeda's Seitenhime of Aunso (Satori's Mama). Kaze, who also had several prestigious wins in international shows in 1983 and 1984, was Best of Opposite Sex at this show.

The SCA suffered from the usual growing pains of rare breed clubs, but it continued to attract new members and to hold shows. From 1986 to 1990, SCA held its National Specialties in conjunction with the BSA (see below). Participants were primarily from the West Coast, with a few people from the Midwest. Each National Specialty featured a seminar and an elaborate picnic lunch, and many friendships were formed. Jean Atkinson was

Standard seemed to follow the AKC Standard for the Akita in some respects. The NSCA Standard allowed a wider size range, specified a heavier body type than desired in Japan, and allowed all colors and markings.

NSCA held its first two specialties in June of 1984, in conjunction with the Hudson Valley Rare Breed Dog Club shows in New Jersey. Best of Breed at the Saturday morning show was Fred Duane's Mokusei Takeshi of Mokuseiso (Sam), and Best of Breed at the Sunday morning show was Kinkajou Mitsu. Two more shows were held that fall in Baltimore with Shosha Cinnabar of Deer Lace winning on both Saturday and Sunday. The 1985 and 1986 specialties were held once again in New Jersey. In 1985 Graham Uchida's Kimiko of Deer Lace won both events and in 1986, Yukihime of Gardenso took Best of Breed on Saturday and was best opposite to Minimeadow's Dreamer on Sunday.

NSCA members gather for the first pair of specialties held by the club in the summer of 1984. M. Lacey.

In 1987, NSCA's officers felt that the club had grown large enough to hold its first National Specialty. The show was organized by Richard Atkinson and held at the Montgomery County Park in Conroe, Texas. Nineteen Shibas competed under Judge Dr. Arthur Reinitz. Dr. Reinitz chose Kinouk Airwolf, owned by Joan Young, for Best of Breed and Uchida's Mayumi, owned by Richard Atkinson, for Best of Opposite Sex.

The AKC board voted in 1991 to take the Shiba into the miscellaneous class effective June 1, 1992, designating NSCA as the parent club. Permission to compete in championship classes as part of the non-sporting group was granted effective June 1, 1993.

On June 11, 1993, the Evergreen Shiba Club hosted the first National Specialty in which AKC points were awarded. The entry was the largest ever for an NSCA event, with fifty-nine Shibas present. Judge Mary Ellen Compagnon chose Frank Sakayeda's import male Toyojiro of Nidai Maneiso

(co-owned by Carol Parker and Camille Wong) as her Best of Breed and the red bitch San Jo's Carrot Top (owned by Desmond and Mary Cole and bred, shown, and co-owned by Leslie Ann Engen) for Best of Opposite Sex.

Beikoku Shibainu Aikokai—During the mid-1980s, the Beikoku Shibainu Aikokai (BSA, meaning "American Shiba Fancier's Club") was pioneered by a California group of native Japanese, including Kaiji and Toshiko Katsumoto. The BSA works closely with Nippo in Japan, and members register their dogs in Japan. On January 26, 1986, the club held its first Nippo-style show, which used the Nippo Standard and Japanese judging procedure. Best Male and Best in Specialty was the Katsumotos' Fujio of Sagami Ikeda Kensha (Yuki), and Best Female was Ayame of Kenwaso, owned by M. Satake. The judge was Nippo Chief Judge Gayu Ishikawa. The 1987 BSA show was held on January 11, and the judge was Etsuo Yamamoto, a Nippo judge from Japan. Best Female and Best in

Specialty was the Katsumoto's Aya of Fussaen; Best Male was her son, Tiare Arndt's Beniwashi of Kenwaso. This show has become a yearly tradition, and SCA considered the show to be its national specialty from 1986 to 1990.

The BSA continues to hold specialty shows and, at the time of this writing, it holds the record with 70 entries, the most Shibas ever assembled for an American specialty. It has also continued the tradition of bringing over a Nippo judge each year. Twice the BSA has been especially honored by the presence of Nippo's chief judge. A seminar is generally given by the judge in association with the shows, and this has proved invaluable for the Americans in attendance. One year the judge showed more than two hundred slides of correct and incorrect Shibas, and the question-and-answer sessions that followed helped to clarify some of the points that are not explained in detail in the Nippo Standard.

Many BSA members have not registered their Shibas with AKC but choose to maintain their Nippo registrations instead. Currently, only Nippo-registered Shibas may participate in their annual show. However, some fanciers maintain dual registration, and many of the top-placing dogs in the 1994 BSA show were also new AKC champions.

Shiba Ken Club—Meanwhile, a fourth American breed club was formed in 1987. Suki Mahar and Susan Houser founded the Shiba Ken Club (SKC) in the fall of that year after becoming frustrated with the lack of information about the Nippo Standard and Japanese history of the breed as well as the lack of shows in the Midwest using the Nippo Standard. Ms. Mahar had traveled to Japan and imported several Shibas, including the JKC Champion Taketora of Yodaso, for her Aoyama kennel. Susan was a former Akita breeder with an interest in the Japanese native breeds. SKC was the original publisher of *The Shiba Journal*, which serialized a summary of various commentaries on the original Nippo Standard. (In 1991 *The Shiba Journal* became an independent magazine.) SKC also began its own stud book and registry, following AKC guidelines.

The main goals of SKC were to educate breeders about the Shiba with translations of Japanese books and articles and to encourage AKC to accept transfer registrations from either JKC or Nippo so that breeders could continue to import Shibas after AKC recognition. SKC was also the original founder of the national Shiba Rescue. (Breed rescue organizations find new homes for purebreds whose owners can no longer keep them.) In an

Shiba Ken Club members at a regional specialty held in Ohio in 1987. B. Gilmore.

attempt to discourage breeders who sold Shibas to pet stores and dog brokers, SKC limited registration privileges to members who signed a strict code of ethics, and no Shiba that had been owned by a pet store or wholesaler, even temporarily, could be registered.

The first SKC National Specialty was held on May 22, 1988, in Greenfield, Indiana, with sixteen Shibas in competition. Judge Tim Catterson named Kodomo of Aoyama Mahar, owned by Suki Mahar, Best of Breed and Kuma Mitsu of Aoyama Mahar, owned by Bill and June Gilmore and Suki Mahar, Best of Opposite Sex.

Shiba Club of America, 1991 to 1996—In 1991, the SKC and the SCA voted to merge SKC into SCA. The SCA still uses the Nippo Standard as its breed standard, including all of the pertinent information from the Nippo Judging Resolutions. The first post-merger National Specialty (the 10th for SCA) was held on May 3, 1991, in Walnut, California. Twenty-nine Shibas were judged by Betty Claus. Best of Opposite Sex was Laura Perkinson's Homaretennome of Gishi Fujiso, and Best of Breed was Fred Lanting's BEEF of Willow Wood.

Ch. Foxtrot Technical Knockout. First black-and-tan AKC champion Shiba. P. Doescher.

Ch. Tanasea's Toyonaka Sama was awarded three Best In Shows in 1993, the first year the Shiba competed for points in the American Kennel Club. L. Sorensen.

After the AKC named the NSCA as the parent club, the SCA continued to exist with a focus on education. In May of 1992, Terukuni Uki, the Director of Nippo, was invited to judge the SCA National Specialty in Connecticut and to give a judging seminar. Mr. Uki awarded Best of Breed to Jeri and Bruce Braviroff's Fukuryu Beikokusekiryuso and Best of Opposite Sex to Blue Mountain's Schnookey, owned by Chip Miller. Ten Shibas were rated "excellent" out of a field of forty-six. Exhibitors were thrilled with the opportunity to see how their dogs measured up to Japanese standards and returned home with a new resolve to work to improve color, missing teeth, and structural problems in future breedings. The SCA board once again invited a Nippo judge to do the honors for the 1993 national. In 1994, the Colonial Shiba Club, host club for the 1992 and 1993 SCA specialties, renamed the show the Shiba Classic and began to offer certificates with the approval of Nippo. Currently SCA offers educational material and breeder referral through its mailing address.

All in all, the Shiba breed seems destined for great popularity. There is concern that this popularity may create for the Shiba the same problems found in other highly popular breeds, where the lure of quick dollars has attracted puppy mill breeders with no regard for producing healthy, high-quality animals. If Shiba fanciers can maintain the breed's most desirable traits—intelligence, hardiness, and simplicity—and stick to the Nippo Standard for the breed, the American Shiba of the future will rival the quality of its Japanese ancestors.

AMERICAN SHIBA STANDARD

As can be seen from the history of American Shiba breed clubs presented here, the Shiba standard has been a source of ongoing controversy. Originally, SCA, BSA, and SKC adopted the Nippo Basic Standard and Judging Resolutions, while NSCA adopted a standard similar to that for the American Akita.

As the text of the Nippo Basic Standard and Judging Resolutions and the commentaries by Japanese experts on the breed were translated and made generally available to Shiba fanciers in the mid-1980s, the Nippo Standard became increasingly popular among breeders. The standards of the American clubs were revised as more information became available, and all of the standards, including NSCA's, have become more similar to the Nippo Standard and to each other. The membership of NSCA eventually voted by a 2/3 majority to adopt a version of the Nippo Standard, and the AKC adopted that standard as the official standard of the breed in 1997.

UNITED STATES FOUNDATION BLOODLINES

This section presents a detailed look at the early Shiba kennels and their imported dogs. The information is designed for Shiba breeders and other Shiba lovers who have a special interest in the history of the Shiba in America.

It is not known when the first Shiba came to the United States. In 1955, Linda Handy and her family brought back to the United States a small dog they found and adopted while living in Japan. Their Japanese neighbors and friends told them that the dog was a Shiba, and photos show that the dog did strongly resemble a Shinshu Shiba or the related Mikawa dog. John H. Staub wrote in a letter published in the October 1992 *Shiba-E-News* (official publication of the National Shiba Club of America) that he received his first pair of JKC-registered Shibas in July of 1955. There may well have been other purebred Shibas or Shiba-type dogs brought over before 1955 by Japanese immigrants or returning U.S. servicemen, but none of the national breed clubs has any record of them.

1973 to 1985

The first imported Shiba with U.S.-registered descendants was a red male named Nidai Akajishi of Sagami Ikeda Kensha (whelped January 1973, died 1985), brought to the United States in April 1973 by Kaiji and Toshiko Katsumoto. The Katsumotos, who were originally from Japan, admired the breed in their native country, and when they had the opportunity to import some high-quality stock, they took advantage of it and established Kenwaso kennel. The Katsumotos also imported a female named Tenshome, who produced four litters by Nidai Akajishi (in March and October 1974, July 1975, and March 1976). As there were no organized Shiba activities in America at the time, all eleven puppies were sold as pets.

In March 1980, the Katsumotos received Kuromatsume of Sagami Ikeda Kensha from the same kennel that had produced Nidai Akajishi. Kuromatsume (her call name, Chibi, meaning small, is a common call name for Shibas) was born on January 2, 1980. This black-and-tan bitch was a daughter of the black-and-tan Japanese male, Kuroichi of Rozanso. Her first litter, sired by Nidai Akajishi, was born on November 20, 1980. This litter contained a red male named Shishi of Kenwaso (Bell), who became a well-known sire, and a red female named Shishihime of Kenwaso, the dam of Janice Cowen's Yukihime of Gardenaso. The Katsumotos also imported a red male named Fujio of Sagami Ikeda Kensha (Yuki) in early 1982 and the red

Kuroichi of Rozanso figures prominently in the pedigrees of several early imports.

bitch Aya of Fussaen (Sai) a year or so later. Sai is a daughter of a top Nippo family of show dogs and herself was the dam, grandam, and great-grandam of several Beikoku Shibainu Aikokai (BSA) specialty winners.

In the mid-1970s, an American woman named Julia Cadwell became involved with the Shiba breed in an unusual way. Ms. Cadwell rescued a little red stray from probable death on a highway near her home in Santa Rosa, California, and named the dog Rusty. Later, she discovered the dog was not a Basenji mix, as she had guessed, but a purebred Shiba. She began to research the breed, and her efforts eventually led to an examination of Rusty by an official from the JKC, who pronounced him a purebred Shiba. Rusty was issued a registration certificate by the JKC in 1977. In 1978 Ms. Cadwell succeeded in importing a female named Shina no Ichihime of Shinshu Mitamuraso (Kojika). On Thanksgiving Day of 1978, Rusty and Kojika had a litter of four puppies—the first litter for Shosha Shibas. Rusty lived to a ripe old age, dying in 1990.

In October of 1981, Ms. Cadwell received three more imports from Japan. These were the red male Ginzakura of Chiba Yoshizenso (Senshi); the red female Tsubaki of Chiba Shiraneso (Shana); and the male Tetsumaru of Ichikawa Aoki (Keidai).

Ms. Cadwell subsequently completed her kennel of imports with the red female Haya no Kiyohime of Akanuma Hayasakaso (Issei), and the red male, Horyumaru of Saisho Kensha (Joe Joe). She also imported several dogs for other Shiba breeders. Ms. Cadwell worked hard to promote the Shiba breed, and her efforts included putting out newsletters and fliers in the late 1970s and marching with her Shibas in the Cherry Blossom Festival in San Francisco for the first time in April 1979.

Among the people who saw her fliers were Merry and Frank Atkinson. The Atkinsons were Akita fanciers whose kennel, Golden Sun, was well known in Akita circles. They were naturally intrigued with the latest Japanese import, and in 1979 they contacted Ms. Cadwell for more information on the breed. They decided they wanted to import a female, and Ms. Cadwell put them in touch with Ben Sasaki in Japan, who made the arrangements for them to import Benitakehime of Dairy Farm (Termite). Despite the American-sounding name, Dairy Farm is a Japanese kennel.

The Atkinsons were introduced to Kaiji Katsumoto by Ms. Cadwell and they were greatly impressed by Mr. Katsumoto's knowledge of the Shiba and the quality of his stock. They asked him to help them import another Shiba and in late February 1981, a black-and-tan male puppy arrived from Japan. This dog was Kuroyuki of Nanko Suzuki Kensha, better known as Kaze, who was born on December 29, 1980, and was just about eight weeks old when he arrived in America. Kaze (like Chibi) was sired by Kuroichi of Rozanso. Frank and Merry Atkinson received their last import with the addition of the red sesame female, Tetsutakame of Saisho Kensha (Hime), brought from Japan by Mr. Keiche Jige, a JKC judge.

In 1982, the Atkinson's breeding program got under way. The kennel name they used for their Shibas was Ogon Taiyoso, which is Japanese for "golden sun." Kaze sired two litters that year with Termite. Ogon no Yukihime of Ogon Taiyoso (Strawberry), a female from the first litter, had a good international show career and was eventually sold to a fancier in England. A female from the second litter, Ogon no Ichime of Ogon Taiyoso, was sold to Sheryl Langan and became one of the foundation Shibas for Langans Brushwood kennel, along with Shosha no Sarasu Kitsune Drift of Shosha Shibas whom Ms. Langan acquired from Julia Cadwell.

The Atkinson's next litter was out of Hime sired by Bell. A pup from this litter (Ogon no Takahime of Ogon Taiyoso) and a pup from Kaze and Termite's second litter (Ogon no Beniichi of Ogon Taiyoso) were sold to Bob and Julie Jennings, who had just started their Maran Atha kennel in Ohio (their kennel name is usually spelled "Maranata" on Nippo pedigrees). The Atkinsons were to breed only a few more litters during the next three years, with puppies from these litters going to Ed and Tiare Arndt (Shogun Hisuiso, or Jade Shogun), Clarence Trebell of Canada (C.R.T.), and the Jennings, among others.

Kaze also sired litters with two of his half sisters, Katsumoto's Chibi and Curtis Van Allen's import bitch Kayame of Chigasaki Moroboshi (also known as Mokusei's Magic). Magic produced Mokusei Takeshi of Mokuseiso (Sam), a Shiba specialty winner for Fred Duane of Frerose kennels, while Chibi produced Kurotake of Kenwaso (Bamboo), a black-and-tan male that was acquired by Mary Malone and became well known as a sire in the Midwest.

In 1981, Frank and Alice Sakayeda became involved with Shibas. Mr. Sakayeda, a native of Japan, had been familiar with the breed for some time. As an importer of dogs from Japan, he used his knowledge of successful Nippo and JKC bloodlines to purchase a daughter of the famous black-and-tan stud, Kotetsu of Kohtokuso. An unremarkable red male puppy was thrown in as a bonus. As happens too often with a prized Shiba puppy, the bitch's bite went off. The little red male that no one thought much of grew up to be a solid little dog, Teruarashi of Fuji Itohso (Kaizo), who sired two litters for the Sakayedas before heading to Canada to become Sheryl Langan's foundation stud.

On his next trip to Japan, Mr. Sakayeda returned with Cha Cha of Hayakoso and Seitenhime of Aunso (Satori's Mama). Shortly after her arrival in California, Mama produced Tsuru, Matsu, and Hana of Satoriso. The pups from this litter are technically considered imports, having been bred in Japan. Matsu of Satoriso (Kamikaze) was sold to Nancy Baugus of Gento kennel along with the black-and-tan bitch, Kuronana of Hayakoso (Kabuki), that the Sakayedas had imported for her. Tsuru (Shuu) was sold to Ms. Langan. Hana of Satoriso (Ginger) was bred to Kaizo and produced Kintaro of Satoriso, who sired several litters after

Monica Flynn and Rudy (Foxtrot Fan the Flames CDX) give a demonstration at the Shiba Classic. Rudy was the first Shiba to earn an Open title. G. Haskett.

his purchase by Frerose kennel. Ginger was sold to the Arndts as foundation stock for their Jade Shogun (Shogun Hisuiso) kennel.

Mama was eventually sold to Mary Malone and produced five litters for Ms. Malone's Minimeadow kennel and one for Jane Vanderpool. The AKC Studbook Vol. 12 shows that by 1992 Mama had been bred eight times for a total of 30 puppies. Mama and her offspring appear in the pedigrees of approximately fifty percent of the Shiba foundation stock registered by AKC.

The Sakayedas in the early 1980s imported and bred a number of other Shibas that proved to be successful as show dogs and producers for various kennels: Haru Sakura of Kagawa Shichihoso (Amber), Taro of Satoriso (Dynamite), and Mitsutamahime of Awa Azumaso (Mitsu) were sold to Jade-Shogun; Gangu no Gen of Sanuki Ganguso (Tomo) to Minimeadow (Tomo went on to win best of breed twice at the Kennel Review Tournament of Champions); Daichi of Toyonaka Okomotoso (sire of Debbie Meador's group-winning male Ch. Kinouk's Road Warrior Tanasea and BIS Ch. Tanasea's Toyonaka Sama) and Top Gun of Satoriso to Joan Young of Kinouk; and Joh of Awa Azumaso to Sue Barnett. Katsura no Miyahime of Izumi no Motoso (Miya) went to Carolyn and Bert Kaufmann of Windcastle, where she became the first Shiba to earn the NSCA Registry of Merit (R.O.M.) title. (In order to qualify for the Registry of Merit, a female must have four AKC champion offspring, and a male must have eight.)

Another early Shiba breeder was Jean Uchida of Graham, Washington, who also owned Akitas. She imported three Shibas to form the foundation of her Graham Uchida kennel. These were the red male Soto no Gyokuryu of Sotoso (Ryu), the red female Tamashibame of Sotoso (Tama), and the red female, Rikihome of Yoshizen Kotobukiso (Hanako).

Joan Young of Kinouk was another Akita breeder who, searching for a smaller animal to breed, selected the Shiba. Ms. Young's first purchase was Graham Uchida's Mischief Maker (Chippies), a product of Jean Uchida's first litter born in August of 1981. Ms. Uchida was the source of another bitch, Porsche of Kinouk. The single pup of Mary Malone's first litter, Fire Fox of Minimeadow, was Ms. Young's first stud. Another bitch of Minimeadow lines, Jazz Dancer of Kinouk, was purchased from Wanda Herbert.

Around 1983, interest in the Shiba really began to explode. Previously, the breed had been popular primarily on the West Coast, but in 1983 Shibas began to attract attention throughout the country. We have already mentioned the establishment of the Maran Atha kennel in Ohio, whose stock included an import female named Tega no Namiyo of Dainana Kashiwayamaso (Sassy) as well as the stock they had purchased from Ogon Taiyoso. Ms. Malone, also in Ohio, imported Haya no Kiyomi of Akanuma Hayasakaso (Cinnamon) and Haruka of Hadano Nagoroso (Yoshi) at around this time.

1985 to 1996

Several new Shiba kennels were established in the mid-1980s. Janice Cowen started her Cowen III kennel with puppies from Kenwaso, Maran Atha, and Gento. The Foxtrot kennel of Kathleen Brown-Truax and Bruce Truax was formed in 1986. Ms. Brown-Truax was not new to dogs, as she had successfully bred and shown Poodles. Foxtrot's first Shiba was from Minimeadow, and they

also acquired a bitch from Karen Raisanen that traced back to Jean Uchida's imports. Three Shibas from Cowen III, including Akira of Cowen Third (also known as Cowen's Patent Pending), completed Foxtrot's original foundation stock, which produced several top-rated dogs and National Specialty winners. Ms. Brown-Truax continued to purchase imports and puppies out of import parents, and bred to imports in an effort to further improve her stock. The black-and-tan import male Fukurinmaru of Gunma Fukuda Kensha (Toy) produced several winning puppies for Foxtrot kennel, some of them out of the red import female Royal Blood Benihana (Su). Toy is now owned by Francis Attridge's O'Date Shibas, a kennel primarily known for its American-breds. Jane Chalfant of Justa kennel also became involved with Shibas in the mid-eighties, and has participated in Shiba events in nearly every region of the country.

Richard Tomita is another Shiba breeder who came to Shibas having already had success in an AKC breed. His Jacquet kennel has produced more than 100 AKC Champion Boxers and many foreign title winners. Mr. Tomita, whose parents are from Japan, imported his Shiba breeding stock with the help of a Japanese friend who is a veterinarian and JKC judge. His fifteen Shiba imports included five from the same kennel: Musashi no Yoshihime of Oikawa House; Minamoto no Haname of Oikawa House (Akemi); Minamoto no Benihime of Oikawa House; Minamoto no Hanagiku of Oikawa House (Mariko); and Ch. Katsuranishiki of Oikawa House (Chibi). Chibi had an outstanding show career at matches and rare breed shows in the East. In an effort to widen his gene pool, Mr. Tomita also imported four Shibas from two different lines: Kuromarihime of Kunimutsuso; Fuji no Kiyohime of Kunimutsuso; Ryutaro of Yamazakiso Kensha; and Kurotomi of Ome Shinjoso. Most of his original Shibas are now owned by his sister—Christine Tomita Eicher (Akemi kennels)—and Don Robinder (Robmar).

Another breeder who imported his foundation stock is Chris Ross (Reno Sakura Shibas), of Reno, Nevada. Mr. Ross' thirteen-year involvement in a Japanese university's exchange program with the University of Nevada resulted in his getting to know several Japanese veterinarians and breeders who helped him select and import his stock. He has imported Tsumigi no Konatsu of Rokumonsentsumugiso (Summer), Ch. Shinshu Chibisuke of

Shinshu Ueda Tenguso R.O.M. (Chibi), Ten of Rokumonsentsumugiso (Hiro), and Ch. Shinshu Benime Rokumonsentsumugiso R.O.M. (Plum Blossom). He works primarily with Jacey Holden (Mokelumne kennel), whose wonderful "Of Shibas" articles are famous among Shiba owners.

Yuko and Gino Salvadori of Connecticut (Avon-Koyukiso kennel) own the red import bitch Aki-Go and the recent import Ch. Eikichi of Dairy Farm (Jiro), a red male. With Vivian Miller, they have played a vital role in the Colonial Shiba Club. Ms. Miller (Yukii kennel) is the owner of Tamabeni-Go Banrakuso (Tama), who was Best of Breed at the 1996 Colonial Specialty and Tama's full brother Tamariki-Go, who were imported by the Salvadoris.

Bruce and Jeri Braviroff of LaVerne, California, are Samoyed breeders who have fallen under the spell of the Shiba. The Braviroffs are active members of the BSA club and are founders of Shiba Rescue of Southern California. In 1987, they acquired their first Shiba, Fukuhime of Kenwaso (Uni) from the Katsumotsos. Since then, they have been extremely successful at BSA, SCA and rare breed shows with Uni and her son, Ch. Fukuryu Beikokusekiryuso R.O.M. (Sumo). Sumo and the Kaufmann's Miya are a well-known "nick," in that they have produced several outstanding puppies.

Also in 1987, George Heath, an Army veterinary technician stationed in Japan, contacted Nancy Russell of Storm Kloud kennel about purchasing a Malamute when he returned home. Ms. Russell responded with a request that he look for two Shibas for her. With the aid of a Japanese veterinarian he was able to purchase a young male, Tetsuryu of Hikari Kaidaso (Shogun) and two bitch puppies, Midorihime of Igaguriso CD and Ch. Miyukihime of Iwakuniso. George had seen numerous pet and stray Shibas in his work at the base animal hospital and had been unimpressed. His visits to the Japanese breeder to arrange the purchase of the puppies gave George his first glimpse of a Nippo show-quality Shiba. He was so enamored with the dogs he saw that he decided against purchasing a Malamute and instead bought Shogun for himself. The two bitches were sent to Ms. Russell in Wisconsin, as promised. Shogun, now a Registry of Merit sire, made a name for himself as a stud and show dog in the Northwest before moving to Minnesota to become the foundation stud for Doug and Evelyn Behrens' Blue Loon kennel. He is the sire of Hansha's Remote Control, R.O.M. (R.C.), who sired numerous outstanding puppies for Foxtrot kennel. R.C. was bred by Bill and June Gilmore of Hansha kennel and was out of Kuma Mitsu of Aoyama Mahar (Kuma), the descendent of Shibas imported by Suki Mahar. Hansha kennel is also the home of a red import female, Hitachi Mikigo Hitachi Hakuyuso.

The late 1980s saw the formation of several more Shiba kennels. Laura Perkinson (Taichung kennel) met her first Shibas at a match in Washington state in 1986. Having already formed contacts with dog lovers in Japan through her Chows, she felt confident she could acquire quality foundation stock directly from that country. Ms. Perkinson has made several trips to Japan, returning with Shibas from the prestigious Fussaen and Fujinomiya Kensha lines, including the lovely Ch. Homaretennome of Gishi Fujiso (Willow) and Shoguniemitsu of Gishifujiso (Casey), who is now owned by the Gilmores.

Nick Marinos of Texas has been a Shiba breeder since the early 1980s and owns the import Musashi no Takamaru Showmakoto Kensha. Another Southerner, AKC judge and German Shepherd breeder Fred Lanting of Alabama, owns the red import male BEEF of Willow Wood. BEEF is possibly the most titled Shiba in America. His titles include International Champion, Champion of the Americas, Puerto Rico, Bahamas, South America, States Kennel Club, and Mexico. Mr. Lanting is a leading proponent of Orthopedic Foundation for Animals (OFA) certification of Shibas and has had the opportunity to observe Shiba classes while judging JKC shows in Japan.

Chip Miller acquired his first Shiba in 1989 and has been an influential supporter of the Colonial Shiba Club show, with several major wins there. His Blue Mountain kennel foundation stock was acquired in part from Foxtrot, Reno-Sakura (a Chibi-Summer daughter), Blue Loon, and Taichung (a Willow son).

Gretchen and Tim Haskett of Foxfire Shibas (Kitsunebiso) have three imports. Mai of Kasaokaryuohso is a black-and-tan bitch who was given to Ms. Haskett by a Japanese breeder, Mr. Morimine, when she traveled to Japan in 1991. In 1992, Mr. Morimine sent a pair of red Shibas to Foxfire: Ch. Heki no Ken of Daini Hekihoso (Kenny), a group placer, and Ch. Azusakikuhime of Matsunaga Ono Kensha (Suzi), a daughter of the 1989 Nippo National Show Best of Breed

Combined SCA/SKC National Specialty (1991) BOB BEEF of Willow Wood with owner Fred Lanting (right) and BOS Homaretennome of Gishifujiso with owner Laura Perkinson (left), both Japanese imports.

Camille Wong and Ch. Matsukiyome of Nidai Maneiso CD go High In Trial at the first NSCA National obedience trial in 1995 with a score of 192.5. C. Parker.

Shiba. Kenny and Suzi produced the group-placing littermates Ch. Kori Bushi of Kitsunebiso (owned by Pat Doescher) and Ch. Kure No Hikari Kitsunebiso (owned by Yori Green).

In 1989, Leslie Ann Engen and her mother, Marianne Nixon, established the San Jo kennel. The easy care, hardiness, and size of the Shiba appealed to Ms. Engen, who was looking for a second breed that would be easier to maintain than Lhasa Apsos, with which she had experienced considerable success. Her original Shiba stock was from Jacquet, and her male, Ch. Jacquet Baron, won a Best in Show from JKC judge Dr. Hideaki Nakazawa at the Hudson Valley Rare Breed Club in June 1990. Her foundation bitch, Ch. Jacquet Thu Ru Hime, was Best of Breed at the National Shiba Club of America (NSCA) National Specialty in June 1990.

Since the early 1990s, Frank Sakayeda has been importing outstanding Shibas from the Nidai Maneiso kennel in Japan. American, Mexican, Japanese, and International Ch. Toyojiro of Nidai Maneiso (Toki) was imported in 1992 at the age of two years, and is co-owned with veteran Akita breeders Carol Parker and Camille Wong. His accomplishments include Best in Specialty Show at the first NSCA National Specialty after AKC recognition, an all-breed AKC Best in Show over 2,500 dogs, and the #1 breed ranking for 1993 and 1994, all systems. Carol Parker, Camille Wong, and Bill Bobrow own four bitches imported by Mr. Sakayeda, including a Toki daughter bred in Japan, Ch. Matsukiyome of Nidai Maneiso CD (Kiku), who was the high scoring Shiba in obedience at the first AKC-recognized NSCA obedience trial. Two of these bitches have already produced champion offspring. Frank Sakayeda and Sharon Lundberg are the co-owners of the import bitch "Happy."

Laura Payton's Fanfair Farms is the home of five Shibas (four males and one female) imported by Frank Sakayeda. All are AKC champions. Four, including Ch. Koryu of Nidai Maneiso, R.O.M. (Guru), the #2 Shiba in 1994, were bred by Nidai Maneiso kennel, and the fifth is Ch. Kotobuki No

MACH2 Kirinji Kashushibaso CD, ADCH, EAC, EGC, EJC, ADC, U-AG1.
Kiri was recognized by AKC as the MACH Shiba of the Year for 2001 and 2002.
Kiri is also the 2001 USDAA Grand Prix Veteran National Champion for the 12" height category.

Kuroichi of Tosa Otaniso. "Kogen," a litter brother of Guru, went to Tanasea kennel. Mr. Sakayeda imported a red male, Ch. Genta Go Gold Typhoon (Cutter), and a black-and-tan bitch, Ch. Kurokomame of Gold Typhoon, for San Jo Shibas (also the breeder of group and specialty winner Ch. San Jo Wise Guy (Guy), a Toki son). Another outstanding male import from Nidai Maneiso is group winner Ch. Kotoyomaru of Nidai Maneiso (Stimpy), owned by Lillian Kletter and Alice Sakayeda. Mr. Sakayeda has also imported three bitches for his own kennel. Needless to say, he has made a great contribution to the breed. Most recently, he has imported two males who are co-owned with Leslie Engen. Sho Go Gold Typhoon finished in three shows, including BOW at the 1996 National Specialty, and earned a Group I in his first show as a special. As this book goes to print, Ms. Engen is awaiting the arrival of Tetsuyuki of Sanuki Mizumotoso, an 18-month-old red male.

Many American Shiba fanciers have invested time and money in importing high-quality stock from Japan, and the import trend seems to be increasing. This demonstrates that the breed is in good hands with people who care about preserving the wonderful qualities that made us all fall in love with the Shiba.

NATIONAL SPECIALTY SHOWS

1981	SCA	BOB-Kuroyuki of Nanko Suzuki Kensha
		BOS-Benitakehime of Dairy Farm
1982	SCA	BOB-Kuroyuki of Nanko Suzuki Kensha
		BOS-Ogon no Yukihime of Ogon Taiyoso
1983	SCA	BOB-Seitenhime of Aunso
		BOS-Kuroyuki of Nanko Suzuki Kensha
1984	SCA	BOB-Taro of Satoriso
		BOS-not recorded
1986	BSA/SCA	BOB-Fujio of Sagami Ikeda Kensha
		BOS-Ayame Kenwaso
1987	BSA/SCA	BOB-Aya of Fussaen
		BOS-Beniwashi Kenwaso
	NSCA	BOB-Kinouk's Airwolf
		BOS-Uchida's Mayumi

1988	BSA/SCA	BOB-Nobumitsu Komiya Watanabeso
		BOS-Benizakura Beikokusoenso
	NSCA	BOB-Taka Justa Bold N Brassy
		BOS-CRT's B's Kogyukuhime
	SKC	BOB-Kodomo of Aoyama Mahar
		BOS-Kuma Mitsu of Aoyama Mahar
1989	BSA/SCA	BOB-Jyo Kenwaso
		BOS-Hidemi Tomonso
	NSCA	BOB-Daichi of Toyonaka Okamotoso
		BOS-Graham Uchida's Mischief Maker
	SKC	BOB-Foxtrot Sizzling Sin-Sation
		BOS-Kinouk's Airwolf
1990	BSA/SCA	BOB-Fukuhime Kenwaso
		BOS-Fukuryu Daitaso
	NSCA	BOB-Jacquet's Thu Ru Hime
		BOS-not recorded
	SKC	BOB-Foxtrot Chip of Chaz
		BOS-Fukuhime Kenwaso
1991	SCA/SKC	BOB-BEEF of Willow Wood
		BOS-Homaretennome of Gishi Fujiso
	BSA	BOB-Akanehime Kashu Yamanakaso
		BOS-Fukuryu Beikokusekiryuso
	NSCA	BOB-Jacquet's Baron
		BOS-Taketomi of Chita Mochizukiso
1992	SCA	BOB-Fukuryu Beikokusekiryuso
		BOS-Blue Mountain's Schnookey
	BSA	BOB-Fukuryu Beikokusekiryuso
		BOS-Katsura no Miyahime of Izumi no Motoso
	NSCA	BOB-Kinouk's Road Warrior Tanasea
		BOS-Homaretennome of Gishi Fujiso
1993	SCA	BOB-Yukii Beniko of Sparrows
		BOS-Kurofuko Hitachi Kubonso
	BSA	BOB-Fujou no Yuuki Fujouso (Windcastle's Free Spirit)
		BOS-Shiokaze no Takame Kanagawa Shiokazeso
	NSCA*	BOB-Toyojiro of Nidai Maneiso
		BOS-San Jo's Carrot Top
1994	Classic	BOB-Jacquet Ryuo
		BOS-Blue Mountain's Yasashii

denotes 1st AKC Sanctioned National Specialty

AMERICAN KENNEL CLUB STANDARD FOR THE SHIBA INU

GENERAL APPEARANCE

The Shiba is the smallest of the Japanese native breeds of dog and was originally developed for hunting by sight and scent in the dense undergrowth of Japan's mountainous areas. Alert and agile with keen senses, he is also an excellent watchdog and companion. His frame is compact with well-developed muscles. Males and females are distinctly different in appearance: males are masculine without coarseness, females are feminine without weakness of structure.

SIZE, PROPORTION, SUBSTANCE

Males, 14½ to 16½ inches at withers. Females, 13½ to 15½ inches. The preferred size is the middle of the range for each sex. Average weight at preferred size is approximately 23 pounds for males, 17 pounds for females. Males have a height to length ratio of 10 to 11, females slightly longer. Bone is moderate. *Disqualification*—Males over 16½ and under 14½ inches. Females over 15½ and under 13½ inches.

HEAD

Expression is good natured with a strong and confident gaze. *Eyes* are somewhat triangular in shape, deep set, and upward slanting toward the outside base of the ear. Iris is dark brown. Eye rims are black. *Ears* are triangular in shape, firmly pricked and small, but in proportion to head and body size. Ears are set well apart and tilt directly forward with the slant of the back of the ear following the arch of the neck. *Skull* size is moderate and in proportion to the body. *Forehead* is broad and flat with a slight furrow. *Stop* is moderate. *Muzzle* is firm, full, and round with a stronger lower jaw projecting from full *cheeks*. The bridge of the muzzle is straight. Muzzle tapers slightly from stop to nose tip. Muzzle length is 40% of the total head length from occiput to nose tip. It is preferred that whiskers remain intact. *Lips* are tight and black. *Nose* is black. *Bite* is scissors, with a full complement of strong, substantial, evenly aligned teeth. *Serious Fault*—Five or more missing teeth is a very serious fault and must be penalized. *Disqualification*—Overshot or undershot bite.

NECK, TOPLINE, AND BODY

Neck is thick, sturdy, and of moderate length. *Topline* is straight and level to the base of the tail. *Body* is dry and well muscled without the appearance of sluggishness or coarseness. Forechest is well developed. Chest depth measured from the withers to the lowest point of the sternum is one-half or slightly less than the total height from withers to ground. *Ribs* are moderately sprung. Abdomen is firm and well tucked-up. *Back* is firm. *Loins* are strong. *Tail* is thick and powerful and is carried over the back in a sickle or curled position. A loose single curl or a sickle tail pointing vigorously toward the neck and nearly parallel to the back is preferred. A double curl or sickle tail pointing upward is acceptable. In length the tail reaches nearly to the hock joint when extended. Tail is set high.

FOREQUARTERS

Shoulder blade and upper arm are moderately angulated and approximately equal in length. Elbows are set close to the body and turn neither in nor out. Forelegs and feet are moderately spaced, straight, and parallel. Pasterns are slightly inclined. Removal of front dewclaws is optional. Feet are catlike with well-arched toes fitting tightly together. Pads are thick.

HINDQUARTERS

The angulation of the hindquarters is moderate and in balance with the angulation of the forequarters. Hind legs are strong with a wide natural stance. The hock joint is strong, turning neither in nor out. Upper thighs are long and the second thighs short but well developed. No dewclaws. Feet as in forequarters.

COAT

Double coated, with the outer coat being stiff and straight and the undercoat soft and thick. Fur is short and even on face, ears, and legs. Guard hairs stand off the body and are about 1½ to 2 inches in length at the withers. Tail hair is slightly longer and stands open in a brush. It is preferred that the Shiba be presented in a natural state. *Trimming of the coat must be severely penalized. Serious Fault*—Long or woolly coat.

COLOR

Coat color is as specified herein, with the three allowed colors given equal consideration. All colors are clear and intense. The undercoat is cream, buff, or gray.

Urajiro (cream to white ventral color) is required in the following areas on all coat colors: on the sides of the muzzle, on the cheeks, inside the ears, on the underjaw and upper throat, inside of legs, on the abdomen, around the vent and the ventral side of the tail. On *reds*: commonly on the throat, forechest, and chest. On *blacks and sesames*: commonly as a triangular mark on both sides of the forechest. White spots above the eyes permitted on all colors but not required.

Bright orange-red with urajiro lending a foxlike appearance to dogs of this color. Clear red preferred but a very slight dash of black tipping is permitted on the back and tail.

Black with tan points and urajiro. Black hairs have a brownish cast, not blue. The undercoat is buff or gray. The borderline between black and tan areas is clearly defined. Tan points are located as follows: two oval spots over the eyes; on the sides of the muzzle between the black bridge of the muzzle and the white cheeks; on the outside of the forelegs from the carpus, or a little above, downward to the toes; on the outside of the hind legs down the front of the stifle broadening from hock joint to toes, but not completely eliminating black from rear of pasterns. Black penciling on toes permitted. Tan hairs may also be found on the inside of the ear and on the underside of the tail.

Sesame (black-tipped hairs on a rich red background) with urajiro. Tipping is light and even on the body and head with no concentration of black in any area. Sesame areas appear at least one-half red. Sesame may end in a widow's peak on the forehead, leaving the bridge and sides of the muzzle red. Eye spots and lower legs are also red. Clearly delineated white markings are permitted but not required on the tip of the tail and in the form of socks on the forelegs to the elbow joint, hind legs to the knee joint. A patch or blaze is permitted on the throat, forechest, or chest in addition to urajiro.

Serious Fault—Cream, white, pinto, or any other color or marking not specified is a very serious fault and must be penalized.

GAIT

Movement is nimble, light, and elastic. At the trot, the legs angle in towards a center line while the topline remains level and firm. Forward reach and rear extension are moderate and efficient. In the show ring, the Shiba is gaited on a loose lead at a brisk trot.

TEMPERAMENT

A spirited boldness, a good nature, and an unaffected forthrightness, which together yield dignity and natural beauty. The Shiba has an independent nature and can be reserved toward strangers but is loyal and affectionate to those who earn his respect. At times aggressive toward other dogs, the Shiba is always under the control of his handler. Any aggression toward handler or judge or any overt shyness must be severely penalized.

SUMMARY

The foregoing is a description of the ideal Shiba. Any deviation from the above standard is to be considered a fault and must be penalized. The severity of the fault is equal to the extent of the deviation. A harmonious balance of form, color, movement, and temperament is more critical than any one feature.

DISQUALIFICATIONS

Males over 16½ and under 14½ inches. Females over 15½ and under 13½ inches. Overshot or undershot bite.

Approved by NSCA November 1995 and AKC February 1997.

Malin Skjervik with an arm full of puppies by Int. Ch. Glendalin Burande and out of Int. Ch. Erai Imoto Av Enerhaugen. The litter was bred by Christen Lang of Norway.

Selecting a Shiba in the United States or Japan

ONCE YOU'VE DECIDED THAT A SHIBA is the dog for you, it's time to do some homework. Perhaps you have already met a reputable local breeder from whom you can obtain a puppy. Shibas are still relatively rare in the United States, but there are always plenty of pups available for sale as family pets and show prospects. If you are looking for a breeder, your first step should be to contact one of the Shiba breed clubs. These clubs are listed in the chapter "Other Sources of Information" in this book. The breed clubs should have available a list of Shiba breeders who subscribe to the club code of ethics. Another source of information is a breed magazine such as *The Shiba Journal*, which has many full-page photo ads from breeders with listings of their Shibas' accomplishments.

Of course, Shibas are also available through pet stores, but investigative reporters in the print and broadcast media have brought to light the fact that many pet store dogs are purchased through puppy mills. Often these puppy mill dogs are of poor health, questionable background and inferior quality, and are sold at highly inflated prices. The price of a pet store Shiba puppy in many cities is currently higher than the price a breeder will ask for a top-quality, show-potential puppy with veterinarian-certified, champion parents.

Make a list of questions to ask the breeder, including the following:
- Will the litter be registered with the American Kennel Club (AKC), the United Kennel Club (UKC), the Japan Kennel Club (JKC), or the Nihon Ken Hozonkai (Nippo)?
- Have the parents' eyes been tested for inherited diseases and given a CERF (Canine Eye Registration Foundation) number?
- What shots will the puppy be given?
- Does the breeder offer a contract with a health guarantee?

If possible, take a look the puppies. Do they appear healthy, active, and outgoing, with eyes and noses free of discharge? Are you able to see the pup's mother? Is she also healthy? (Be aware that mama will have lost her coat and will not be looking her best.) Does the owner of the litter also own the father or have a photo available for you to view? Are the premises clean? If satisfactory answers to these questions are not forthcoming, do not purchase your Shiba puppy from this breeder.

It is purely a matter of your own personal preference whether to select a male or female puppy for a pet. Some breeders feel that their females are more aggressive, while others are sure the males are feistier. Whichever sex you choose, do not take a puppy home with you before he has reached eight weeks of age. A younger puppy has not developed mentally or physically to the point where he can safely leave its mother and litter mates. Do not be surprised if the breeder asks you to sign a spay/neuter contract when you purchase your puppy. (Veterinarians now recommend that both male and female pets be altered to prevent accidental breedings and to lengthen the lives of the individual animals.)

Although Shibas in general are healthier than many more familiar breeds, they do have a few hereditary problems for which an informed buyer should be on the lookout. Unfortunately, hip dysplasia (HD) is a common problem. It is a bit too early to get a reliable average percentage figure for HD incidence in the Shiba, but we know that the number is high; perhaps as many as 30 percent are affected to some degree. Because of their small frames, most Shibas with HD generally will not suffer the crippling effects that plague larger breeds. However, the fact that HD is not always obvious in Shibas makes it imperative that all breeding stock be tested and receive a number from the Orthopedic Foundation for Animals

(OFA). Under no circumstances should you purchase a puppy unless both parents have received an OFA certificate with a non-dysplastic rating. When dogs are under two years of age, OFA issues a certificate with a temporary rating but no OFA number; when the dog reaches two years of age, the owner can have the dog x-rayed again and receive a certificate with a permanent rating and a number.

Among Shibas, patellar luxation is also a common problem, in which the kneecap on one or both of the rear legs is not firmly anchored. The condition is graded with four levels of severity. In the least severe grade, the kneecap will not move out of position unless force is applied. In the most severe manifestation, the kneecap will not remain in the correct position. Dogs with mild or moderate patellar luxation in one knee typically can run and play, but they may misstep with the affected leg or hold it off the ground while moving. The more severe grades can cause serious impairment in the dog's gait. Patellar luxation can be detected by your veterinarian and treated with surgery.

Occasionally a breeder will have a puppy or young dog that has developed either HD or patellar luxation to a degree that he should not be bred but will still make a healthy, happy companion. Families looking for a pet might be able to purchase one of these Shibas at a reduced price, and they will be getting one that is probably more beautiful than the average puppy because it was originally chosen as a show prospect. Breeders are always happy to find a good family for these dogs rather than euthanize them or keep them in a kennel run where they would not receive the attention typically given to show dogs.

As with any puppy or dog you purchase, take him to your veterinarian for a checkup within the first few days of purchase to make sure you are getting a healthy pet that will remain with your family for years to come. A reputable breeder will give you a health certificate signed by his or her veterinarian stating that the pup is in good health; that the stifles, heart, and bite have been checked for abnormalities; and that the puppy is of sound temperament.

Think carefully about the temperament you are looking for in your Shiba. The sweet little lapdog that is ideal for one family may not have the show attitude to win in the ring, and the gentle nonaggressive male may not have the gumption it takes to serve as a stud dog to bossy Shiba lady visitors. Similarly, the alpha male that performs so wonderfully at dog shows may be a nightmare for the novice to handle at home.

SELECTING A SHOW PUPPY

Selecting a show puppy is a very difficult task. In reality you are selecting a puppy with show potential. So many factors go into the making of a good show dog that it is impossible to determine a sure-fire winner at eight-to-ten weeks of age. At eight weeks of age a show-potential Shiba puppy will be very agile and possess surprisingly good coordination. Although still a baby, the puppy should be able to trot briskly towards you when called and stop foursquare with an alert look when tempted with a bit of food. Look first for soundness, coordination, and alertness.

Type (the physical characteristics and attitude that distinguish the Shiba from other breeds) is somewhat more difficult to select for. Look for a broad skull (especially in males) with small ears slanting forward and set farther apart than in other dog breeds. Dropped ears (ears that are folded over to some extent rather than completely erect) could develop into ears that are too long in the adult and should be very carefully evaluated. In general, the Shibas with the best ears never have dropped ears as puppies, although some puppies with dropped ears can grow into adults with ears within the acceptable range. It is also possible to end up with ears that are too small for a large head.

Missing teeth are a serious problem in the Shiba, and too many missing teeth can reduce the chances that your dog will be successful in the show ring or desirable as a stud. It is impossible to know how many adult teeth an eight-week-old puppy will be missing, but check to make sure the puppy has a good scissors bite and all of his puppy teeth. Be warned that a puppy with full dentition will not always have full dentition as an adult and that a good bite can go bad. Ask the owner of the litter how many teeth each parent is missing and find out about the grandparents as well, if possible. It is best not to purchase a puppy for show if either parent is missing more than four teeth. Of course the ideal is to find a puppy with parents having full dentition. If you are looking for a show prospect, you may wish to ask the breeder for a guarantee of dentition. (No more than four missing teeth would be a reasonable request.)

Most Shibas settle down as they mature, but one busy young Shiba can sometimes seem like ten dogs.
C. Ross.

The Shiba's clean habits and ability to make himself at home in small places make him an excellent companion for the road.
P. Doescher.

Check for a good tail length. A short tail is a fault in the Shiba. When the dog is full grown, the tail should reach almost to the hock joint. Shiba puppies generally curl their tails between six and twelve weeks of age, so at eight weeks it can be difficult to determine what the adult tail will look like. A double-curled tail is cute, but a single curl (making one circle) or a sickle is more correct.

Show-potential puppies should have very dark brown, slightly triangular-shaped slanted eyes. Puppies with very round or "bug eyes" should be sold as pets. Eye rims, lips, nose, paw pads, and anus should be black. Nails should be black also, except in the case of Shibas with white paws.

Red and red sesame puppies at eight weeks are generally a bronze color with black hairs on their faces and bodies, although a few red Shibas are born without any black at all. If you look carefully at the skull of a puppy you may be able to guess at the adult color by the slight tinge of red you see there. Experienced breeders will use this method to predict the depth and shade of red. A too-heavy black overlay on red sesames is a fault in Shiba coat color. More than 50 percent black hairs or a black saddle pattern on a puppy is too much.

Black-and-tan puppies will be nearly solid black at birth with only a few tan hairs on the legs and the muzzle, but by eight weeks the tan and white markings should be well defined. Look for a rich, deep red in the tan areas on the legs and sides of the muzzle. In addition to the black-and-tan base color, there should be white trim in the form of a bow-tie on the chest, a white face bib, and perhaps some white socks and the required underbody shading. It is important that there be a black strip down the bridge of the nose with tan on the sides of the muzzle between the black strip and the white bib. It is equally important that there be tan on the legs between the black upper arms and any white socks. A pure black Shiba or a black-and-white Shiba with no tan markings is not proper.

Watch for white hairs on the top of the muzzle on red and red sesames, and tan or white hairs in the same place on black-and-tan puppies. These hairs could be a sign that as adults the faded tan or white color will spread to cover the bridge of the nose and the Shiba will become mismarked. As a rule Shibas lighten with age, so evaluating depth and richness of color is a big part of selecting a show-potential pup.

Say cheese! This handsome fellow is owned by Kim Carlson. Studio II.

Both red and black-and-tan Shibas are often born with black muzzles. This black mask should completely fade by the age of eighteen months at the very latest. It is impossible to judge whether the mask will fade properly by looking at the puppy. This is best predicted by asking to see the parents and older relations in the family line.

Height is also a very important consideration in choosing a Shiba that you intend to show. The ideal height for the Shiba is in the middle of the allowed range—neither too tall nor too short. If possible, ask the breeder for the measurements of the parents and grandparents.

As you can see, there are no guarantees that the puppy you purchase will grow to be a "top ten" Shiba. The best advice for purchasing a show prospect of any breed is to study the standard and talk to as many breeders as you can before you make your choice. Serious breeders should consider purchasing older dogs so that dentition, type, color, and soundness will not be a gamble. Remember that no dog is perfect!

Top breeders will often require a deposit of $50 to $100 toward the purchase of a show prospect. This deposit will put you on a list of potential new owners for the best puppies in a particular litter. The average Shiba litter is only three or four pups, so it is not unusual to wait awhile, especially if you specify male or female or a particular color. You may wish to ask how many champions the breeder has produced. If the answer seems high, you can bet that you will have to work hard to convince the breeder that you deserve the pick of the litter. Some breeders require a puppy back, stud rights, or co-ownerships as part of the sale. Before entering into a co-ownership make sure you have a good business relationship with the breeder and complete understanding of a contract that spells out every conceivable eventuality.

REGISTRATION

A registration certificate serves no purpose for a pet owner other than to ensure that the breeder and stud owner have signed a litter registration application stating that the litter is the product of two specific AKC-registered purebred dogs. However, if you want to show your Shiba, proper registration is essential. If you wish to show your dog in AKC conformation events, you must have an AKC registration number. *Not all U.S.-born Shibas are AKC registered.* Many members of the BSA choose to register only with Nippo.

If your puppy is AKC registrable, your breeder will provide you with a blue AKC registration application. You must fill in the puppy's name and send the form along with the required fee to the American Kennel Club. The address of the AKC is listed on the form if you have any questions. Shibas without registration papers may still compete in non-conformation events if they have an Indefinite Listing Privilege (ILP) number. ILP applications are available from the American Kennel Club.

The two choices for registering Shibas in Japan are Nippo and JKC. Nippo is the primary registering and showing body for Shibas in Japan. However, many Americans are more comfortable registering with the JKC, since its registration process is very similar to AKC and the forms are partially in English. The JKC has the added attraction of being a member of the Fédération Cynologique Internationale (FCI), the primary international dog-registration body, so the registrations of these dogs are easily transferred to FCI-affiliated countries around the world.

A Nippo registration will enable your Shiba to participate in the prestigious Beikoku Shibainu Aikokai (BSA) Specialty, held in California with a top Nippo judge and bronze Shiba trophies flown in from Japan. Many Shiba breeders maintain their Nippo registrations so they can continue to participate in this yearly event. You will need the aid of someone with knowledge of the Japanese language to fill out the Nippo forms. At the time of this writing the BSA has members available to help newcomers with Nippo registrations. Nippo members receive a stylish membership pin and a subscription to its magazine, which contains photos of the best Japanese Shibas in the world. The Nippo registration certificates are made of handcrafted blue rice paper and are beautiful and suitable for framing. A Nippo registration certificate means that your Shiba is part of the world's oldest and largest Shiba registry.

The Colonial Shiba Club holds a show in the Northeast each year with a judge from Nippo. Shibas are not required to be Nippo registered to participate in this show, and it is a wonderful opportunity for those who do not have Nippo registration to have their dog evaluated by one of the most knowledgable Shiba judges in the world.

IMPORTING A SHIBA

Good Shibas imported from Japan can do much for an individual breeding program, and they are having a major influence on the development of the breed in America. Of course, without our original imports we would have no breed at all, since every Shiba currently in America is descended from imports. But looking beyond this obvious factor, what can we say about the quality of the import stock that has formed the breed in America? Now that we have a fair number of Shibas in the United States, is it really necessary for us to keep importing, and, if so, what problems does that bring up? Where can we go from here?

The original Shiba imports were a mixed bag of high-quality stock and, inevitably, pet-quality stock

A matched pair of Shibas from Norway.
C. Lang.

that should not have been in any breeding program. This was the case because most people knew very little about type in the early days of the breed in the United States. Available source material on the breed was in Japanese, and there were few pictures to guide the new Shiba fanciers.

As time went on, more and more information about the breed was translated and made available to Americans. Shiba fanciers developed more contacts in Japan. The consistency and quality of imports began to improve, and in recent years, a higher percentage of imports have been of respectable quality. The total number of imports and their descendants that have been used in American breeding programs is very difficult to assess, since a fair number of imports were not registered with the American Kennel Club. It would be a good guess that so far there have been perhaps two hundred imports into this country from Japan that have been used for breeding.

The offspring of some of the original imports have been phased out of most breeding programs, while offspring of others are being widely bred. Some of the more recent imports will leave an

important mark on the breed, while others will fall by the wayside.

One of the major reasons why some of the first American Shiba fanciers were opposed to AKC breed recognition was that before 1992 the AKC did not recognize any Japanese registry. This would have meant that imports from Japan would have been cut off after the AKC took over the breed registry. Fortunately, that obstacle was removed when the AKC recognized the JKC's registry. But JKC recognition has not completely solved the problems brought by AKC recognition for those who want to import Shibas, since most high-quality Shibas are not registered by the JKC but by Nippo. Fortunately, importers of Nippo-registered Shibas can apply for and receive the JKC export pedigree required for AKC recognition.

There is another danger in AKC recognition that is more subtle. As the number of American-bred Shibas increases, people may come to feel that imports are no longer needed. New people will be coming into the breed, and until they have a chance to learn about the breed, they may not be able to see the ways in which Japanese stock can be used to improve type in this country. If imports from Japan become less frequent in the future, two big problems may arise:

1. The quality of Shibas imported to the United States has, in some cases, been less than desirable. Because some pet-quality imports were used in breeding and because of the inevitable lack of detailed knowledge of proper type in this new breed, the American Shiba today is lacking in overall consistency when compared to Shibas found in Nippo conformation events. Recently, some tremendous strides have been made in quality; more high-quality imports are becoming available for breeding, and more breeders are coming to understand breed type. But, this improvement is a slow process and will take years to complete. So far, we have not even been able to utilize truly top-winning Japanese stock because this stock is simply not available for export. In the future it may be possible to use frozen semen from top stud dogs in Japan, but this option is not currently approved by Nippo.

2. The genetic consequences of fewer imports could be disastrous. Some imports have been widely used for breeding, while others have barely been used at all. Successful lines tend to become more widely used, resulting in concentrated bloodlines and increased inbreeding. Since all U.S. Shibas are descended from imports, the imports used in our breeding programs represent the sum total of genetic material available to our breed. If this genetic material gets too concentrated or too limited, we can run into problems. For example, a widely used stud dog that is a carrier of progressive retinal atrophy (PRA), a common eye disease that often leads to blindness, may spread the defective gene throughout an entire population before it can be determined that the problem originated with him. Unfortunately, the carrier state of PRA in the Shiba cannot be detected by any test.

In general terms, it is better to retain as much genetic variability as possible for the maximum health of a breed. If imports are reduced, the wealth of genetic variability present in the Japanese Shiba population will be lost to us, and we will be limited to what was present in our original number of imports.

AKC recognition of the Shiba is bringing about many changes in the breed. Shiba fanciers should not allow the emphasis on import stock from Japan to be downplayed. We have a long way to go to achieve the best possible Shiba, and the fastest way to get there is to continue to import the finest stock we can from the breed's native country.

The Importing Process

Virtually every Shiba fancier has a dream of importing his or her own Shiba from Japan. The reason for this is very simple—Japan has the highest quality and greatest number of Shibas of any country in the world. There is no quicker way to establish a high-quality breeding line or to improve existing stock than by bringing in high-quality Shibas from Japan. Their quality is so superior that using them in breeding almost invariably leads to a dramatic improvement in the type of Shibas produced.

Barriers to Importing

So why aren't we flooded with imported Shibas, and what is standing in the way of all those people who would like to own an import? If you want to import a Shiba, what problems should you expect? There seem to be three main areas of concern:

1. The cost of high-quality adult Japanese Shibas is higher than what we are accustomed to paying for show stock in this country. It is almost impossible to buy a Nippo winner, because their owners typically don't want to part with them, and even if one were for sale, the cost could range from $30,000 to $100,000! Very few JKC champions have been imported, and to this date no American has been able to both afford and arrange the purchase of a Merit Award winner from a Nippo National—although several now reside in Taiwan. Top Nippo Shibas currently enjoy the same celebrity and investment status as national champion Arabian horses have in America. Therefore, most people who import bring in puppies or young dogs rather than proven adult Shibas, because these dogs are more affordable. (Males are usually available in better quality than females.) Good quality puppy and young adult Shibas have been purchased in the price range of $1,000 to $20,000 and these dogs and their offspring have proven quite competitive in U.S. shows.

Top show quality puppies are rarely available but occasionally can be purchased for around $8,000 or more. As soon as the adult teeth come in the price will rise rapidly for a show quality dog with full dentition and a few wins at local and regional shows to its credit. Prices can be significantly lower outside of the greater Tokyo area. Of course, economic conditions and exchange rates make the cost of a Japanese Shiba quite variable in terms of American dollars. You may hear stories of people purchasing quality Shibas in Japan for very low prices, but don't take these stories too seriously. Although a few quality Shibas have been sold to Americans for low prices, these sales were really more in the nature of gifts to Americans from Japanese breeders who were friends or who just have a desire to see the breed successfully established in America. Most cheap imports were inexpensive because they were pet-quality dogs.

2. The language barrier is quite an obstacle to building up the Shiba stock in America because so few Americans speak Japanese. Most younger Japanese have studied English in school but aren't able to speak it any more fluently than you are able to speak the language you may have learned in high school. If you don't speak Japanese and you want to import a Shiba, you will need to find someone who does speak the language and who has contacts in Japan to serve as an intermediary. Selecting your intermediary can be the most critical part of the whole importing process, since your intermediary will probably determine which kennels in Japan you are to contact.

3. Cultural differences between Japan and the United States can cause problems when importing. In Japan, business tends to be done more on the basis of personal contacts, goodwill, and trust, rather than by the written contract we are familiar with in the United States. Insisting on a contract with health guarantees, breeder and buyer stipulations, and so on, is not common practice in Japan and might be seen as insulting by a Japanese breeder.

Procedures

Let's say that you are aware of the challenges of importing a good Shiba, but you have thought long and hard about it and have decided that you want the best for your breeding program and are willing

Although they are not natural retrievers, Shibas can be trained to enjoy a game of fetch. G. Haskett.

to do what is necessary to get it. What is the best way to proceed? First, you must familiarize yourself totally with proper Japanese type, which may be very different from what you are used to seeing in the show rings in your area. Study the Nippo Standard and commentaries and all the pictures you can find of top-winning Japanese Shibas. Some of the American breeders who are breeding to the Japanese standard can be helpful here. *The Shiba Journal* features photos of Nippo National Merit Award winners, and the judges' comments about each dog. You can familiarize yourself with successful kennels by reading these results.

When you feel confident in your ability to evaluate a Shiba, begin to look at the ones that other people have imported. It is better to see the Shibas in person than in pictures because a skilled photographer can make a mediocre dog look good, whereas a great dog may not be photogenic. Also, in person you will be able to evaluate the dog's temperament and movement—both very important aspects of the Shiba. Different Japanese lines have different characteristics and you should try to familiarize yourself with their strengths and weaknesses.

The best sources for finding people who have imported Shibas are ads in the breed magazine, ads in general interest dog publications, and breeder referral lists furnished by the Shiba breed clubs. These sources will give you the names of Shiba breeders to contact about any imported stock they may possess. Ads in the breed magazine may be particularly useful, because they generally show a picture of the dog and state whether or not it is an import.

When you have found some breeders who have imported Shibas you believe to be of high quality, talk to them and ask for their advice and help in importing your own Shiba. Good breeders who have the welfare of the breed at heart will be happy to give you all the assistance they can, and with any luck you will be able to find your intermediary this way. Remember that just because someone says they can import a Shiba for you, you are not guaranteed a good dog. There are pet-quality Shibas in Japan just as there are in the United States, so it is best to work with someone who has a proven track record of importing show-quality Shibas, preferably one or more that you've seen with your own eyes.

The least expensive method of shipping a Shiba is to visit Japan and to bring it home as excess baggage. Tickets for people are usually discounted in the fall, which is a very convenient time to travel if you plan to make a trip to the Nippo National show. You will be asked to declare your Shiba to customs on your return just as you would declare any other item purchased or received as a gift in a foreign country. Many Shibas have been brought to the United States by Japanese judges and students or by friends returning from business trips. Having a Shiba shipped directly from Japan is far more expensive and will probably require the services of a customs broker to navigate your dog through the paperwork. Japan requires that dogs receive a rabies shot not less than thirty days prior to leaving the country. Very young puppies under three months are excluded from this regulation. Japan is a rabies-free country, so rabies shots are not generally given to pets. This makes it extremely difficult to simply visit Japan, purchase a dog, and return home with it. You will need a signed certificate or letter from a Japanese vet stating that the dog has received the vaccination. Verify current regulations with the Japanese consulate in the nearest city *before* leaving on your trip!

A few puppies imported to the United States have died of parvovirus or distemper shortly after their arrival. It is not known if these puppies were vaccinated at all in Japan or if the vaccination they were given was not constructed to resist U.S. strains. Perhaps the stress of the trip contributed to their deaths. At present, most importers will not guarantee the health of your puppy, just as you will generally not receive a guarantee of hips, eyes, or dentition. Purchasing a healthy older dog with full dentition is fairly safe, but unless you have a good relationship with the Japanese breeder, it will be difficult to receive a hip rating before you make your purchase. Japan does not have an independent organization equivalent to the OFA in the United States to rely on for the evaluation of radiographs. A hip radiograph could be taken in Japan and mailed to the OFA for evaluation. Be warned that this request is likely to be taken as an insult if the breeder is not familiar with using hip radiographs to determine hip dysplasia. Most Japanese breeders rely on heavy exercise and roadwork to determine the presence of hip and knee abnormalities.

If you visit Japan yourself, there are three sources from whom to purchase Shibas. The first is through a private breeder. However, unless you have done some homework or have an intermediary, it is extremely unlikely that you will be invited to the home of a private breeder on a short trip to Japan. A second way to buy a Shiba is from one of several dog centers that specialize in the breeding and sale of Japanese native dogs. Most of these store owners participate actively in dog shows, and most puppies available are sired by winners. Unfortunately, it is unlikely that you will be able to purchase anything other than a pet-quality puppy without establishing a relationship prior to your trip, and some of these places do not have a much better reputation than the usual pet store or puppy mill. The third place to buy a Shiba is a pet store. There are puppy mills and breeders in Japan that provide animals to these stores in much the same way as do their counterparts in the United States. As with pet shops in the United States, it is highly unlikely that you will find a suitable puppy in these places. Human nature is the same everywhere in the world, and you will find both reputable and disreputable breeders in Japan. Be sure you make it very clear to the beeder that you intend to breed and/or show your new import. Most Japanese breeders take great pride in their dogs, and the authors know of one breeder who was angered to hear that a dog he sold as a pet was bred and shown in America.

Before you bring your dog home, there is the important matter of registration to consider. AKC recognizes the JKC registry but does not directly recognize Nippo. JKC accepts Nippo pedigrees into its studbook and will also provide export pedigrees for Nippo-registered dogs. Nippo will issue temporary pedigrees to JKC-registered dogs, but three generations must be registered in this manner in order for a bloodline to be reinstated to full Nippo registration. Many JKC-registered Shibas are also registered with Nippo.

AKC requires that you submit a JKC pedigree or an export certificate listing the transfer date and your name as owner before they will consider registering your dog. The transfer date is vital, and AKC will not register the dog without it. If the dog you wish to import is registered with Nippo but not with JKC, submit the Nippo pedigree to JKC, along with JKC registration forms, to get a JKC pedigree certificate or an export certificate. To avoid disappointment, make sure that your intermediary is able to advise you on this crucial point. You should also call the AKC before you import your dog to determine exactly what the current requirements are. Don't rely on word-of-mouth or on what someone who imported their Shiba some time ago did. AKC regulations can change and you should be sure you have the latest information and forms.

All of this may sound discouragingly difficult, but keep in mind that many people have successfully imported beautiful Shibas from Japan. Although importing a Shiba is not as easy as buying an American-bred dog, it can be done. With persistence and a little homework you will see the day when you have your own treasure from Japan.

Austin and Kogata enjoy the July 4 parade in Deerfield, Illinois. G. Haskett.

The Ideal Shiba

A Commentary on the Japanese Standard for the Breed

INTRODUCTION

In this chapter, we present a detailed discussion of Shiba type, based on knowledge gathered from translations of the Nippo magazine and Japanese books (listed in the Bibliography) by experts on the Shiba. The Nippo Standard (see the chapter on Japanese History) is divided into numbered sections. We reprint each section of the Nippo Basic Standard, then discuss that section in depth, drawing on the Judging Resolutions and breed commentaries.

COMMENTARY ON THE STANDARD

Essence and Its Expression

The first section of the Japanese Dog Standard is titled "Essence and Its Expression" and is worth 15 percent of the total score in judging the Shiba. This is a higher percentage than that given to any other numbered section in the Standard. What is meant by "essence" is temperament, the entire personality and nature of the dog. How that dog shows its nature to the world is the expression.

The Nippo Basic Standard states:

"The dog has a spirited boldness with a good nature and a feeling of artlessness. It is alert and able to move quickly with nimble, elastic steps."

The Nippo Standard uses three words to describe the temperament of the Japanese dog: spirited boldness (kan-i), good nature (ryosei), and artlessness or unaffected forthrightness (soboku). These are the three mental characteristics that the Japanese dog must have.

What is *Kan-i*?

Kan-i is considered to be the most important characteristic of the Japanese dog. In his book *Nihon Ken Hyakka*, Mr. Hajime Watanabe states that *kan-i* is bravery and calmness, boldness and alertness, all tempered with obedience. In other words, the dog with *kan-i* is brave without being foolhardy, bold but alert to danger, and always under the control of the master. In the dog that has these characteristics, dignity and power will appear automatically.

To determine if a dog has *kan-i*, remember to look for the qualities of mental strength and strong purpose. In the show ring in Japan the dogs are faced off against one another in a similar fashion to terrier sparring in the United States. In a face-off, the dog that has *kan-i* will face its opponent and stare without turning away. Turning the eyes away from the opponent, showing the whites of the eyes, or looking at the opponent and then looking away shows a lack of *kan-i*.

The dog that has *kan-i* will normally hold its tail strongly in a curled or sickle position. A slight quiver of the tail due to strong emotion is to be expected, but if the tail drops between the legs, this shows a great lack of *kan-i*. Good *kan-i* means the dog will stand with its head held high, and there will be no breaking of the body pose (in the Japanese show ring the handler stands behind the dog and is not allowed to touch it). *Kan-i* shows a vigorous will combined with a calm demeanor. The dog that attacks an opponent for no reason, provokes a fight, or doesn't pay attention to its master may be a bold dog, but since it is not obedient, this behavior should not be mistaken for *kan-i*.

What is *Ryosei*?

The literal translation of *ryosei* is "good nature." The things that come from good nature are a gentle disposition, faithfulness, and obedience—all the qualities of a good watchdog and companion dog.

To be a good watchdog and companion and obedient to the wishes of its master, the dog must be intelligent; so, it is of the utmost importance that the Japanese dog be clever and have good habits and a tame nature. The dog with a good nature works quickly in response to commands. The complete submission to the master's will does not imply a cowardly temperament, though. For example, it may be necessary for the dog to respond to a command that requires fighting spirit and courage, in which case the dog must obey instantly and fearlessly.

This discussion of good nature shows that *kan-i* and *ryosei* are really yin and yang—two sides of the same coin. The Japanese dog with proper *kan-i* will have proper *ryosei*—one can't exist without the other.

What is *Soboku*?

The Japanese word *soboku* is defined as "naiveté, artlessness." Artlessness means without artifice; that is, sincere, genuine, and uncomplicated. It implies the charm of a simple, open spirit that is appealing because of its very nature and not because of any attempt to be so. According to Mr. Watanabe, "*soboku* is modesty and gentleness, with character and grace which must be shown spontaneously. Said another way, *soboku* means without pomp, without vulgarity; the word speaks of a simple appearance." *Soboku* is not mere physical beauty, but the combination of *kan-i*, *ryosei*, and *soboku* into a harmonious whole produces the natural beauty of the Japanese dog, and these three traits produce the essence that the Japanese dog must be endowed with.

The second sentence of section 1 of the Japanese Dog Standard states: "It [the dog] is alert and able to move quickly with nimble, elastic steps." The dog must be aware of what is going on around it at all times and so must have keen senses. Keen senses are a requisite for the Japanese dog because its very survival depends on them. For the hunting dog, which must fight bear, wild boar, or deer, without regard for its own life, these senses are its weapons and its only defense. For the watchdog, keen senses are a prerequisite to carrying out its duty.

A dog can be overly alert to the point of having a nervous temperament—getting excited over nothing and showing cowardice. The Japanese commentaries say that this is a most serious defect for a Japanese dog. The opposite of extreme alertness is dullness, stupidity, slowness, or lethargy. The ideal for the Japanese dog is the mean between

Fujihana of Shibainu Rensei Kai owned by Y.S. Chuang of Taiwan. 85th Nippo National 1st place Sokensho.

these two extremes. The dog that is properly alert is calm and steady, has reliable responses and is capable of immediate, decisive action—whether it be attack, defense, or warning.

In order to put the keen senses into practice, the Japanese dog must be "able to move quickly with nimble, elastic steps." Its agility is expressed by the saying that in the forest it should be able to be as still as the trees, then in an instant be able to move like a flash to catch its prey. All three gaits—walking, trotting, and running—should be smooth, although the small- and medium-size breeds have more of a spring in their step than the large Akita. This nimble gait depends on physical structure, but good structure alone is not enough. The body must be trained and conditioned to achieve the necessary flexibility and strength. Japanese breeders generally condition their show dogs by running them, with a commonly recommended distance being 20 kilometers (about 12.5 miles) most days. Showing a Shiba in Japan in "soft" condition would probably be a waste of time.

Proper mental qualities, keen senses, and agility combine to allow the Japanese dog to perform its work, whatever that work may be. All these things make up its temperament (i.e., "essence"), which is the single most important characteristic in the judging of the Shiba.

General Physical Characteristics

The Nippo Basic Standard states: *"Males and females are obviously distinct with proportioned bodies. The frame is compact with well-developed muscles. Males have a height to length ratio of 10 to 11; females, slightly longer. The height for males is 39.5 cm, for females 36.5 cm. A range of 1.5 cm taller or shorter is allowed."*

In saying that the male and female should be obviously distinct, the Standard is not referring to merely the external genitalia. In the correct Shiba, the male is masculine in its entire appearance, and the female is feminine in her entire appearance. A female Shiba that appears masculine, a male that appears feminine, or a dog of either sex that appears neutral in gender is not correct. The distinction between male and female is said to be an important characteristic of higher animals, and Mr. Watanabe notes that the more highly developed a species is on the scale of all animals, the more pronounced are the differences between the sexes. Therefore, the requirement that Shibas have distinct

sexual differentiation reflects the view that the dog is one of the most highly developed of animals.

In evaluating what the Japanese judges call the "gender signs," the first consideration is that the sex of the dog should be obvious at a glance. The features of the male Shiba should show a masculine dignity and nobility. The head, skull, and facial bones are wider, longer, and thicker than in the female. The forehead is flat and wide, the cheeks are very full (with a "pouched" look), the muzzle is thick and strong, and the eyes should have an expression of strength. In comparison to the male, the female's head is slighter and narrower, and the expression of the eyes shows delicacy. The features of the female should show gentleness.

In physical structure, there is a distinction in most species between what can be called the robust vitality of the male versus the feminine refinement of the female. In the case of the dog, the male physique should be brawny, with the muscles and tendons well developed. The bone of the female should be lighter and her body more delicate. Body height, weight, and volume also differ for the male and female, and on the whole, the ratio is as 110 to 100 (i.e., the male should be 10 percent larger in each of these measurements).

The second important item in the General Physical Characteristics section of the Standard is the very important question of ratio, or proportion. This has to do with the body parts fitting together into a harmonious whole. "Proportion" of build is mentioned in the Standard, and this is commonly known in English as balance. Balance is *harmony* and *equilibrium* in the dog's structure, and comes from the proper relation between all the parts of the dog's body—the head, neck, trunk, and four legs. The head itself must have balance between the forehead, muzzle, eyes, and ears.

Harmony means that all the parts of the dog's body blend together well. For example, long legs don't harmonize with a cobby body, and small ears are in disharmony with a large head. Harmony must apply to the whole dog, from the skeletal construction to the fine details of the body. Proper ratios of all the parts means that the dog can function efficiently. If the trunk is too short in relation to the height, the gait will be cramped.

Equilibrium means that the amount on one side of the scale equals the amount on the other side, so any difference of weight from left to right, top to bottom, or front to back harms the equilibrium of the dog. For example, if the head and shoulders of the dog are well developed and the rear quarters are thin, the dog does not have good equilibrium.

Rules have been developed for the Shiba to indicate the ideal ratios of the various parts of the body to one other. These rules are shown in Diagram 1, but it should be remembered that the dog's body is in three dimensions and is kinetic. The height of the Shiba is given in the Standard as 38-41 cm (14.96-16.14 inches) for the male and 35-38 cm (13.77-14.96 inches) for the female (note that American measurements, taken at the high point of the withers, will be somewhat higher because Nippo judges measure height just behind the point of the shoulder). In addition, the average weight of the Shiba should be 10 kg (22 lb.), with the male dog about 10 percent more, and the female about 10 percent less.

The angles of the dog's body should also be balanced. The correct angles are grounded on the basic principles of motion in the dog and give the greatest mechanical efficiency to the gait. In this respect, the angles of the four legs are the most important. Also to be considered are the angles in other parts of the body (such as the inclination of the ears and eyes), which will be discussed in the following sections.

To sum up, we can say that balance, which appears at first to be a simple topic, is really quite complex. Diagram 1 gives a framework for balance, but there are many other considerations (e.g., joint angles, muscle development, and facial expression) that are not covered in it. For example, a dog with a sullen or mean facial expression cannot be considered to have an expression that is in harmony with the rest of his parts. Why do we pay

---

DIAGRAM 6-1: THE PROPORTIONS OF THE JAPANESE DOG

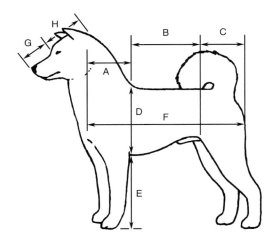

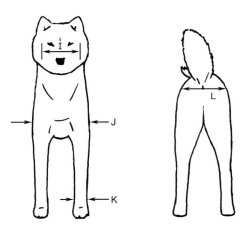

A: fore-body
B: mid-body
C: rear-body
D: chest depth
E: elbow to ground
E+D: height
F: body length
G: muzzle length
H: backskull length
G+H: head length
I: face width
J: chest width
K: pastern circumference
L: hip width

Ratios

If height = 100
    Length = 110
    Pastern circumference = 19-20
    Hip width = 28-30
    Chest depth = 45-50
    Chest circumference = 116-120
    Chest width = 36-38

If length = 100
    Fore = 28.5
    Mid = 43
    Rear = 28.5

If head length = 100
    Muzzle length = 40
    face width = 56-58

© M. Flynn

so much attention to balance? Balance is critical in allowing the dog to perform up to its capabilities. Correct balance produces the natural beauty of the Shiba because it is a functional breed.

The Ear

The Nippo Basic Standard states: *"Ears are the shape of a small triangle, leaning forward slightly and standing up firmly."*

The erect ears are one of the hallmarks of Shiba type, and their importance cannot be overemphasized. Along with the tail carried over the back, the ears serve to define the look of the Shiba, and a Shiba with drop ears can hardly be called a Shiba at all.

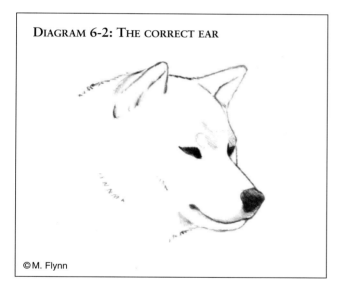

DIAGRAM 6-2: THE CORRECT EAR

©M. Flynn

Size

The easiest way to determine if the ears are the proper size is to judge whether or not they are in harmony with the head. An ear that is too large on one dog might be perfectly correct on another dog with a larger head. Since correct ear size is a matter of proper proportion with the head, no absolute measure for length and width of the ear can be given. You must study dogs that have proper ear size and use your own aesthetic sense. Generally speaking, ears that are too large are much more common than ears that are too small.

Shape—It is imperative for good ear type that the ears be triangular. In general, the proper triangle is an isosceles triangle (the two equal sides being the sides of the ear), because it gives an overall impression of balance and stability. Because the

ear extends down farther on the outer side of the head, these two sides will not actually be of identical length, but the appearance should be equal when viewed from the front. A vertical line down the center of the ear should bisect the ear into two approximately equal parts. If you draw an imaginary pair of parallel vertical lines tangent with the widest part of the face, the outer edges of the ears should not stick out beyond these lines.

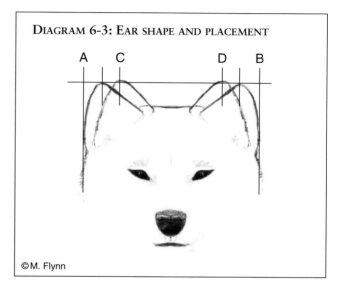

DIAGRAM 6-3: EAR SHAPE AND PLACEMENT

©M. Flynn

Common faults include ears that stick out to the side of the head, ears that lean in toward each other, a diamond-shaped ear that contains a dogleg curve at the base that sticks out to the side of the head (common with small ears), an ear tip that bends backward or flaps a little when the dog moves, a round ear that lacks a distinct point at the tip of the triangle, and an ear with a narrow base that distorts the triangle. An ear type that is not faulty unless carried to an extreme is the cupped ear. The opposite of this is the flat ear, where there is virtually no "pouch" inside the ear. An extremely flat ear is less desirable than an extremely cupped ear, but the average between the two is ideal.

Forward Tilt

The Standard says that the ears should lean forward slightly. When one looks at the dog from the side, the ear line should not be perfectly vertical to the ground, and there will be an angle between the line of the forward leaning ear and the vertical. Viewed from the side, the back line of the ear will

DIAGRAM 6-4: COMMON EAR FAULTS

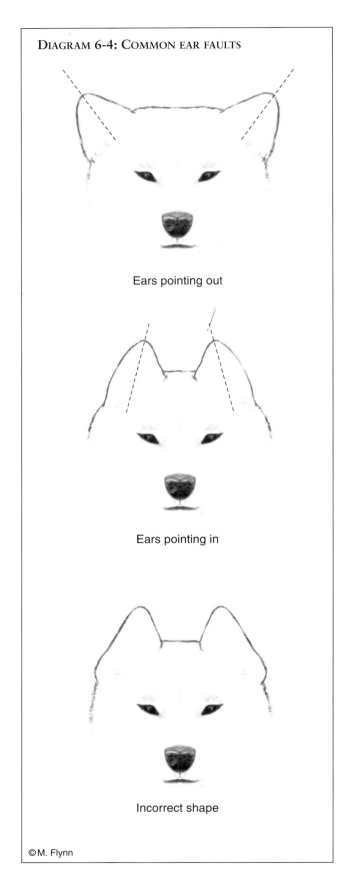

Ears pointing out

Ears pointing in

Incorrect shape

lean forward 30 degrees from a perpendicular line from the plane of the forehead or about 60 degrees from a plumb line to the ground. The front line of the ear will make a right angle (90 degrees) with the plane of the forehead. Of course, these angles cannot be measured exactly due to the slight roundness of the backskull and irregularities in the shape of the skull. An occasional Shiba will have too much forward inclination of the ears, but it is much more common to see dogs whose ears do not have enough forward inclination. Since the proper degree of forward inclination is so important in the appearance of the dog, it must be given serious consideration in the evaluation.

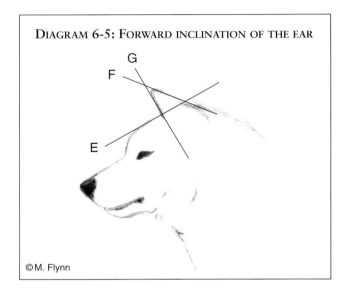

DIAGRAM 6-5: FORWARD INCLINATION OF THE EAR

Erect Carriage

"Standing up firmly" means that the ears should stand rigidly erect. When the dog moves, the ears should not sway or flap back and forth. The mental state of the dog can have a considerable effect on ear carriage. A dog that is relaxed may carry its ears more out to the side; some dogs have this tendency more than others. A fearful dog will flatten its ears, which is also a way of showing submission. The proper ear carriage for the Shiba reflects the idea that this breed should always demonstrate calmness and courage.

Other Factors—Two other factors that are not specifically mentioned in the basic Standard are attachment and thickness of the ears.

Viewed from the front, the ears must not be attached either too high on the skull or too low on the side of the head. If the ears are set too high, this leaves too small a gap between the ears and disturbs the harmony of the features. If the ears are set too low (too far toward the side of the head), the natural, rounded line of the skull between the ears is visible instead of being covered by the ears, and this gives an apple-headed appearance. The skull, viewed from the front, should appear level between the ears. Viewed from the side, the ears should not be attached either too far forward or too far back. If the ears are too far forward, the occiput (back of the skull) appears to jut out behind the ears, and the ideal smooth curve of the line from the ears to the neck is destroyed. If the ears are set too far back, this inevitably means ears that are too flat (not cupped enough).

There is a greater impression of thickness if the ears stand up strongly. The appearance of thickness is also influenced by the length and density of the fur on the ears. Occasionally, a dog will have a heavy growth or fringe of long hair inside the ears. This is called a *sasa* (bamboo grass) ear. A proper ear gives a feeling of harmony to the features because the isosceles triangle is a very stable shape. When the thickness of the ear is increased, it enhances this look of stability. Therefore, it is desirable that the ear be thick. Although thinness of the ears is a more serious fault, the ear is too thick if it gives an impression of stolidness. Once again, the ideal is between the two extremes.

The Eyes

The Nippo Basic Standard states: *"Eyes are somewhat triangular and slant upward toward the outside corner of the eye. The color of the iris is very dark brown."*

Shape

The shape of the eye is determined by the shape of the upper and lower eyelids; that is, the shape is the result of the opening created by the eyelids. In various emotional states, the shape of the eye opening changes with the movement of the eyelids. For example, if the dog is hunting and sees some game, his eyes may get very big and round as he watches. But in the normal, tranquil state of mind, the eyelids should present a somewhat triangular shape. The upper eyelid is a little longer than the lower lid due to its up-and-down movement over the eyeball. When open and when the dog is in a relaxed state, this upper eyelid has a distinct arch, and this is what gives it the "somewhat" triangular

shape. This arch is a little closer to the inside corner of the eye than the outer corner. So, if we view the three sides of the triangle as being made up of the two lines on either side of the arch (the upper eyelid) and the line formed by the lower eyelid, we can see that the triangle is not a perfect equilateral triangle but is somewhat extended on its outer side.

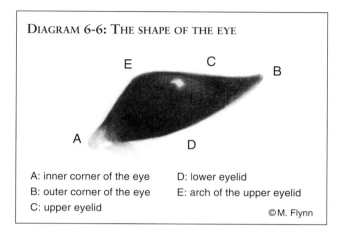

DIAGRAM 6-6: THE SHAPE OF THE EYE

A: inner corner of the eye   D: lower eyelid
B: outer corner of the eye   E: arch of the upper eyelid
C: upper eyelid

©M. Flynn

It is equally important for the shape of the eye to have the proper upward slant toward the outside corner of the eye. Too much of an upward slant produces a severe expression, while too little results in a soft appearance. To picture the proper angle of upward slant, imagine a straight line going from the inner corner of the eye to the outer corner of the eye, continuing until it touches the ear. If the line touches the side of the head at just about the lowest point of attachment of the ear's outer edge to the side of the head, this is the correct degree of upward slant of the eye.

Size

Small eyes are preferred in the Shiba. It is possible for the eyes to be too small, but this is unusual. It is far more common for the eyes to be too large. Because of the Shiba's small size, its eyes are relatively larger in proportion to head size than in the larger Japanese breeds. This is why the Shiba is especially prone to the fault of large, round eyes. Large eyes are somewhat round and protuberant, whereas small eyes seem to be set deeper into the head. This makes sense when you consider that dogs with large and small eyes probably have eyeballs that are of similar size; it is the size and arrangement of the forehead bones and the eye

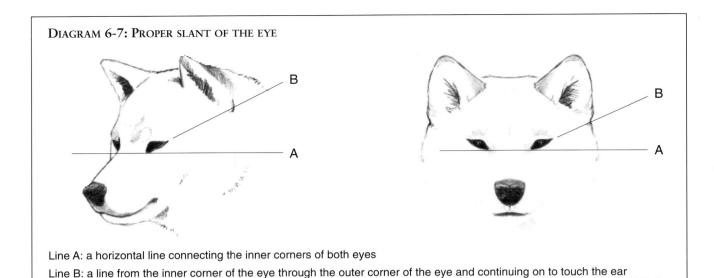

DIAGRAM 6-7: PROPER SLANT OF THE EYE

Line A: a horizontal line connecting the inner corners of both eyes
Line B: a line from the inner corner of the eye through the outer corner of the eye and continuing on to touch the ear

©M. Flynn

DIAGRAM 6-8: PROPER SLANT OF THE EYE FOR THE VARIOUS NATIVE JAPANESE BREEDS

Line A: for the Kishu, Shikoku, Kai and Hokkaido
Line B: for the Shiba
Line C: for the Akita

©M. Flynn

socket, and particularly the size of the opening formed by the eyelids, that determine the "size" of the eyes. The female's eyes often appear larger, due to the smallness and fineness of her bone structure. The most important point to remember in evaluating the size of the eyes (as with evaluating the size of the ears) is that they must harmonize with the rest of the head.

Position
Position of the eyes involves two factors: the distance between the eyes, and how deeply the eyes are set in their sockets. The proper distance between the eyes depends on the structure of the forehead, and varies with the breadth of the forehead. If the eyes are too far apart, the features seem to "fall apart," and the expression does not show the proper spirit of the Shiba. On the other hand, if the features are too close together, the expression has a harsh, wily look.

Being set into the eye socket at the proper depth is very important for the correct eye. If the eye socket is too shallow, the eyes protrude, and probably appear too round as well. This is commonly called a bulging eye. How do we distinguish eyes that are too deep set from eyes that are set too shallow? If the highest point of the round surface of the eyeball protrudes beyond the plane of the eye socket, then the eyes are protruding. If the highest point of the eyeball does not reach this plane, then the eyes are too deep set. Ideally, the highest point of the eyeball should be at the plane of the eye socket, but again, consideration in judging must also be given to the factors of expression discussed above. Other factors that can affect the appearance of deep-set or protruding eyes are the condition of the fur, the health and nutritional status of the dog, and the muscles of the face.

Color
Eye color is determined by the number of pigment granules (called melanin) that are present in the iris. These granules are always a brown color, but variations occur because of differences in their number and density. The ideal, very dark brown color (it has a hint of black) comes from pigment

granules that are numerous and densely arranged. When the granules are fewer, the color will be light brown or light yellow, and when the number and size are extremely small, gray or light blue eyes are produced.

The color of the iris is important not only for the aesthetic quality of the eyes but also for its impact on the proper expression of the dog. When the eyes are very dark brown and blend with the color of the pupil, they give the face a composed expression. On the other hand, when the eyes are a light color, the contrast with the black pupil gives a flighty, unreliable appearance, and the dog's eyes look unpleasantly like those of a bird of prey. There are four general levels of eye color that occur in the Shiba:

Very Dark Brown. With this ideal color, the iris and the pupil give an impression of one dark color. If you look closely, you will see that the iris is not quite identical in color to the pupil because the pupil is black and the iris is a very dark, rich, brown. But the colors of the pupil and the iris are similar enough that they appear to blend into one another and the appearance of one color tone is given.

Dark Brown. Eyes that are a little lighter than the ideal very dark brown color, but are nevertheless a dark brown color, are acceptable. If two dogs are the same in all respects except that one has very dark brown eyes and the other has dark brown eyes, the one with the darker eyes would win. However, the dog with merely dark brown eyes will not be penalized in ordinary judging. Eyes that are dark brown can be distinguished from eyes that are the ideal very dark brown because with merely dark brown eyes, the iris and the pupil do not appear to blend together in one color tone, but instead can be easily seen to be somewhat different colors.

Light-brown or yellowish. These colors are more lacking in pigment than the dark brown color, and are faults. The iris is light enough that it presents a clear-cut contrast with the black pupil of the eye (enough to give a bull's-eye pattern). If the iris is lighter than the pupil but not enough to be obviously different, and the eye has the basic brown color, then it is classed as acceptable brown.

Gray, light yellow, or light blue. These colors are major faults and are obviously undesirable in the extreme. Though very rare in the Shiba, they are seen occasionally.

Expression

The eyes can express emotion in the following ways: Joy is shown by narrowing of the eyes; rapture by shining eyes; surprise by round eyes; grief by tearful eyes; and anger by sharp eyes and bristling eyebrows. In humans, the eyes are as good as words for expressing emotions. In the dog, the eyes are also very expressive, and this is one reason why dogs make such good companions to humans. The expression in the eyes of a Japanese dog is expected to show the important characteristics of spirited boldness, composure, obedience, loyalty, and high intelligence. Conversely, poor temperament is reflected when a dog looks away, rolls the eyes so that the whites show, or looks restlessly from place to place. Such eye movements indicate that a dog is suspicious or servile.

The Muzzle

The Nippo Basic Standard states: "*Muzzle: The bridge of the nose is straight, the sides of the mouth firm, the nose hard, and the lips are tight.*"

Judging from the amount of space devoted to it in the Nippo Standard and Judge's Resolutions, the muzzle is very important. The muzzle consists of the nose, bridge of the nose, upper and lower jaw, lips, and oral cavity. It is defined as the area from

Azusaichihime of Sanuki Mizumotoso, owned by Morihito Ono. 86th Nippo National Bunka Chokansho.

the middle of the stop to the end of the nose. The length of the muzzle should be two-fifths of the total length of the head (40 percent of the total head length), with the total length measured from the tip of the occiput to the end of the nose.

It is specifically stated in the Nippo Standard that the bridge of the nose should be straight. In the Judging Resolutions, it is also specifically stated that "a bulge on the bridge of the nose is a fault." Any unevenness of the bridge of the nose, whether convex (a protuberance) or concave (a scooped-out appearance), is a serious fault.

The width and depth of the muzzle should be moderate. A long, thin, shallow muzzle is inappropriate because it is weak and lacks sufficient biting power, while a short, stumpy muzzle mars the appearance of the features. The width and depth of the muzzle, and the appearance of strength, are somewhat different in the male and the female in accordance with the principle that the male must be masculine and the female feminine.

The muzzle should taper somewhat from where the stop begins to the end of the nose. A muzzle that doesn't taper is called a "tube mouth" and is incorrect. This even, gradual, tapering gives the muzzle a wedge-shaped appearance. However, it should not taper so much that the end of the muzzle appears pointed. The end of the muzzle must have enough depth and breadth to maintain the appearance of strength. A muzzle that tapers enough to make the face look snipy or weak in any way is incorrect.

The muzzle should be firm, well-knit, and with tight lips. Dewlap in the Shiba is specifically mentioned in the Judging Resolutions as a fault and is considered very atypical of the Shiba. The pigment of the lips should be black, although this black color should be restricted to the lips themselves and not extend to the hair around them. The Judging Resolutions imply a contrast between the muzzle (firm) and the cheeks (full). The cheeks of the Shiba are properly very full, giving a pouched-out look. This fullness contrasts with the firm tightness of the lips and the muzzle in general, and as stipulated in the Judging Resolutions, the muzzle appears to jut out from the cheeks. The sides of the muzzle should be "thick, full, and round." In most dog breeds the sides of the muzzle are somewhat flat; looking at these dogs from the front reveals a somewhat rectangular shape to the muzzle, with the sides of the muzzle being the long sides of the

rectangle. In the Shiba, you should see a more circular shape, the rounded sides of the muzzle giving an impression of strength. The Shiba's nose is quite hard to the touch, and the pigment must be black.

The pigment of the tongue is also important, but the desired pigment is the reverse of what is wanted for the nose—the tongue should ideally be pink with no black spots. The Standard specifies that very small black spots (no bigger than a fingertip) are allowed on the tongue, but it also says that the allowable size of a spot depends on the size of the dog. This means that the smaller the dog, the smaller the allowable tongue spot. If the largest dog (the Akita) is allowed to have tongue spots no bigger than the size of a fingertip, then the smallest dog (the Shiba) would have to have very small tongue spots indeed to be acceptable!

There should be white markings on the sides of the muzzle and under the jaw. The fur on the bridge of the nose should be red in red and red-sesame dogs and black in black-and-tan dogs. The black-and-tan dog will have clearly defined tan markings between the black bridge of the nose and the white markings on the side of the muzzle. Red dogs should have no black hair on the muzzle, although the nose and lips should be black.

Under no circumstance should the white markings on the sides of the muzzle extend across the bridge of the nose. This fault usually occurs in conjunction with white which completely surrounds the eyes as well as covers the cheeks (the reverse mask).

A black mask and dewlap are two characteristics that Japanese breeders believe indicate cross-breeding, and when they appear it is a very bad sign. These characteristics are not thought to have been in the gene pool of the native Japanese dog. It should be noted that red and red-sesame Shibas often will be born with a black mask and occasionally will carry some black hair on the muzzle throughout puppyhood.

In summary, the following points are important regarding the muzzle: it evenly tapers into a wedge shape; it is firm and round; it is in the proper proportion to the head; the nose and teeth are correct; the lips are tight; the lip and nose pigment is black; and the muzzle is strong.

Teeth

The Nippo Basic Standard states: *"Teeth are strong with a scissors bite,"* and the Judging Resolutions establish limits for missing teeth. Three characteristics—strength, scissors bite, and correct number of teeth—are the essential requirements for the dentition of the Shiba. The Japanese word we have translated as "strong" also carries an implication of health.

Of the modern Japanese breeds, the four medium-sized breeds are said to have the best teeth, followed by the larger Akita. The small-sized Shiba is known for having the worst teeth—the main problem being a high number of missing teeth. Japanese experts cite the cause as the extensive inbreeding of Shibas that occurred after World War II.

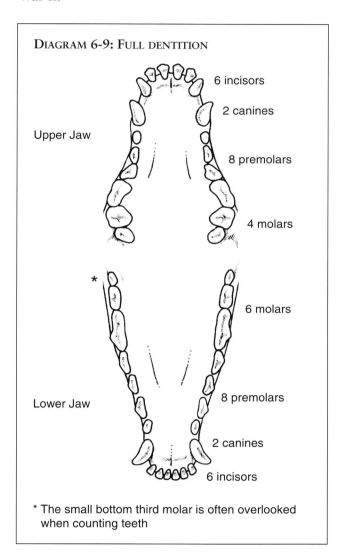

DIAGRAM 6-9: FULL DENTITION

6 incisors

2 canines

Upper Jaw

8 premolars

4 molars

*

6 molars

Lower Jaw

8 premolars

2 canines

6 incisors

* The small bottom third molar is often overlooked when counting teeth

The Nippo point system of minus marks for missing teeth in the Shiba has gradually been tightened up over the years as the dentition of Japanese

Shibas improved, and today in Nippo shows Shibas are no longer allowed to have any missing teeth. Shibas in America still have a problem with missing teeth, however, and Nippo judges who judge here have graciously agreed to use the Nippo point system that was in place from approximately 1985 to 1994, so that is the point system that we will discuss.

Missing teeth have the following deductions: First premolars—one minus mark for each tooth. Second premolars—three minus marks for each tooth. Any missing teeth other than first or second premolars—five minus marks for each tooth. The point system is based on the relative importance of the teeth in question. The first premolars are very small and, even when present, are not very helpful to the dog whereas the canines and the carnassial teeth are extremely important. In Nippo shows before 1994, a Shiba could win an "excellent" rating with up to two minus marks (one or two missing first premolars), and a "very good" rating with up to four minus marks (up to four missing first premolars or one missing first and one second premolar). A Shiba with more than four minus marks could not win an award.

Acquired missing teeth (teeth that the dog once had but lost) are penalized the same as congenitally missing teeth. One reason for tooth loss is poor structural quality of the enamel. Since strong enamel and bone are both formed from a proper balance of calcium and phosphorus, poor tooth structure is generally associated with poor body structure. Poor tooth quality can mean brittle enamel, resulting in cracks in the teeth from everyday wear and tear which eventually leads to tooth loss. Weak teeth decay very early in the dog's life. Discolored teeth, which can result from distemper or poor diet, are also more easily worn down and broken than normal teeth.

The normal bite of the Japanese dog is described as the inside edge of each incisor of the upper jaw just covering the outside of each incisor of the lower jaw, in a scissors appearance. The canine teeth of the lower jaw are in front of the canine teeth of the upper jaw, and the premolars and molars must engage correctly. This type of bite gives the most biting power and the least wear on the teeth.

The irregular or abnormal bites are overshot, undershot, and level. Bad bites usually have nothing to do with the teeth themselves but result from

Scissors bite: Top incisors just overlap bottom

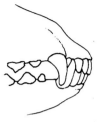

Overshot bite: A gap between incisors due to face too long or jaw too short

Undershot bite: A gap between incisors due to face too short or jaw too long

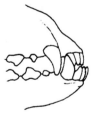

Even bite: Incisors meet level or even

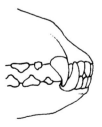

DIAGRAM 6-10: CANINE OCCLUSION

incorrect jaw structure. The undershot bite (also called reverse bite or scoop teeth) is caused by underdevelopment of the upper jaw—as in the short-faced breeds—and this is the most common irregular bite in the Shiba. The undershot bite is undesirable not only because it is deficient in biting power but also because it gives the face a sullen, ugly expression.

The overshot bite is generally due to poor development of the lower jaw. At first glance it may appear to be a normal bite, but the falling away of the lower jaw gives a weak appearance as well as a weak bite.

The third type of abnormal bite, the level bite, occurs when the incisors meet at the tips instead of overlapping. This puts remarkable stress on the teeth, resulting in much quicker wear than normal.

The incisors should be in a neat row. Sometimes the incisors may be turned a little to one side or the other, or they may be pushed forward or toward the back of the mouth. This disorder is sometimes called crowded mouth because it can result from insufficient room in the jaw, and it is common in some of the undershot breeds. It occurs frequently in the Shiba due to the small size of the mouth.

Under the Nippo Standard several years ago, a slightly overshot or undershot bite was allowable, whereas markedly overshot or undershot was disqualified. Now, the Nippo Standard states that "noticeably" overshot or undershot is a disqualification, which presumably means any degree of overshot or undershot that can be noticed, no matter how small that amount may be.

The Head

The Nippo Basic Standard states: *"Head: The forehead is wide, the cheeks well-developed, and the neck sturdy."*

The head is an extremely important part of the type of the Japanese dog. It is important not just in the general appearance and structure of the dog but also for two more specific reasons. First, the expression of the face is critical in determining if the dog has proper temperament (i.e., the "spirited boldness, good nature, and artlessness" mentioned in the Standard and discussed earlier). Second, the structure of the head determines to a great extent if the dog has the proper gender signs.

In evaluating the head, there are two general considerations:

1. The easily quantifiable, structural items (e.g., length, width, and shape)
2. The more subjective items (e.g., features, character, and expression)

Structure

The structure of the head is derived from the bones of the head, which consist of the cranium (forming the back part of the head and containing the brain) and the facial bones (including the bones of the bridge of the nose and the jawbones with their movable joint). The back of the skull has a prominent bump called the *occiput* that can be felt between the ears; this marks the end of the skull, and it is the point from which the length of the skull and the total head length are measured. The bones of the head give the basis for the quantities that we can measure, such as the length and width of the head, the cheeks, the stop, and the muzzle.

The total length of the head is made up of the combined length of the muzzle and the backskull. The length of the backskull is measured from the tip of the occiput to the middle of the stop, while the length of the muzzle is measured from the middle of the stop down to the end of the nose. The ratio of the two parts is very important, with the backskull and muzzle making up 60 and 40 percent respectively. An imaginary line drawn between the two inner corners of the eyes can be used to indicate the middle of the stop.

The width of the head is determined by the spread of the cheekbones. The Shiba has very full cheeks, and this can give the impression that the head itself is wider than it actually is. These full cheeks not only make the head appear wider than

in other breeds of dogs, but also give the head an impression of ruggedness.

Although no specifics are given regarding forehead width, the Standard does say that the forehead should be broad. It is rare to see a Shiba that has too broad a forehead. A narrow forehead can result from a narrow bone structure; or, regardless of the actual skull width, from ears that are too close together. A narrow forehead gives a cramped appearance to the face and greatly mars the dignity of the expression.

In addition to the width of the forehead, the following points should be considered. First, the forehead must be flat. Viewed from either the front or the side, there should not be a noticeable bulge in the forehead. A rounded forehead produces an apple-shape head, which is a common fault among Shibas. Second, while there should be no wrinkle on the head of the Japanese dog, there may be a shallow groove down the center of the forehead, ending in the stop. This groove may be scarcely visible, depending on the coat, and should never be a deep groove in any case.

The full cheeks of the Shiba—like the ridge of the Rhodesian Ridgeback or the tulip ear of the Collie—are a special characteristic of the breed, as are spirited boldness of temperament and erect ears. Therefore, full cheeks are very important. Words like plump, very round, and pouched-out are used to describe the cheeks. The tight, tapering muzzle contrasts with the very full cheeks, and it is this contrast that gives the face much of its characteristic expression. From the front, the Shiba resembles a badger because of the wide cheeks and tapering muzzle.

DIAGRAM 6-11: THE HEAD AND MUZZLE

A: Forehead is broad and flat. A rounded "apple head" is incorrect.

B: Cheeks are full.

C: The stop is neither shallow nor deep. It is moderate.

D: The bridge of the nose is straight, not convex or concave.

E: The nose is black.

F: Both the upper and lower lips are black, tight, and make a straight line.

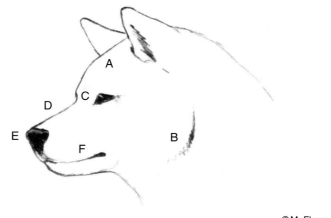

©M. Flynn

Chisato of Sanuki Mizumotso, owned by Yasuke Doi. 92nd Nippo National Naikaku Sori Daijinsho.

DIAGRAM 6-12: THE HEAD IN PROFILE

This face is too flat. The line of the forehead (A) and the line of the muzzle (B) are too close together.

This face is too steep. The lines of the forehead and the muzzle are too far apart, while the line of inclination of the stop is too steep.

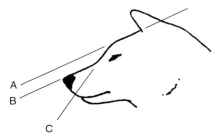

This shows the correct profile, with the proper stop.

The stop is the dividing line between the muzzle and the backskull. Because it marks the transition from the broad forehead and the full cheeks to the contrasting tight, tapering muzzle, the stop should be clear-cut. This does not mean it should be abrupt. In the area between the inner corners of the eyes there will be a gentle downward curve. This curve must be clear, but it must be gentle: in other words, a moderate stop. A particularly shallow stop is singled out in the Nippo judging resolutions as a fault, but an excessively deep stop is also undesirable.

Features and Expression

The Japanese native dog has proper expression when there is harmony in its features. All the items discussed so far—the eyes, ears, muzzle, backskull, stop, lips, and nose—together form the appearance of the face, and if any one of them is out of proportion or out of harmony with the rest, the result will be a coarse or unpleasant expression. With something such as facial appearance, which evokes a subjective reaction, we must consider the overall impression that is produced, as well as the individual parts.

According to Japanese breed experts, wrinkles on the forehead seriously mar the overall expression of the face. Wrinkles are commonly figure-8, V-shaped, or parallel lines. If the groove in the center of the forehead is too deep, it is considered a wrinkle and therefore faulty.

In expression as in structure, the distinction between male and female must be readily apparent. The expression of the male should convey rugged boldness, while the expression of the female may be softer and more refined. The dog expresses its feelings with its entire body, but as with people, it is in the face that the emotions are most clearly seen. Eye and ear movements and vocalizations such as barking and whining can show alertness, fear, happiness, anger, and many other emotions. For this reason, the facial appearance is crucial in evaluating the Shiba for proper temperament.

In conclusion, the head is a very important part of the Shiba and should have great weight in the judging of the breed. In judging head type, the maturity of the dog must be considered. It is a big mistake to judge the younger dogs—in which the process of development is not complete—by the standard of head type expected of the fully mature dogs.

The Neck

The neck should be somewhat thick in circumference. The neck is biggest at the point where it connects to the shoulders, then gradually tapers as it rises up to the head. The hair grows thicker on the neck than on other parts of the dog's body and is denser on the sides and back of the neck, so one should try to part the hair to get an idea of the true thickness of the neck.

When a dog is standing at attention, it naturally holds its head high. In this stance, the line of the back of the neck forms a 50-degree angle, approximately, with the line of the back. The line of the ears' forward inclination carries through the line made by the neck in a smooth curve, seemingly without a break in the outline as seen from the side. When a dog stands naturally like this in the show ring, with the head up and the profile of the neck and the ears forming one smooth line, it a very good pose.

When the Shiba walks and trots, the head is carried somewhat lower than when standing at attention, but when the dog is sprinting as fast as it can go, the neck is extended almost parallel to the ground. This extension of the neck while the dog is running is necessary to move the center of gravity forward. When the body weight is mostly on the forelegs, the rear legs are able to move more freely and propel the body faster.

The neck also supports the head and gives strength to its movements, such as biting and carrying prey. This is why the Standard says the neck must be sturdy, and this strength is reflected in the thickness of the neck. In a dog with a proper, sturdy neck, the transition from the neck to the shoulder is not noticeable. Dogs that show a definite line where the neck ends and the shoulder begins are usually slender with thin necks.

There is no definite measure for correct neck length because correct length depends on the thickness of the neck for any given dog. A thin neck gives the impression of too much length whether or not it is actually very long, whereas a very thick neck may give the appearance of shortness. Therefore, the ideal length of the neck cannot be reduced to a mathematical quantity. The Shiba appears to have a somewhat shorter neck than the medium-sized Japanese native breeds. Japanese commentaries on the Shiba attribute the Shiba's short neck to the type of hunting it does. This may be a reference to the type of cover in which the Shiba usually hunts (low, thick brush and forest), or it may reflect the fact that Japanese dogs are expected to be sturdy enough to subdue game that is considerably larger than they are (for example, there are reports of Shibas holding bears at bay).

The skin of the neck should appear closely attached to the underlying muscle. When the skin of the neck is slack, it gives the impression that the dog is old or out of shape. Slack skin in the neck of some dogs, particularly on the underside of the neck, can cause wrinkles in the throat or a droop in the line of the throat. This not only looks bad but also is a sign that the dog may not be of pure blood. Hanging skin on the neck is completely atypical of the Shiba.

The Forelegs and Hind Legs

The Nippo Basic Standard states: *Forelegs: The shoulder blade has moderate angulation and is well-developed. Forearms are straight with paws well knuckled-up. Hind legs: Hind legs are strong with a wide natural stance. The hock joint is strong and the paws well knuckled-up.*

In general, the legs serve to support the body and provide mobility. The forelegs and hind legs perform these functions differently. The forelegs support approximately 60 percent of the weight of the dog's body, and the hind legs support about 40 percent; therefore, the forelegs should be thicker than the hind legs in order to bear this extra weight, and the circumference of the hind foot should be about three-fourths that of the front foot.

The fact that the forelegs carry more weight means that they will not move as freely or be as flexible as the hind legs when the dog is in motion. The hind legs propel the body forward and are said to start the movement, while the forelegs complete the movement. In starting movement, the hind legs stretch and grasp the ground, then dig in, raise up, and transmit forward motion to the back. This forward motion of the back creates stress on the shoulder joint, which is relieved by the forelegs carrying through the forward motion.

Because the forelegs and hind legs work together to move the body properly, a balance between them is very important. This harmony is shown in three ways:

1. The angulation of the forelegs must be appropriate for the hind legs. For example, while a dog that is overangulated in both front and rear will not move very well, he will move better than a dog that is overangulated in the rear and too straight in the front.
2. The legs must have harmonious length and muscle development. For example, if the hind legs are too long compared to the forelegs, or if the hind leg muscles are strongly developed while the front legs are weak, movement cannot be good.
3. If the legs harmonize well, the dog will naturally assume a four-square pose when it stops.

The Standard states that the shoulder blade should have moderate angulation (the ideal is 105 to 110 degrees, which corresponds to a layback of about 30 degrees). The angle in question is formed by the shoulder blade (the scapula) and the upper arm (the humerus). The upper arm is connected to the foreleg by the elbow joint; therefore, the upper arm must adhere closely to the trunk. If it does not, the dog will be out at the elbows, which is a common fault in the Shiba. Elbows that are too close to the body and appear to be squeezed in are also occasionally seen but are a much rarer fault.

DIAGRAM 6-13: LEG JOINT ANGLES
FOREARM JOINT ANGLES / REAR LEG JOINT

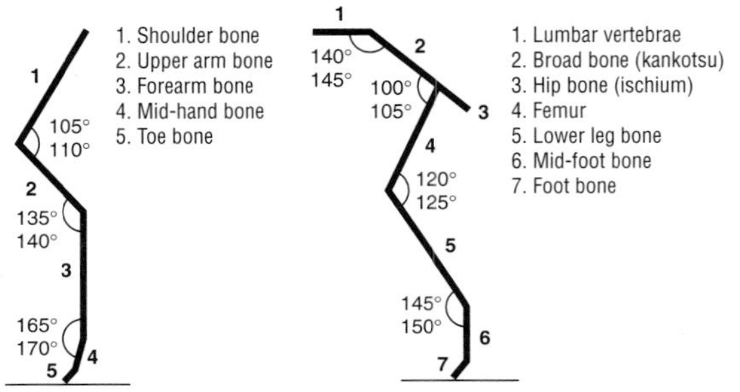

1. Shoulder bone
2. Upper arm bone
3. Forearm bone
4. Mid-hand bone
5. Toe bone

1. Lumbar vertebrae
2. Broad bone (kankotsu)
3. Hip bone (ischium)
4. Femur
5. Lower leg bone
6. Mid-foot bone
7. Foot bone

Note: Modern cineradiology indicates that the angle between 1 and 2 is closer to 150° and that between 5 and 6 is more likely to be 143°. See text.

©M. Flynn

Viewed from the front, the forelegs must form a straight line from the shoulders to the ground, and they must be parallel. Since the leg should be neither out nor in at the elbows, the outer line formed by the leg will be continued by the outer line formed by the chest. Thus, looking at the dog from the front, we should see an H shape, with the "cross" of the H being the underside of the dog's chest.

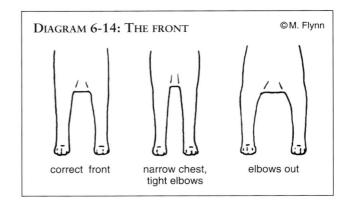

DIAGRAM 6-14: THE FRONT

©M. Flynn

correct front   narrow chest,   elbows out
                   tight elbows

The pastern should be neither long nor short, but moderate in length. The ideal Shiba has a slight forward slant of the pastern, so that (when viewed from the side) the pastern connects to the foot slightly forward of where it connects to the foreleg. The angle of the pastern should be 10 to 15 degrees. Pasterns that are too short are generally too steep and don't have the desirable spring and flexibility, while pasterns that are too long generally have too much angle and are weak. A common fault in the Shiba is a long, weak pastern that turns out.

The feet should have highly arched toes, giving a moderate thickness to the feet and pads. The toes should not have any gaps between them. If the toes are separated or too long, this gives the foot the appearance of a hare foot rather than the desired cat foot. The hare foot makes the gait unattractive and is undesirable in the Shiba.

The toenails should be short and hard. If the feet and toes are correctly formed, the toenails make direct contact with the ground. This moderate degree of wear and tear tends to keep the nails short and helps with traction. With longer, looser toes, the nails do not contact the ground as well and grow longer from the lack of abrasion. Toenail color generally should be black, but if the area above the toenail is white (as with white socks), then the toenail may be translucent.

Since the hind legs are responsible for the driving power that starts the dog's motion, they must be strong and very flexible. The Japanese term used in the Nippo Basic Standard to describe the rear legs of the Shiba is *chikarazuyoi fumbari*. It is one of the compressed terms common in the Nippo Standard that has several nuances and is not easily translated. The word *chikarazuyoi* means forcible, forceful, and vigorous and presents no great problem of interpretation, but the word it modifies has a somewhat more ambiguous meaning. *Fumbari*, a form of the verb *fumbaru*, means "to brace one's legs, straddle, stand firm, keep one's feet" (*Kenkyusha*). Another, less authoritative dictionary defines the term as "to hold out, hold fast." The image this phrase conveys is of hind legs that are strong enough to grip the ground in a very powerful stance. In this context, the word "straddle" implies that the hind legs should not be close together in the natural stance of the dog, nor should they be excessively wide. Indeed, the ideal stance as shown in Nippo diagrams shows the legs to be parallel when viewed from the rear.

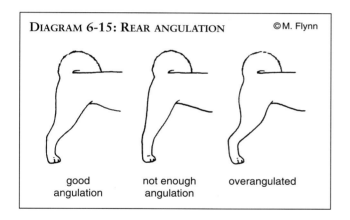

DIAGRAM 6-15: REAR ANGULATION ©M. Flynn

good angulation   not enough angulation   overangulated

One of the important elements that contributes to a strong, natural stance is the flexibility of the hind legs. The hind legs get their greater flexibility from to the croup bone, which is analogous to the shoulder blade of the front assembly. The joint of the croup and the femur is the all-important hip joint, which takes so much wear and tear in the movement of the dog and must be properly constructed. This rotating joint gives the rear legs their extra flexibility. The Shiba Standard specifically states that any weakness or malformation of this important joint is a fault.

The next joint down from the hip joint is the knee joint—the connection of the femur and the lower leg bones. This joint (tibia and fibula) is especially critical in the Shiba, since the breed is very susceptible to patellar luxation.

The hock is actually the connection of the lower leg to the foot (what we commonly refer to as the foot of a dog is really only the toes), and is analogous to the pasterns of the front feet. The hock is particularly important to a strong stance and to powerful driving movement. There should be no loose skin in the hock area and very little fat. In examining the hock, we should see the bone and tendons covered tightly by the skin, giving it a very tough, sound appearance. The feet and nails should follow the description for the front feet.

Viewed from the rear, the legs are parallel, and the width of the stance matches the width of the hips. Some common faults are the narrow stance, the O-shaped stance with legs bowed out, and the X-shaped stance (cow hocks).

Sketches of canine skeletons that appear in older breed books and illustrated Standards such as Nippo's were often based on the artist viewing

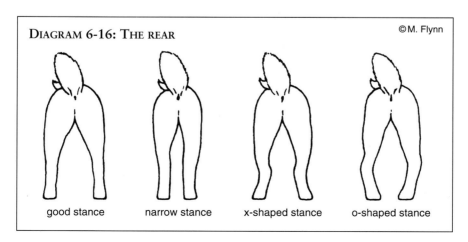

DIAGRAM 6-16: THE REAR ©M. Flynn

good stance   narrow stance   x-shaped stance   o-shaped stance

an x-ray where the dog is positioned on its side on a table or drawn from skeletons that were inaccurately pieced together. The joint angles pictured in Diagram 13 show a femur that slopes more severely than would occur in a standing dog, which throws off the rest of the leg angles. Today dogs are x-rayed standing or moving to provide more accurate information. In 1990 Fred Lanting x-rayed his moderately-angulated OFA Excellent Shiba. His findings were that the shoulder sloped about 30 degrees and the stifle/hock angulation was approximately 143 degrees (in a standing dog the femur and metatarsus are nearly parallel).

The Torso

The Nippo Basic Standard states: *"The chest is deep, with ribs moderately sprung. The forechest is well-developed. The topline is straight, the loin well tucked-up."*

The chest is a very important part of the dog; indeed, it can be seen as the center of its whole body. The chest has a great influence on the appearance of the body, especially as it affects the outline of the body and contrasts with the contour into the tucked-up abdomen. A broad, powerful chest also gives an impression of confident strength.

The chest is made up of two distinct regions. First is the forechest, which is the area bounded by the lower edge of the neck, the sternum, and a plumb line from the shoulder tip. The second region is the thorax or chest wall, which is the area from the shoulder tip back to the loin and contains the ribs.

The width of the forechest is determined by measuring the distance between the left and right shoulder joints. The shoulder joint is located between the shoulder blade and the upper foreleg and is the widest part of the chest (it is distinguished from the shoulder tip, which is the top of the shoulder blade and is the highest point on the back). The structure and especially width of the forechest are very important in determining if the dog will have proper structure and movement in the forelegs.

If the forechest is not correct, then the shoulder blade and upper arm will not be correct, and the dog will not have proper gait. In particular, the reach of the front legs will not be correct. Also, it will not be possible for the dog to assume the correct natural pose when standing.

Because of the importance of the forechest to gait and soundness, the forechest must be well developed. This means that it must have strong bones and tendons, with adequate, well-developed muscles. The muscles of the forechest should be developed enough that the shoulder joint is not prominent as you view the forechest.

The thorax (rib area) begins from a plumb line at the lowest part of the back of the neck (right in front of the shoulder tip) and extends back to the belly. At the top of the thorax are the vertebrae, which support the dog's back. At the bottom of the thorax is the sternum, which runs along the brisket area and to which the ribs are attached. There are thirteen pairs of ribs: the first nine pairs are attached to the sternum; the last four pairs before the abdominal area (the short ribs) are not attached to the sternum.

The ribs enclose the thoracic cavity, which holds the heart and lungs. The size of this cavity has an effect on the size of the heart and lungs, and it is very critical that the thoracic cavity be large enough to contain these organs. The proper chest dimensions—length, width, and depth—are important to form and function and deserve a thorough discussion.

Chest depth is determined by measuring from the highest point of the withers to the bottom of the chest at the point of the elbow. (Note that the Nippo Judging Resolutions specify that height of the body as a whole is to be measured just *behind* the shoulder tip.) Chest depth that is half of the body height is good, and the Standard specifies that chest depth must be 45 to 50 percent of total body height. Chests that are too deep or shallow are common and major faults.

Chest width (as distinguished from forechest width) is taken by measuring the distance between the ribs at the greatest part of their outward curve. Since the proper chest height and length are easily determined by comparing with ratios for the whole body, the major determinant of proper thoracic cavity size is width. The correct shape for a thorax resembles the shape of an egg standing on its small end in cross section, and the widest point of the ribs therefore occurs just behind the shoulder blade.

Flat ribs, the condition of insufficient chest width, cause the elbows to be too close to the body and result in a dog that does not have the correct natural stance. The opposite condition is barrel torso, in which the ribs are overly rounded and the thorax is not properly egg-shaped. In this case, the dog is apt to have turned-out elbows and will not have the nimbleness of gait called for in the Standard.

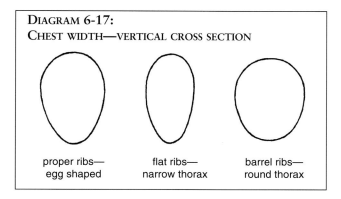

DIAGRAM 6-17:
CHEST WIDTH—VERTICAL CROSS SECTION

proper ribs—
egg shaped

flat ribs—
narrow thorax

barrel ribs—
round thorax

Chest length is determined by overall body length, which is 110 percent of body height for males and slightly longer for females. The thorax must have length that is in harmony with the overall length of the dog. A dog that is too short will have cramped movement. Chest length will be similar in males and females because the extra body length in females comes from a longer loin area to accommodate puppies in gestation.

Long, egg-shaped ribs are the most flexible and provide sufficient room in the thoracic cavity for the lungs to expand and contract in the exchange of large quantities of air—critical to a dog that runs for long periods of time and uses up a great deal of energy. Barrel-shaped ribs provide plenty of room in the thoracic cavity, but they cannot contract as much as the long ribs of the egg-shaped thorax and, therefore, can't pump air as well. Flat ribs constrict the space for the heart and lungs and do not provide good expansion and contraction.

When evaluating the chest, another consideration is the attachment of the forelegs. If the sternum bone is not properly developed, then the angles of connection of the shoulder blade and the upper arm cannot be correct, and the front legs cannot move efficiently. If the dog has a barrel torso as viewed from the front, the H-shape formed by the chest and legs is too wide and the elbows rotate outward, causing the movement to be slow and awkward. In the dog with flat ribs, the H-shape is too narrow, the elbows are too close together, and the dog will not have the endurance to be agile and nimble.

In medical terms, the back runs from the base of the neck to the end of the rib area (the beginning of the belly or loin area). However, when most of us refer to the back, we are referring to the area from the base of the neck all the way to the root of the tail. The Nippo judges have issued a resolution that the back is defined as the entire distance from the base of the neck to the root of the tail (the topline). It is extremely important for the Shiba to have a straight topline from the neck to the tail.

The hip area is formed by the seven lumbar vertebrae and the four sacral vertebrae, and it also includes the loin or belly area. The lumbar vertebrae run approximately from the end of the rib cage to the croup, and the sacral vertebrae run from the croup to the tail root. The hips are not as wide as the thoracic area, but the hip area must have adequate width for proper movement. Overall, strength is the major requirement for the hip area. The muscles of the buttocks must be powerful to propel the dog forward, and the hip joint must be extremely strong to withstand all the wear and tear inflicted on it.

When the back is not straight, the problem usually lies in the lumbar rather than the thoracic vertebrae, and there is a natural tendency for the topline to slant down somewhat from the point at which the curled tail crosses the back. Even though this tendency may be natural, a dropping off of the topline as it approaches the tail is a fault—the ideal in the Standard calls for a perfectly straight back. A dog that is "high in the rear" is also faulty.

Two common faults that affect the entire topline are the roached back and the sagging topline. The roached back (convex back or carp back) is a condition where the entire topline arches upward, with the highest point in the middle of the back. It is rare in comparison with the number of dogs that have sagging toplines, but it does occur. The roached back can be either a structural fault that the dog is born with or a temporary condition brought on by stomachache or nervousness. A dog that has internal parasites often exhibits a roached back, which returns to normal after worming.

The concave or sagging back is much more common and is the opposite of the roached back. The sagging back results in a "fishtail" motion, in which the back and hips swing left and right while gaiting. This happens because the sagging back is not structurally strong enough to efficiently transmit the driving motion of the hindlegs to the front part of the body. This condition is sometimes caused by an excessively long back; the extra length causes strain and loosening of the ligaments that hold the vertebrae together. A sagging back can also be brought on by overfeeding and under-exercise. Both the roached back and the sagging back are extremely incorrect.

The Tail

The Nippo Basic Standard states: *"The tail is thick and powerful. It can be either sickle or curled. In length it reaches almost to the hock joint."*

While the tail may not be of great importance in most dog breeds, it is tremendously important in the Shiba. Among Japanese breeders, a concept called *tokucho* refers to the qualities that make the Japanese dog distinct from other breeds, and Japanese dogs that do not possess these characteristics are said to be of doubtful parentage. Of these characteristics, the tail is considered to be the most important. Indeed, it is said that erect ears and tail carried over the back are the two hallmark traits of the Japanese breeds. The tail must help in the agile and nimble movement typical of the small Shiba, and it helps the dog maneuver while hunting.

As has been written time and time again, the Nippo Standard is not comparable to our concept of standards in America. Here in the United States, the criteria for judging a particular breed should be expressly set out in the standard. In the Nippo Standard, on the other hand, some very important items are considered so obvious that they are not even mentioned. Although a dropped tail is not specifically mentioned in the Standard as a fault, at any Japanese show a Shiba with a dropped tail would stand no more chance of winning than would a dog with an obvious disqualifying fault under an American breed standard.

The most important word used to describe the tail in the Nippo Standard is the Japanese word *chikarazuyoi*, which we translated as "strong and powerful." *Chikarazuyoi* means forcible, forceful, vigorous, virile, reassuring. Although the word means strong, it also has a connotation of action. Thus, the tail should be powerful in a way that expresses the active vigor of the dog as well as its strength. When it is said that the tail should be thick, this does not mean just that the hair coat should be thick. It is true that the tail hair is longer than the hair on the rest of the body, and the impression of thickness is made even greater by the

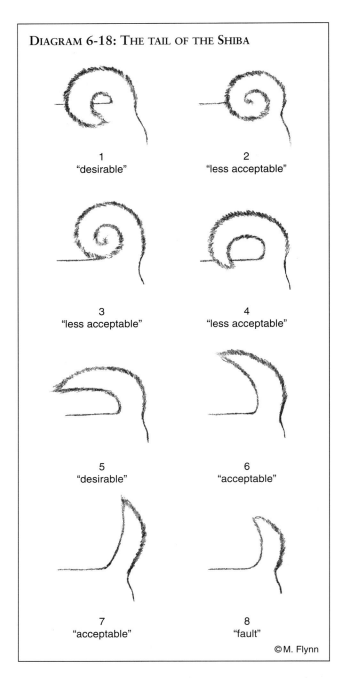

DIAGRAM 6-18: THE TAIL OF THE SHIBA

1 "desirable"

2 "less acceptable"

3 "less acceptable"

4 "less acceptable"

5 "desirable"

6 "acceptable"

7 "acceptable"

8 "fault"

©M. Flynn

hair standing off of the tail. But the thickness of the tail should also come from its bone structure—from the thickness of the tail vertebrae themselves. A thin tail cannot express the strength that the Japanese dog must have.

Tail hair should stand off from the tail bone evenly. Conversely, a tail with hair that converges to form a ridge is not desirable and is considered a sign of poor coat texture. This type of tail is called *ogami* because the hair forms the shape of praying hands.

Bearing in mind that the tail must be carried over the back, there are two categories of permissible tail carriage in the Shiba. These are the *maki-o* (curled tail), and the *sashi-o* (sickle tail). Several subtypes of both curled and sickle tails exist, some of which are more desirable than others, but there is no preference for the direction in which a tail curls. Direction is determined by looking at the dog's tail from the rear: a left curl spirals toward the left hip, and a right curl spirals toward the right hip. From our own observations, left curl seems to be more common than right, but right curl is not rare, and both are equally good.

There are four common shapes of the curled tail, and these are shown in Diagrams 6-18.1 through 4. Diagram 1 shows the most desirable curled tail, the single curl. In terms of beauty, expression of desirable temperamental characteristics, and flexibility for proper movement a single curl is preferred over a double or half curl.

Diagram 2 shows the double curl. While not exactly making a double loop, it is a tight curl that makes more than one circle. The fact that this tail curl is less desirable than the single curl is commonly misunderstood by Shiba breeders and judges outside of Japan. Many people assume that because a drop tail is bad, a tight double curl is best. But in Japan, the double curl is considered less attractive than the single curl and less desirable because the greater flexibility of the single curl makes it a better rudder for the dog's movement.

Diagram 3 shows the *taiko-maki* tail, which is undesirable in the Shiba. (A *taiko* is a big decorative bow worn at the back of a kimono.) The curl of this tail type is tighter than the curl in Diagram 1, but not as tight as in Diagram 2. The distinctive feature of this tail type is that the entire curl is above the line of the back.

Diagram 4 shows a slack-tail curl that is halfway between the curled tail and the sickle tail and is therefore called either half-curled or half-sickle. This type of tail curl is considered weak looking, does not express good temperamental qualities, and is not a very desirable type of tail.

Sashi-o (sickle tail) types are shown in Diagrams 5 through 7. Although not seen as often as the curly tail, the proper sickle tail is considered just as good as the curly tail. Quickness and agility of movement are considered to be extremely important for the Shiba's hunting activities, and the sickle tail—because it expresses great vigor and

quickness and aids in movement—is considered to be a good type of tail.

Diagram 5 shows the type of sickle tail that is most common, one that slants strongly forward and is carried almost parallel to the line of the back. Although Diagrams 5 through 7 are all *sashi-o* tails, Diagram 5 depicts what is most commonly meant by the term. Diagram 6 shows the *tachi-o* tail. A *tachi* is a long sword, and the sword's qualities of vigor and strong carriage should be evident in this type of tail. There should never be anything weak or slack about the appearance of a sickle tail!

The tail type in Diagram 7 is called the *naginata-o*. A *naginata* is a halberd, which is a type of ax. This type of tail should not be confused with the congenitally short tail. Although the carriage is similar, the *naginata-o* is of normal length. Of the sickle tail types shown in Diagrams 5 through 7, the type in Diagram 5 is generally considered the most desirable, but the types shown in Diagrams 6 and 7 are also good if they are strong and thick.

Diagram 8 shows the *tan-bi* or short tail. This very rare type of tail is hereditary and is listed as a fault in the Shiba. It is also called a *chasen* tail, named for a bamboo whisk that is used as a tea-stirrer in Japan. The short tail is seen in artwork from long ago, and so has somewhat of a nostalgic appeal, but in the present, it is considered very undesirable.

The Coat

Quality
The Nippo Basic Standard section on coat states: *"Outer coat is stiff and straight; undercoat is soft and thick. Tail hair is slightly longer and stands off."*

The Shiba has a classic double coat, with an outer coat of guard hairs, and a thick, woolly undercoat. The hairs of the outer coat should be strong and straight and are coarser and stiffer than those of the undercoat. Wave, curl, or soft texture in the guard hair is a serious fault. The undercoat hair (called the "cotton wool coat" by the Japanese) must be very thick, dense, and luxurious, allowing the Shiba to weather wind, rain, and snow. The undercoat should be so thick that it causes the outer coat to stand up at an angle of at least 45 degrees from the body. Guard hair laying down flat on the body due to a lack of undercoat is not proper type.

Because the Shiba is a shorthaired dog, long hair is an extremely serious fault. Due to the thick undercoat, the Shiba appears to have slightly longer hair than most short-haired breeds. The coat is shortest on the head, slightly longer on the body, a little longer yet on the neck and back, and longest on the tail. The tail hair is described as standing open; that is, standing up off the tail. It is also described as being soft and long enough that it "sways like the wind is blowing."

Color

The Nippo Basic Standard states: *"Coat color is sesame, red, black, brindle, or white. The quality and color of the hair should express the characteristics typical of the Japanese dog."*

Not all of the five colors listed above are allowed for all of the six native Japanese breeds. For example, the Judging Resolutions state that the Akita, the largest of the native breeds, must be red, white, or brindle. The Shiba, the smallest of the breeds, must be red, red sesame, or black and tan. In his article on coat in *Shiba Dog*, Mr. Ishikawa states that the color pattern of each individual red or black hair is pale at the root, dark in the middle of the shaft, then either pale or dark at the tip. He says that even if a dog has a beautiful color on casual inspection but has the same color tone on the entire hair shaft upon closer inspection, this is incorrect color and suggests the dog may not be purebred.

Red Coat Color—In Japan, the Shiba is referred to colloquially as *aka inu*—"red dog." The color red is so strongly associated with the Shiba that it is reflected in the most fundamental attribute of the breed—its name. In *Dialogues: Directions For Breeding Shibas*, Mr. Ishikawa and Mr. Watanabe discuss the Shiba's red color. First, they note that the red of the Shiba is a reddish-brown color in general. Then, they discuss the Mino Shiba, which was one of the three founding strains of the modern Shiba and had a coat color that Mr. Ishikawa calls cardinal red. He says this color was red like a flame, extending for about 1 cm on the tip of the hair, and was found primarily on the back. Since the Mino Shiba is now extinct, this cardinal red has become very rare, but it is an excellent color for the Shiba. In *Shiba Dog*, Mr. Ishikawa notes that the overwhelming majority of Shibas in Japan are red. He describes the most intense red scarlet as the most desirable coat color.

So, the picture we get of the best possible coat color for the Shiba (and the historically correct coat color) is an intense red. Many times people apply the term red to dogs that are a fawn color or a brown color, but this is incorrect. True red dogs are neither fawn nor brown but an intense red color that appears almost orange. Proper red color is not dark or dull but rich and vibrant. Although it is a difficult goal, many Shiba breeders are striving to recreate the beautiful cardinal red or flame red of the Mino Shiba.

Sesame Coat Color—There are three types of sesame coloring mentioned in the Nippo Basic Standard. These are *shirogoma* (white sesame), *akagoma* (red sesame), and *kurogoma* (black sesame). White sesame is a white dog with a frosting of black hairs; red sesame is a red dog with a frosting of black hairs; and black sesame is a black dog with a red, fawn, or silver undercoat. The Nippo Judging Resolutions state that the red sesame is the only one of these three sesame colors allowed for the Shiba. The correct red sesame dog does not look black with a red undercoat, but rather gives the impression of a red dog with a light overlay of black hairs.

The correct red sesame has only a small amount of black hair. Red sesame is *not* a brown color with a moderate black overlay, as is sometimes seen. The red should be just as clear, bright, and intense as that of the correct red Shiba, with the frosting of black hairs making a nice contrast. The red sesame should have the same white markings as the red Shiba. The black overlay does not extend onto the white markings. The black hairs are sprinkled over most of the dog's body, usually ending in a distinctive widow's peak on the forehead, leaving the muzzle red. The lower legs are red as well. The black overlay should never be concentrated on the back in the saddle pattern typically seen in red sable German Shepherds. Shibas with a saddle pattern and/or black muzzle are not correct and are generally considered to have mixed blood.

In Japan, a Shiba that is red with a light sprinkling of black hairs down the spine and no black elsewhere is considered to be a mismarked red, not a red sesame. The hallmark of the true red sesame coloring is that black hairs are evenly mixed in with the red over the entire coat, except for the lower legs, muzzle, and the areas of white markings.

Black-and-Tan Coat Color—The color requirements for the black-and-tan Shiba are very strict. If the tan markings and the white markings are not just so, the dog will be faulted. Plain black with no tan markings is *not* an acceptable Shiba color. Also, tan markings that are too extensive are a fault.

In the book, *Inheritance of Coat Color in Dogs*, Clarence Little lists the typical tan points pattern in dogs: on the sides of the muzzle, throat, and belly line; inside the ears; on the chest; over each eye; on all four feet and parts of the legs; around the anus; and on the underside of the tail. He observes that the tan in any or all of these areas may be so reduced that it disappears or the tan may extend outside the usual areas so that the only dark area remaining is a saddle on the back. Restrictions on the tan pattern in the black-and-tan Shiba serve to avoid both these extremes.

The November 1984 issue of the Japanese dog magazine, *Aiken No Tomo*, contained an excellent article about the black-and-tan Shiba by Hideo Motoyama. In it he states that the color should not be a shiny black, but a matte black, with tan in the following pattern: spots over the eyes (the Japanese sometimes call this color pattern "four eyes"), the lower part of the sides of the mouth and both cheeks, the forechest, the ends of the legs, and the undersurface of the tail. The dividing line between the tan and white areas should be distinct, with no fading of the tan into white. In *Dialogues*, Mr. Watanabe and Mr. Ishikawa specifically state that the tan must not cross onto the forehead (from either the small spots above the eyes or from the neck or cheek markings). Mr. Ishikawa jokingly says that some dogs show so much tan they should be referred to as tan-and-black (rather than black-and-tan).

Pictures of top-winning black-and-tan Japanese Shibas usually show a typical color pattern. There is tan inside the ears. On the head, the bridge of the nose is black, with white markings on the lower part of the sides of the muzzle and a fair amount of tan in between. The black color continues to the upper part of the cheeks and around the eyes, covering the forehead and the entire top and sides of the neck area. The white markings on the lower part of the cheeks and the underside of the jaw flow into the white on the underside of the neck, making a bib. There may be some black on the underside of the jaw. The tan spots above the eyes are small and do not stretch out in an eye-

Banshu Kurohime of Banshu Seppikoso, owned by Kazuhiko Nanto.
81st Nippo National Sokensho winner.

brow shape to the side. They may have an area of white or lighter hair alongside. Black hair covers the lower part of the neck's undersurface, between the white hair of the bib and the white hair on the chest. The white hair on the chest is usually in what is called a bow-tie pattern—it stretches from one side of the chest to the other with a narrowed area in the middle. This narrowing may be so extreme that it actually separates the white hair on the forechest into two different patches. It should be noted that the white hair on the chest of some dogs will occasionally extend beyond the bow-tie pattern to form a white blaze on the chest. As long as the white does not go out of the prescribed boundries for white markings, these various chest patterns are acceptable to judges, although breeders generally prefer the bow-tie pattern. There are usually tan socks on all four legs, and if there is white on the legs, it is generally on the toes or feet (occasionally one sees white socks with tan between the sock and the black coat color). There is white on the inside of the legs extending up into the white on the belly and some tan on the tail's undersurface.

The Nippo Judging Resolutions list four items that are faults in the black-and-tan Shiba: the reverse mask, where white hair covers the entire muzzle, the cheeks, and the area around the eyes; tan spots over the eyes that stretch back too far; an excessive amount of tan on the head, neck, back, trunk, etc.; and a gray-black or eggplant body color on maturity (i.e., the fading out of the black color with age).

In addition to a fading of the black color that sometimes occurs as the dog matures, there may be an expansion of the tan areas as the dog ages. Little notes that in many breeds with the tan points gene, the tan points may be very small at birth, but they progressively increase in area. Mr. Watanabe states in *Nihon Ken Hyakka* that because this increase of the tan markings does happen in the Shiba, care must be used in evaluating black-and-tan puppies for proper markings.

White Markings—The white markings, or *urajiro*, are another of the barometers of the Shiba's purebred lineage. A Shiba that has no *urajiro* is probably not a purebred Shiba, Mr. Ishikawa says. The book *Shiba Dog* has one of the best, most concise descriptions of the correct white markings. A properly marked Shiba should have white on the cheeks and the sides of the muzzle, and it should have small round spots on the eyebrow border right above the eyes. There should be white under the lower jaw, under the neck, on the chest, on the underside of the body, and on the underside of the tail. White may also be on the forelegs up to the elbows, on the hind legs up to the knees, and on a few hairs on the tail tip, although the socks and the white on the tail tip are not required.

Although it is an important characteristic of the Japanese native breeds, the *urajiro* must not extend too far. White spots outside of the specified areas, or white markings that extend beyond the proper areas, are severely penalized. In looking at the Shiba from the side, the white above the eyes should not extend over more than one-third of the side of the face that is visible, nor should the white of the chest cover more than one-third of the visible side of the chest. (As stated in the Judging Resolutions, white may extend to the point of the shoulder but not onto the shoulder itself.) White must never extend across the bridge or top of the muzzle but must be confined to the sides of the muzzle, with the base coat color (red or black) down the entire length of the top of the muzzle.

The white spots over the eyes must not stretch back onto the forehead or extend too far around the eyes. White must not extend from under the neck up onto the ears or the upper surfaces of the neck or body.

The Judging Resolutions state that white markings are allowed on the rear legs "up to the knees." Since the knee joint is about halfway between the hip joint and the hock, a literal interpretation of this statement means that white is allowable halfway up the entire rear leg. In fact, we have never seen a picture of a winning Japanese Shiba with such markings. Generally, when a Shiba has white socks on the rear legs, the area of white decreases gradually as it goes up the legs. There may be white at the level of the knee joint, but it is toward the inside of the leg, with the dog's body color generally extending down at least to the hock on the outside of the leg.

Coat Color Faults

Nippo judges use a scoring system which assigns each section of the Standard a certain percentage importance. In addition, particular faults require the judge to make a deduction. The evaluation levels at a Nippo show are "Excellent," "Very Good," and "Good" for awards. The Judging Resolutions state that "a dog having a characteristic that is listed as a fault may not be awarded an 'Excellent' evaluation." Whether a Shiba that has a particular fault can get one of the lesser awards depends on how extensive the fault is. The following are the three general areas of faults in coat color.

Incorrect colors—The Nippo Judging Resolutions list the acceptable Shiba colors as red, red sesame, and black and tan, and they state that "white coat in the Shiba is not desirable and is a fault." Yuko Salvadori attended a large Nippo regional show on April 24, 1988 in Atsugi, Japan that attracted a total entry of 650 dogs, including 451 Shibas. Of those, Yuko noted, there were 401 red, 10 red sesame, and 40 black and tan. The following month at a show in Morioka, Japan, Yuko reported a total entry of 231 Shibas: 198 reds, 11 red sesames, and 22 black and tans. Coat colors such as black with no tan markings, black sesame, and pinto are not approved in the Shiba, are extremely rare, and are not seen in the show ring. Brindle color apparently does not exist in the Shiba today. The recessive gene for white or cream color (the dilution factor) is fairly common, and this is why the Judging Resolutions specifically state that white is not an acceptable color for the Shiba.

The Japanese experts on the breed whose commentaries we have been quoting are vociferously and unequivocally critical of white and brindle as colors for the Shiba. In *Dialogues*, Mr. Ishikawa says these two colors are out of the question for the Shiba and white Shibas should be set apart from the group. Mr. Watanabe adds that a white Shiba should not be a stud dog because its offspring will be carriers of the white gene and may produce white even if they are not white themselves. Mr. Ishikawa states that a brindle color in the Shiba is very undesirable. Both men also consider black sesame undesirable in the Shiba. In *Shiba Dog*, white color is said to be "weak in strength of expression and undesirable."

In *Nihon Ken Hyakka*, Mr. Watanabe states that genetically red dogs that also carry the gene for faded color may be faded red, light fawn, cream, or virtually pure white, and that black-and-tan carriers of the gene can be ash color. The dilution factor also reduces the pigment in the eyes and the skin, and thus the nose, eye rims, foot pads, and so forth may not be the desired black color. Because there are fewer pigment granules in the hair shaft, it is thinner and softer. The Nippo Standard sometimes discusses white color and faded color separately, but it is not clear whether they are caused by separate genes. See the chapter "Genetics For Breeders" for a full discussion of coat color inheritance.

It is not on a whim or just because Japanese breeders and judges don't like the look of the color that white is considered to be unacceptable in the Shiba. There are three reasons why white is not allowed. First, the Shiba in Japan has historically been a red, red sesame, or black-and-tan dog. Since the Shiba is one of the native breeds and is designated as a national treasure, it is not considered proper to try to change the dog from what it has been historically. Second, colored Shibas who have white ancestors are thought to be more likely to have an unattractive, faded coat color themselves or to produce this in their offspring. Finally, Japanese breeders believe that white or faded coat colors are linked to health problems. Mr. Watanabe says: "Faded color shows up in a lack of pigment in the coat and the skin, and is associated with atrophy of the internal organs, poor resistance to disease, and physical and mental weakness." It should be noted that the white or cream Shibas produced in the United States do not appear as yet to have any more health problems than the other colors. However, there are not enough Shibas in the United States to research the subject with any statistical accuracy.

Spots in the coat—The presence of spots (usually white) in the coat is listed at the end of the Nippo Basic Standard as a fault. The Judging Resolutions mention that obvious freckling (usually red or black) in the white markings on the legs is also a fault.

White spots generally occur on the trunk or back of the neck or other area where white markings are not allowed, and sometimes they extend into a streak or band. The Judging Resolutions mention that such spots may be acceptable in an Akita with otherwise correct coat color, if the spots are not unsightly and not large enough to qualify as pinto spotting. However, the Judging Resolutions make no such comment about Shibas. Therefore, it is probably safe to assume that even small, isolated white spots in a Shiba coat are a fault.

Reverse and black masks—The reverse mask (white hair covering the muzzle and extending around the eyes and onto the cheeks) is mentioned in the Judging Resolutions as a fault. This is what is popularly called the ghost mask in America. The Japanese commentators feel that this mask gives the face a clownlike expression that does not go along with the dignity of the Japanese dog. White should never cross the bridge of the nose, and the white above the eyes should be small spots, not spread out along the eyelid in the shape of an eyebrow. White should never totally encircle the eyes. The reverse mask is not thought to be native to the Japanese breeds and is considered a sign of crossbreeding. In *Dialogues*, Mr. Ishikawa states that the reverse mask still occurs but is steadily decreasing in numbers as the correct white markings replace it.

A black mask is also considered incorrect in the Shiba. Although Shibas are usually born with some degree of black on their muzzles, they lose this as they grow older. A black mask retained into adulthood is not desirable. The black mask covers up or replaces the desired white markings on the muzzle and cheeks and is, therefore, not correct even on a red sesame or black-and-tan Shiba. Ideally, a red Shiba adult should have no black hair at all.

Two lovely Shibas. Ch. San Jo Satori My Oh My, and 4-month-old daughter, Ch. San Jo Scandalous. © S. Evans.

Care and Management

ONE OF THE MOST IMPORTANT THINGS you must do before you bring your new puppy home is select a veterinarian. An area breeder may be able to supply the names of vets familiar with the Shiba. Some people insist that their veterinarian's facility be approved by the American Animal Hospital Association (AAHA), which inspects facilities and certifies those that meet its standards. Other people seek a vet who has graduated from a prestigious college of veterinary medicine or had a high class ranking. A vet who also teaches veterinary medicine is likely to be a highly knowledgeable person. And, of course, you should ask your friends for their recommendations. Doctors and nurses who own pets can be good sources for your list of possibilities.

Once you have made a preliminary selection, you should call and ask if you can visit the facility and talk to the veterinarians and staff. When you arrive at an animal clinic, ask a staff member for a tour. Cleanliness of the waiting and examining rooms is obviously important, but be sure to check the rest of the facility as well. Are the animal pens clean, secure, and well supervised? Is there an enclosed area for surgery that is clean and roomy, with modern equipment and good lighting? Is medicine properly labeled and stored? Do staff members seem to love animals and enjoy their work? Is there respect and good communication between the staff and the vets? Are your questions answered openly and completely? Do you feel rushed?

Important items to discuss include hours of business, arrangements for emergency care, areas of specialization, availability of referral to specialists, and policy on phone consultations. You should be able to get an idea of the amount of diagnostic-testing equipment the facility has and its state of upkeep. Does the veterinarian send tests to a local laboratory or do them in house? (Most vets do the more common tests in house and send the rest to a local laboratory.) Many animal clinics today have more than one veterinarian, and the vets rotate duties. Make sure that your pet will have one vet primarily responsible for its care, and that the other vets on staff (who may treat your pet in an emergency or when your regular vet is on vacation) are competent.

When you have decided on a veterinarian, arrange to bring your puppy in for an examination within twenty-four hours of the puppy's arrival. Ask the vet to verify that your new puppy is in good health, and make a second appointment for the followup puppy shot, usually given between ten and twelve weeks of age.

In many cases your Shiba will be the first patient of this breed for your vet. *It is imperative that you warn your vet that a few Shibas have had near fatal anaphylactic reactions to common vaccinations so that he or she will have epinephrine on hand in the event of an emergency.*

VACCINATIONS

A responsible breeder will already have made at least one trip to the vet with your puppy for its first vaccination and physical prior to shipment. This first visit should be made when the pup is between six and eight weeks of age. The breeder's vet should check for general health, run a stool test for worms and prescribe worming medication, check the bite, palpate the puppy's stifles, and check for heart murmur. It is not unusual for a six-week-old Shiba pup to have slightly wobbly knees or a slight juvenile heart murmur. In many cases, these conditions will clear up within two or three weeks; however, the breeder should pass this information on to you, so that your veterinarian can keep an eye open for the occasional serious case. Your puppy will receive a shot, which vaccinates against Distemper, Adenovirus 2, Parainfluenza, Parvovirus, and Coronavirus. These diseases are very serious in adult dogs and often deadly to puppies.

Your puppy should visit the veterinarian again at about sixteen weeks of age to receive a DA2PP+CvK/LCI vaccination, which includes protection against all of the above diseases plus Leptospira Canicola and Icterohaemorrhagiae. The first rabies shot will also be given at this time. Many dog training clubs and boarding kennels also require vaccination against Canine Bordatella, a bacterial infection that can occur simultaneously with other respiratory infections. By four months of age your Shiba should have outgrown any juvenile patellar luxation or heart murmur.

Often dogs are placed on preventative medication appropriate for the area of the country in which they live. For example, in regions where mosquitoes are present, dogs are given a blood test for the presence of heartworm in the early spring and placed on daily or monthly medication until the first frost (in areas of the country where there is no extended cold season, dogs are given the preventative medication year round, but still must be tested yearly). In some parts of the country ticks can carry Lyme disease, and owners of dogs that make frequent trips to wooded areas may wish to have them vaccinated. Dogs residing in warmer climates are often given medication to guard against flea infestation. Wherever you live, it is important to discuss with your vet the kind of activities your dog is likely to participate in so that he or she can choose the vaccination and medication program best suited to you and your dog.

Although three-year rabies vaccinations are available, yearly booster vaccinations are required to protect against most other diseases. Some veterinarians recommend parvovirus booster shots at five and six months of age (in addition to the regular puppy shots), and every six months thereafter. A good veterinarian will give your dog a complete physical and may spot potential health problems that you have not noticed. If you plan to show and breed your Shiba, your vet should also keep an annual record for you of the dog's dentition and patellar status, as these can deteriorate with age. He or she can also run health tests to certify that your dog is in the normal range for thyroid hormone and canine von Willebrand's factor. Most veterinarians have the equipment needed to take hip and elbow radiographs for certification by the Orthopedic Foundation for Animals, and, if not veterinary ophthalmologists themselves, can recommend a certified individual to administer an eye test.

Many Shibas are prone to flea allergies or have allergic reactions to tree and grass pollen in the spring and ragweed and leaf mold in the fall. If you live in an area where humans are bothered by hay fever, you can bet that your Shiba will have itchy and runny eyes when humans do. If your Shiba seems to be rubbing away the hair around its eyes or scratching more than usual, make an appointment with your vet to check out the cause. Allergy tests are now available for dogs. A Shiba with a mild reaction to pollen can be given a course of over-the-counter Benedryl for a few weeks during the height of the allergy season. The dosage for an average-size male of about 25 pounds would be half a tablet (12.5 mg) given three times a day. However, you should consult your veterinarian before offering this or any home remedies to your dog, since medication can be harmful if given in the wrong dosages or to an individual sensitive to it.

NUTRITION

Some dog breeders believe that heavy doses of certain vitamins will improve coat and bone development. In fact, if the dog is getting a proper diet, supplementation is not likely to benefit the dog and may cause serious harm. For good coat and bone, there is no substitute for proper breeding, a quality dog food, and plenty of fresh air and exercise. A premium brand of dog food such as *Science Diet, Iams,* or *NutroMax* will supply all of the requirements necessary for a balanced diet. Most regular brands will also supply all recommended ingredients but watch for unnecessary additives such as fillers and food coloring.

If you are feeding your Shiba a premium food but don't see the healthy glow you want, first check with your veterinarian. If there is no medical problem, try another premium food. Shibas sometimes do somewhat better on one food than they do on another, and a bit of experimenting may be required. In addition, the stage of the dog's life is important. The premium brands have different formulations for puppies, overweight or inactive dogs, seniors, and so on. In addition to its regular prod-

Whether the day is hot or cold, your Shiba should always have access to fresh water. C. Kaufmann.

uct line, *Science Diet* makes a wide variety of special diets used in the treatment of medical conditions, and these must be prescribed by a veterinarian. If your dog is on a prescribed special diet, it is important to follow that diet strictly.

CONDITIONING

A Shiba puppy up to six months of age needs no more conditioning than that provided by several hours a day of free running and playing in a large, securely-fenced area with human companions and friendly dogs. After six months of age, you may want to start your Shiba on a more structured conditioning program. If you want to show your Shiba, conditioning will help the dog's gait and appearance. Dogs are like people, and exercise will help your dog maintain proper weight and a happy state of mind. Indeed, exercise can be even more important to the mental health of a dog than it is to a human, because dogs do not have the rewards and distractions of earning a living!

Common-sense rules must be followed in any exercise program. First, start slowly and build up very gradually. Do not expect a Shiba couch potato to go out and run a marathon. Exercise should be fun for your dog, not an ordeal. Pay attention to your dog, and if he acts tired, let him rest. Shibas have heavy coats, and can very quickly become overheated on a warm day.

Some methods of exercise are inherently more dangerous than others. Riding a bike while pulling a Shiba along on a lead is dangerous for two reasons. One is that the Shiba may pull the bike over and injure both of you. The other is that bikes go fast, and a Shiba that might do fine running ten-minute miles with a jogger may not be able to do five-minute miles with a biker. A safer exercise method is walking, jogging, or hiking with your dog. Remember that most Shibas are not reliable off-lead (although early, consis-

A walk in the woods is a favorite Shiba treat. P. Doescher.

Make sure your Shiba is in good condition before setting off on a cross-country run.

Carry plenty of water and give him a chance to rest periodically. C. Ross.

tent training may work). In addition to a lead, be sure that your Shiba is always wearing a collar with identification tags, in case the worst happens and he slips his lead and disappears. If you are on a bike path or sidewalk, be sure that your Shiba does not dart out into traffic or get tangled up with a bike.

Another good way to exercise with a young Shiba is a game of "fetch." Most Shibas will quickly become bored with the owner standing in one place and throwing things, so some ingenuity and owner participation are called for to make the game fun and keep your Shiba running. One of the authors has a Shiba bitch that will not fetch at all, but loves to play "catch me." She starts the game by racing past the author, who lunges out to grab her; then she speeds up and zooms to the other end of the yard, wheels around, and makes another pass. The idea is for her to get as close to the author as she can with-

out getting caught. It is a little like bullfighting with a 17-pound bull. A word of caution—this game should not be tried with an "alpha" Shiba or a Shiba under two years of age, because they might interpret the game as showing their dominance over the owner. It is a game best suited to a Shiba with a mild temperament.

A companion Shiba should have a minimum of thirty minutes a day of moderate to active exercise such as walking, running, playing catch, or hiking, and should have more exercise if he shows signs of mental stress due to frustration (e.g., obsessive or destructive behavior) or has weight gain unrelated to a change in diet or health. If you are conditioning your dog for show, you may want to do a little more than thirty minutes a day. Japanese breeders typically run their adult show Shibas up to 20 kilometers (about 12 miles) per day. One Japanese Shiba expert stated that it is almost impossible to give a Shiba too much exercise after it reaches the

The Shiba is perfectly sized to enjoy family outings of all kinds. C. Ross.

GROOMING

Grooming your Shiba will not take much effort, but you will have to spend time training it to enjoy the attention. Puppies generally will not need brushing, but as newborns they should be stroked gently with one finger and then, as they get older, with a soft brush every few days so they become used to the feel. Teeth should be cleaned on a regular basis if needed.

A dog's toenails should be clipped frequently. Be sure to trim the nails on the front dewclaws. (Rear dewclaws are extremely rare and should be removed.) Shibas hate having their toenails clipped more than just about anything, so it is a good idea to make toenail trimming into a game while they are young. For example, one of the authors sings "It's puppy cookie time" to the tune of "Howdy Doody" while clipping the nails of her oldest bitch, who lies perfectly still on her back and watches intently while each paw is taken care of. After the last nail is cut, the author yells "cookie time!" and her Shiba flips over and dashes to the kitchen counter, where she gets a reward for being so good. It may look silly, but the job gets done without any fussing or struggling.

If your Shiba lives outdoors, it should be brushed with a slicker every few days to keep dust away from the skin. Shibas shed or "blow" their soft undercoats about twice a year. During the rest

age of six months. However, even though the Shiba may be capable of impressive athletic feats, it is important to keep the safety and comfort of your dog in mind at all times. To condition your dog for an AKC show, you will not need to run it for twelve miles per day. If you can walk or jog with your dog for five or six miles at least four times a week, both you and your Shiba will be in shape for the shows!

Some dog-show exhibitors exercise their dogs by driving a car slowly in an area with no traffic and holding the dog's leash while the dog runs or trots beside the car. This method may work for a large, reliable older dog, but is dangerous for the small, agile, quick-moving Shiba. Another method used by some is the treadmill. The authors believe that this method is dangerous and cruel, because paws could get caught in the mechanism and because the dog cannot control the treadmill speed.

Shiba feet are very sensitive. Training your puppy to calmly endure nail trimming once a week is an important part of raising a well-behaved dog. L. Engen.

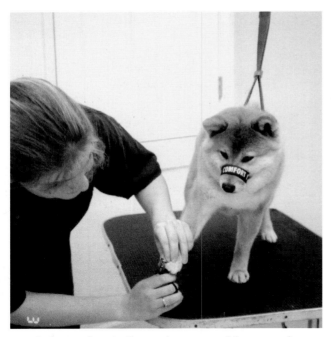

Soft muzzles similar to the one used here may be purchased from any pet supply store or catalog. Cat clippers are ideal for cutting the softer nails of puppies. L. Engen.

The difference between a Shiba "in coat" and "out of coat" can be alarming. Don't worry — the hair always grows back! G. Haskett.

of the year they shed very little. When they do, they should be combed daily with a Teflon undercoat rake and an English comb (one with both medium and fine steel teeth) to avoid matting. This is also the best time to bathe your dog; the undercoat is thin or completely gone, so you have a chance to get through the guard hairs to clean the skin. A warm bath will loosen up the remaining hairs and speed up the shedding process. A good all-purpose dog shampoo is best. Shampoos with special colors for red or black dogs don't have much effect other than staining the grout in your bathroom and putting a hole in your pocketbook. Don't be worried if your fluffy dog turns into a scraggly little coyote when all the undercoat is blown; a beautiful new coat will come in before you know it.

Grooming your Shiba for a show takes only a little more effort than taking care of your pet. Even show Shibas should not be bathed more than four times a year unless they are really dirty. This is almost never the case unless they are kenneled in a very windy area of the country where sand and dirt blow into their run regularly. Bathing a Shiba too often will ruin the coat by softening it and can damage the skin by stripping away natural oils. Going over the feet and white areas of the body with a wet washcloth is normally all that is needed. Dampen the coat very slightly with a spray bottle of water, then comb backward from the head and brush forward from the rear to remove any loose hairs. As with any northern breed, special care should be taken not to damage the skin by pulling. Some breeders use a blow dryer to blow away loose hair and dust. A final touch-up with a slicker and polish with a chamois cloth before entering the ring will help to show off a flaming red or glossy black stand-up coat. If the coat has grown dull from exposure to the sun and wind, a light application of mink oil brushed through the coat will restore the shine somewhat. Black-and-tan Shibas should not

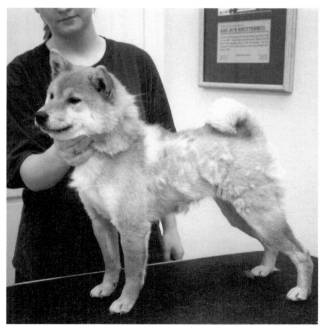

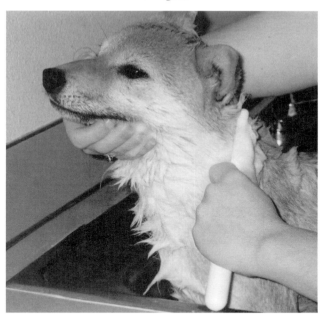

Much of the loose hair can be removed by combing while the dog is still in the tub.
L. Engen.

Shibas do not normally shed year-round, but instead "blow" their coats twice a year. This young bitch is ready for a bath and combing out! L. Engen.

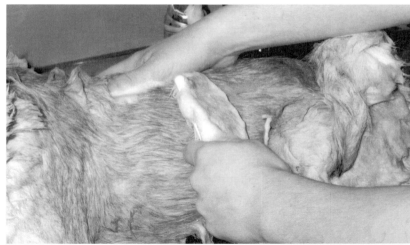

Comb the hair from front to back while your Shiba is wet and lathered with shampoo.
L. Engen.

Training your dog to stand and stay will make bathtime easier for both of you. Look at all the hair that came out!
L. Engen.

be kenneled in direct sun for long periods of time even in cooler weather, because black hairs can be sunburned to a rust color from the light.

The coat should *not* be trimmed at all. A small section of the guard hairs over the withers will stand up in a fanlike pattern on a dog with plenty of spirit. Although some groomers unfamiliar with the breed may be tempted to trim this area, they should be dissuaded from doing so, as a clipped coat is easily detected by a sharp-eyed judge and can cost the Shiba a victory. In the same vein, whiskers should *not* be trimmed. Although the Japanese Standard does not specifically state that a Shiba with clipped whiskers should be disqualified, an experienced Shiba judge may pass one over when the competition gets tough.

To sum up, the Shiba should be shown *au naturel*, with a clean, healthy coat and neatly trimmed nails. Its appearance should never be altered by artificial means. The use of chalk and coat stiffeners are at odds with the unspoiled character of the Shiba and in direct conflict with the appearance of artlessness called for in the Japanese Standard. Cosmetic alterations are for glamour breeds, and the Shiba has proven itself capable of winning without any outside help, thank you very much!

TRAINING

Your Shiba puppy will need training whether it is destined for the show ring, the obedience ring, or will spend most of its time at home. Before you bring him home, purchase or check out from your local library several books on dog training. You will probably find a multitude of training methods. Shibas are extremely quick learners but do not perform with unquestioning obedience. They are a hound/spitz breed and were bred for primitive style hunting and independent thought. Most Shibas will do what you want them to do only when they decide it is in their best interest to do it. A Shiba is quickly bored with training drills, so practice sessions should be kept short (no more than ten to fifteen minutes without a play break) and varied.

Visit training schools in your area and interview the trainers. An instructor with award-winning Golden Retrievers and Shelties may not understand your Shiba. Ideally your trainer will have achieved obedience titles with northern, spitz, hound, or terrier breeds.

All Shibas should go through at least two eight-week training sessions. The first should be a Kindergarten class, which will give your puppy the basics and expose him to humans and other dogs. The second class should be taken when your dog reaches adolescence—especially if it begins to exhibit dominance "alpha" behavior (e.g., food guarding, warning growls or snaps, refusal to obey commands). These sessions will reinforce your place as the one in charge. Extra sessions may be necessary with alpha Shibas. Under no circumstances should you ignore a problem with a disobedient Shiba. Shibas can lose their natural bite inhibition if allowed to believe that they are the dominant member of the household. One easy method of training a Shiba to accept its owner's leadership is to require the dog to sit before he gets fed, goes for a walk, or gets petted. The simple act of responding to a command to earn a reward, when repeated over and over, will engrain in the Shiba's mind the idea that the owner is dominant.

Leash training is probably the first step you will take toward obedience, companion, or show training your Shiba. Many Shiba puppies show their independent streak early and would rather do just about anything than go in the same direction you want to go. Wearing a collar or dragging the leash is not often the problem; it is the tug on the neck that upsets the puppy. Many Shiba owners will tell you that the first time they heard the "Shiba scream" was during their first attempt to take their new puppy for a walk! The screaming can be very embarrassing—to suburbanites and city-dwellers especially—but you can use a few tricks to help your puppy learn to walk on a leash. The first is to take mom Shiba or another older dog for a walk and connect the puppy to the older dog's leash with a brace coupler. The pup will be so busy aggravating the older dog that he will not notice the leash. (Make sure the older dog is very tolerant of puppy antics!) A variation of this method is to have someone walk slightly ahead with the older dog while you follow close behind with the puppy.

If you do not have a reliable older dog around, neighborhood children can be used as a substitute. Shiba puppies are usually crazy about children of any age and will tolerate a little neck pulling just so they can play with a child. Do not, however, leave your puppy to play unsupervised! Children are not always as gentle as they should be and

Leash training can be a frustrating experience. Jeni demonstrates a few typical moves. J. Holden.

Scream!

Flip!

Drop!

Ta Da!

small children have a short attention span and may run off and leave your puppy alone in the yard.

Bribing the puppy with special food treats or a squeaky toy works in a few cases, but your puppy will probably be too upset with the leash to take a bribe. Use a wide flat ribbon collar and leash for a little puppy. This kind of collar will distribute the pressure over a wide area of the neck. Use short gentle leash pops (i.e., short tug and release of the leash) to get your puppy moving forward. If you pull the puppy along by the leash in a continuous manner you will soon find the puppy has collapsed and you are dragging him along on his back. Do a little leash training everyday, even if you have a big fenced yard for your puppy to play in. Sooner than you think, the screaming and fussing will stop, and your puppy will be trotting happily along beside you to the amazement of the neighborhood!

Shibas can be aggressive towards other dogs, and you may have to make a little extra effort if you want your pet to be friendly with strange dogs. A Kindergarten class that offers puppy play time is an excellent beginning. However, a puppy that seems happy and confident in its relations with

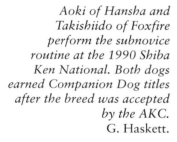

Obedience training is an essential part of Shiba ownership. The down-stay command creates time for tempers to cool after a multi-Shiba fracas over a prized toy. G. Haskett.

strange dog. If a friendly neighborhood dog approaches your puppy while on a walk, allow your puppy some slack and talk to both dogs in a confident, happy manner.

Sometimes, in spite of all your efforts, your Shiba will dislike unfamiliar dogs. Don't feel guilty about it or ashamed of your Shiba; his job is to love you and your family and not the Poodle next door. This does not mean that your dog should be allowed to embarrass you in public. Some Shibas derive a great deal of pleasure from challenging other dogs. You might not be able to eliminate this behavior, but you should not let this king-of-the-hill display continue without a few good leash pops and some choice words. Try placing your dog on a sit as another dog passes in front of him and reward him with praise and a treat if he stays put quietly. If for some reason it is absolutely necessary

Aoki of Hansha and Takishiido of Foxfire perform the subnovice routine at the 1990 Shiba Ken National. Both dogs earned Companion Dog titles after the breed was accepted by the AKC. G. Haskett.

other dogs will often behave aggressively a few months later. Make sure your puppy has *regular* contact with friendly dogs throughout puppyhood and adolescence. One unpleasant experience during this critical learning period can trigger a Shiba to behave in a dog-aggressive manner for his lifetime. Many Shibas have difficulty with the social sniff greeting that is well developed in more domesticated breeds. When he is restricted on a leash, your Shiba may feel uncomfortable and forced to defend himself when approached by a

for your dog to get along with all other dogs, you may wish to consider another breed or the purchase of a nonaggressive adult Shiba.

The types of corrections you use should be carefully modified to fit the individual personality of the dog. Many Shibas cannot take a harsh correction and will give an Academy Award-winning imitation of a sullen cat when punished. Others can handle a good leash pop and any amount of yelling and still come up kissing. After any correction, be sure to remind your dog that you still love him!

Shibas have not competed in obedience in great numbers thus far. In 1992 (the first year Shibas were eligible for AKC obedience competition), eight Shibas earned qualifying scores, and seven earned their Companion Dog titles. The highest individual score was a 189.5, earned by Aoki of Hansha, CD. As Shibas and their owners become more familiar with obedience, we look forward to higher and higher scores!

BREEDING

Are you thinking of becoming a Shiba breeder? If so, the authors hope that you will endeavor to become an *ethical* Shiba breeder. Just what does that entail?

National dog breed clubs publish codes of ethics that members must promise to adhere to as a prerequisite of joining the club. These codes may differ slightly from one club to another but the principles are the same. An ethical breeder will follow the code of ethics for his breed regardless of whether he or she belongs to a national breed club. Most AKC champions are also loved family pets raised in homes and backyards across the U.S. Even if you own just one female Shiba you can be just as ethical as the best professional show kennels. The 14 items listed in Table 7-1 make up the NSCA Code of Ethics.

An ethical breeder is never a "backyard breeder" or a "puppy miller." You may have heard these terms before but what do they really mean? A backyard breeder is an individual who breeds his pet dog without regard to genetic health, soundness, or breed type. He has not paid for hip or eye certification for his dog prior to breeding and has no idea if his dog is a good representative of the breed or not. He is not familiar with the genetic problems of his dog's family tree nor does he have any intention of working to eradicate them. He sells his puppies to whoever has the price and does not require a spay/neuter contract. If the puppies run into difficulties in their new homes, he has no intention of taking

---

TABLE 7-1

The NATIONAL SHIBA CLUB OF AMERICA establishes this CODE OF ETHICS, which states the minimum responsibilities and practices that shall be maintained by all of the members of this organization. As a member of the National Shiba Club of America I will

1. agree to follow the regulations as set forth by the American Kennel Club as they pertain to my purebred dog operations.
2. agree to abide by and uphold the principles of the Constitution and By-Laws and this Code of Ethics of the National Shiba Club of America.
3. as a breeder, furnish with any Shiba sold a certificate stating that the dog in question is in good health.
5. maintain the best possible standard of health and care in all of my dogs and see that the puppies are immunized and checked for parasites. I will furnish complete health records, care, feeding and grooming instructions with each puppy sold.
6. encourage spaying or neutering of animals not desirable for breeding.
7. refuse to knowingly sell dogs to wholesalers, retailers, puppy mills, dog fighters or any other where there is reason to suspect that the Shiba will not receive proper care or may be used in any way detrimental to the breed or to the dog itself.
8. establish a reputation of trust and honor among my fellow club members and all interested parties.
9. adhere to ethical breeding practices, striving to achieve the maximum ideal of the breed.
10. in my breeding program keep alert for and work to control and/or eradicate inherited problems and conditions that are particular to my breed, and breed as closely as possible to the standard of the breed.
11. represent my dogs as honestly as possible to prospective buyers and try to assist the serious novice in his understanding of the breed.
12. try at all times to show good sportsmanship and keep in mind that the good of the breed comes before any personal benefits.
13. refrain from deceptive or erroneous advertising.
14. not knowingly falsify any records, pedigrees, or registrations and acknowledge that if so proven, I will have my membership privileges revoked.

Shiba bitches are not always easy to breed and can be very choosy about their mates. This courtship was successful and produced four black and tan puppies.
G. Haskett.

them back and finding different homes for them. He is either unconcerned or unaware that the puppies he produces may find their way to dog pounds or puppy mills. The backyard breeder produces puppies to provide cheap pets for friends and relatives, to allow his children to witness the "miracle of birth," or in an attempt to make a few dollars' profit.

A puppy miller, on the other hand, is all of the above, but also usually owns many dogs of many different breeds. He produces puppies strictly as a business. Puppies are usually sold to a broker, who in turn sells them to pet stores. Ethical breeders know that breeding dogs properly is very seldom profitable. Even without the cost of a good quality foundation puppy factored in, there are genetic health tests, dog show expenses, and the cost of stud service, all of which usually mean that you will be lucky to break even. Dog breeding is a hobby — not a profession or a supplemental source of income. Ethical breeders that turn a profit generally either have a sideline, such as dog show training, grooming or handling, or have been fortunate in

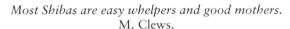

Most Shibas are easy whelpers and good mothers.
M. Clews.

the ownership of an exceptional dog that regularly produces high-quality offspring.

Before you breed your Shiba, you should consider becoming a member of the national breed club. We have described in this book some of the genetic problems that occur in the Shiba, but you will need to become familiar with your dog's family tree before you choose a stud dog. The best way to do this is to join the club and talk to as many breeders as possible. Experienced club members can tell you the strengths and weaknesses of your dog's relatives.

If you have never bred or whelped a litter of puppies, we would also suggest you purchase a book solely devoted to breeding dogs. One that the authors can personally recommend is *Canine Reproduction* by Holst (1985, Alpine Publications, Inc.). Shibas can occasionally be difficult to breed. Stress can sometimes cause the female to go out of heat when shipped and a few bitches cycle only once a year. Some dominant bitches are very selective about their mates and will fight rather than accept a male not of their choosing. Some males will refuse to breed a bitch that is being restrained and some bitches will not stand for breeding without restraint.

Shiba litters are usually small. Three to four pups is the norm and a litter of one is not uncommon. Large litters of six or more are rare. Puppies average about 300 grams at birth. Female Shibas are usually excellent mothers. They are easy whelpers and keep the puppies and whelping boxes clean with minimal or no human assistance. A mother will help train her puppies to eat solid food by regurgitating her food into their mouths when they reach about seven to eight weeks of age. This instinctive reaction is triggered by the puppy licking the dam around the mouth, a behavior of wild canids that has been lost in many familiar breeds.

A mother Shiba seems to prefer her little sons and sometimes develops an intense dislike for a daughter when she comes in season for the first time. This should be taken into consideration if you are planning to keep a puppy from her litter. As for male Shibas, many enjoy playing with their sons until the onset of puberty when the puppy begins to lift his leg or a bitch in the household comes in season. Then, watch out! A mother-daughter or father-son relationship can change from being congenial to adversarial in less than twenty-four hours.

The bottom line is, dog breeding should never be undertaken in a casual manner. A dog breeder is ultimately reponsible for the life of every puppy he produces. Only the best dogs should be allowed to produce offspring. The AKC now offers a limited non-breeding registration certificate and ethical breeders should take advantage of it by providing this type of registration for the pets they sell. If you have purchased your dog from a pet store or backyard breeder it is highly improbable that your dog is of breeding quality. Please do the ethical thing and spay or neuter your canine friend. If you are sincerely interested in breeding, become an active member of the national breed club and familiarize yourself with U.S. and Japanese pedigrees. Begin your breeding program with the purchase of a quality, genetically screened Shiba from an ethical breeder and do your best to improve the quality of the breed.

These puppies are the product of a true sesame dam and a black-and-tan sire. It is difficult to distinguish a true sesame from a sable at this age. However, the bitch in the middle is a true sesame and when bred to black-and-tan studs she produced true sesame.
K. Brown-Truax.

Japanese import Ch. Sho Go Gold Typhoon with owner Leslie Ann Engen and co-owner/importer Frank Sakayeda. Sho received three 5-point majors including Best of Winners at the 1996 NSCA National Specialty in his first three shows in the United States. Sho was Westminster Kennel Club BOB in 1998 and 2001 and NSCA National Specialty BOB in 1998 and 2000. © Downey.

Showing Your Shiba

AMERICAN KENNEL CLUB SHOWS

IF YOU ARE A NOVICE SHIBA OWNER and want to show your dog, there are many excellent books available that will tell you all about shows, both breed (conformation) and obedience. Current show regulations are available from the American Kennel Club. There are also books to help you learn how to handle your own dog in competition. In this chapter, we will present a very brief overview of AKC shows and tell you a few things that are more specific to showing Shibas.

AKC shows are generally put on by AKC licensed Superintendents in conjunction with an all-breed club. If you plan to show your dog, you will need to contact the Superintendents who put on shows in your area (the addresses are available from AKC) and ask for "premium sheets" for upcoming shows. Your Shiba must be a minimum of six months of age to be entered. Classes at a typical AKC show are divided by sex, with males shown first, then females. Within each sex, puppies (six to nine months and nine to twelve months) are shown first, then Novice, Bred by Exhibitor, American-Bred, and Open. Sometimes there is a class for 12-18 months. The judge will examine all the entrants, then award first through fourth place ribbons in each class (judges can withhold a ribbon if they think none of the entrants are worthy of the award).

When all the male dogs have been shown, the first-place winners from each class go back into the ring and the Winners Dog is selected. This dog gets championship points, the number of points (one to five) depending on how many males were entered. The number of points awarded differs by region, with more populated regions generally having higher requirements. At the time of this writing it takes an entry of just six male Shibas to earn a five

point major in Illinois. A dog competing in Idaho, a state that has very few Shiba breeders, must find an entry of thirteen males for the same five point major. This is because Idaho is in the same AKC Division as Washington State, where many Shibas are bred and shown.

After the Winners Dog is selected, the other males remain in the ring, and the second-place dog in the class the Winners Dog won goes back into the ring. The judge then selects a Reserve Winners Dog from this group. If the Winners Dog is disqualified for any reason (for example, if he was Canadian bred and was shown in the American-Bred Class), then the Reserve Winners Dog will be awarded the points. Similarly, after all the females have been shown, a Winners Bitch and Reserve Winners Bitch are selected. A dog must earn a total of fifteen points for an AKC Championship, including two "majors" (wins of three to five points) under two different judges.

After the Winners Dog and Winners Bitch have both been selected, they come back into the ring, along with the "specials," for the Best of Breed competition. A "special" is a dog that has already finished its championship. These are typically outstanding dogs that easily finished their championships and are being campaigned for a national ranking. The judge will select a Best of Breed winner, a Best of Opposite Sex, and a Best of Winners. The Best of Breed will then go on to compete in the Group, along with the other Best of Breed winners for all the breeds in that Group. The Best of Opposite Sex is just what the name implies—if the Best of Breed was a female, the Best of Opposite Sex will be a male, and vice versa. The Best of Opposite Sex does not compete in the Group.

The Best of Winners is either the Winners Dog or the Winners Bitch. If the Winners Dog won four points and the Winners Bitch won only two points (because there were more males than females entered at this show), and the Winners Bitch wins Best of Winners, then she will get four points also, in recognition of having defeated the four-point winner. A judge can award the Best of Winners the Best of Breed also, and if so, the Best of Winners will go into the Group. This is a great honor, because it means that the judge thinks the Best of Winners, although not yet a champion, is clearly superior to dogs of established merit.

Group judging is generally held in the mid to late afternoon, and the judges select four placements in each Group. There are seven Groups, and the seven first-place winners compete at the end of the day for Best In Show.

In addition to regular shows, breed clubs sometimes work with an all-breed club to put on a "supported entry" or a "specialty" at an AKC show. A supported entry generally means that special prizes are offered, and a larger than normal entry competes. A specialty show also typically has a larger than normal entry, and special classes may be offered. These can include a Veteran's Class, for dogs and bitches seven years of age and

Graham Uchida's Kimiko swept the 1985 NSCA summer specialty weekend. M. Lacey.

older, and a puppy Sweepstakes or Futurity. Both supported entries and specialties may feature additional activities such as seminars, dinners, and fund-raising.

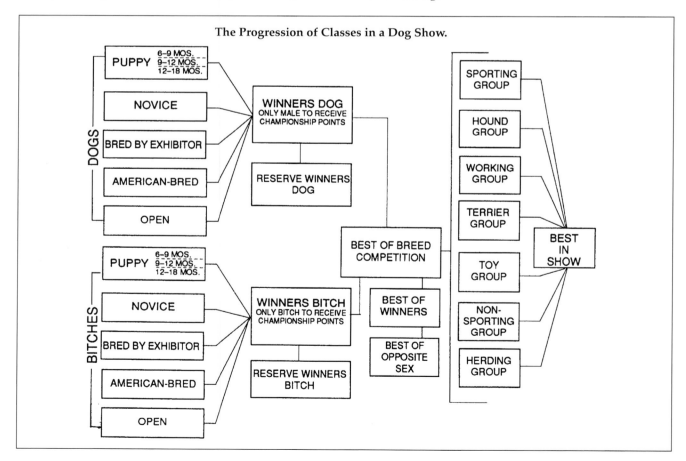

The Progression of Classes in a Dog Show.

DOGS

PUPPY — 6–9 MOS. / 9–12 MOS. / 12–18 MOS.

NOVICE

BRED BY EXHIBITOR

AMERICAN-BRED

OPEN

WINNERS DOG — ONLY MALE TO RECEIVE CHAMPIONSHIP POINTS

RESERVE WINNERS DOG

BITCHES

PUPPY — 6–9 MOS. / 9–12 MOS. / 12–18 MOS.

NOVICE

BRED BY EXHIBITOR

AMERICAN-BRED

OPEN

WINNERS BITCH — ONLY BITCH TO RECEIVE CHAMPIONSHIP POINTS

RESERVE WINNERS BITCH

BEST OF BREED COMPETITION

BEST OF WINNERS

BEST OF OPPOSITE SEX

SPORTING GROUP

HOUND GROUP

WORKING GROUP

TERRIER GROUP

TOY GROUP

NON-SPORTING GROUP

HERDING GROUP

BEST IN SHOW

Midwest black and tans show off at an Illinois rare breed show in 1991. K. Brown-Truax.

Shibas are shown in the "Non-Sporting" Group in AKC conformation shows. This Group also contains Poodles, Dalmatians, Chow Chows, Bichons Frises, Schipperkes, and Boston Terriers, among others. If you go to a "match" (informal shows where no championship points can be won—they generally draw large entries of puppies in training for AKC point shows), the breeds in each Group are generally judged in alphabetical order (although some judges prefer to judge in order of size and speed with the largest breeds first), and Shibas will be judged after most of the other Non-Sporting breeds. At AKC point shows, however, the assigned time can be any time of the day.

Training your puppy for conformation events can be a breeze if you start early and are consistent and regular about training sessions. Your puppy must be leash trained and well socialized. He must be exposed to strange people, places, and noises. Let your puppy play with neighborhood kids. Take him to parks and for walks around the local convenience store parking lot. Craft fairs usually have no prohibition against dogs and are an excellent way to socialize your Shiba. You should also purchase a grooming table or make a reasonable facsimile of one in your home. Although Shibas are shown on the ground in Japan, most AKC judges use a table for the hands-on evaluation. Your Shiba will be asked to tolerate advances from these judges that are against his aloof nature to accept readily. The judge will need to look in your dog's mouth and touch your dog in places that your Shiba may consider off limits, such as feet and testicles. You can

Shosha Cinnabar of Deer Lace was the winner of both of the Fall 1984 NSCA specialties. M. Lacey.

expect that many judges will be familiar enough with the breed to know that your Shiba will not be happy about this examination and will be quick and gentle. However, it is best to prepare your dog for the occasional heavy-handed judge. One AKC judge likes to pick up and squeeze front paws. Dogs who have been acclimated to strangers from birth will endure or even enjoy a handshake.

Like any other breed, Shibas can act up at inopportune moments. Typical Shiba table behavior

This young male has good body proportions and can already assume a show stance unassisted. Y. Green.

problems include: leaning on the handler, squirming, screaming when touched, and even diving off the table. Movement problems include pulling on the lead (dragging, forging, or straining away from the handler), screaming, slipping the lead, the bunny hop, and the "Shiba shake." The latter is probably the most frustrating problem, and can develop at any time in a Shiba's show career. Just when you are rounding the corner for a triumphant trot home to the judge, your Shiba will stop, cock his head, and shake it vigorously. In extreme cases a Shiba will shake his head during the entire circuit of the ring. Some dog trainers attribute this behavior to nerves, and yet it has developed in old pros. The only cure is to watch your Shiba carefully and give him a good leash pop when you sense he is about to get a case of the shakes.

Many of these problems (except for the Shiba shake) can be eliminated by early training. A conformation-class instructor is the best tool available to help cure your Shiba of poor ring behavior and help you prevent quirks from developing. Fortunately, many Shibas are showy by nature and require little training to sparkle for the judge.

NIPPO SHOWS

We are fortunate in this country to have two clubs that hold yearly Nippo-style shows with a judge from Japan: The BSA in California and the Colonial Shiba Club in Connecticut. The following introduction to Nippo shows will allow you to understand the process if you participate in Nippo shows in the United States or have an opportunity to observe Nippo shows in Japan.

In national and large regional Nippo shows, the entry is usually so large and so many high quality Shibas are present that a dog with one of the listed faults is not considered for an award. For this reason a Nippo "fault" can be viewed as roughly equivalent to an AKC disqualification, although in a Nippo show dogs with faults are not dismissed from the ring.

The main purpose of a Nippo show is evaluation. Each dog is judged twice—individual judging in the morning focuses on evaluating the dog's form, while group judging in the afternoon is directed at evaluating the dog's character through interaction and comparison with other dogs.

As the judging begins in the morning, the judge's assistant checks and counts each dog's teeth. Once the teeth have been counted, the dogs may not be touched by anyone—handler or judge. The dog must pose and stand firmly by itself, without the benefit of the handler placing the legs in a proper show stance. No baiting is allowed. It is felt that if the dog has the correct structure, temperament and training, it will assume the show stance by itself. The handler must stand behind the dog holding the leash at a 45 degree angle. The judge then orders the handler to move his or her dog in a triangle pattern at a moderate trot to evaluate physical condition and elasticity of gait. Although Nippo actively encourages women to exhibit their dogs, the majority of the participants are still men. It has long been considered an honorable gentleman's hobby to participate in breeding and showing the Japanese native breeds.

Dogs at Nippo shows are evaluated as *Yuryo* (A–excellent), *Tokuryo* (B–very good), *Ryo* (C–good), or do not receive an evaluation. They are also ranked in numerical order. The results are reported in the Nippo magazine, *The Japanese Dog*, which also contains the judge's comments about the top-rated dogs. Today, the show Shiba has become very standardized in Japan and it can be difficult even in a large class to find an individual that looks significantly different from the other entrants. Balance, type, and soundness are the hallmark of the Japanese show quality Shiba. Because of this, Shiba judging relies very heavily on evaluating the dog's temperament, character and physical conditioning.

In each show, all dogs entered in a class will be placed, from 1st to 50th if necessary. However, if a dog does not perform well in the morning individual evaluation the owner will often pull the dog from the afternoon comparison judging. For this reason national show results might list placings to 30th when the actual entry was larger. A Nippo judge is allowed to examine only 50 dogs at a show. Because of this rule a regular class with an entry of 180 dogs will be subdivided into A, B, C and D divisions. This is not an unusually large Shiba class entry for a Nippo national. Nippo judges are not permitted to numerically rank a *Tokuryo* (B) dog above a dog rated *Yuryo* (A). Today it would be very unusual to see a dog rated lower than *Yuryo* at a national show, because all national entrants must qualify by winning at the local or regional level. But in local show results the placements are often listed A1, A2, A3 . . . B1, B2, B3, meaning that not all dogs entered were of excellent quality. Junior puppies are not placed but are instead given a small "a" in the results if considered potentially excellent. A dog missing a few teeth could not place first in today's Nippo shows no matter how beautiful the dog was in other respects. This dog would be rated *Tokuryo* or lower and there would be plenty of *Yuryo* dogs available to place above him.

In addition to the letter rating and class placements, Nippo Shibas may win a Merit Award. These awards have changed over the decades. At the first Nippo Headquarters show the highest honor was the *Monbu Daijinsho* (Minister of Education Award). The top prize had become the *Nihon Ken Hozonkai Honbusho* (Nippo Headquarters Award) when Naka became the first Shiba to win Best In Show at the 1949 Headquarters event.

In 1964 the Headquarters show was renamed the Nippo National. The top award at the national level today, equivalent to Best In Show, is the *Naikaku Sori Daijinsho* (Prime Minister's Award), the first runner up is awarded the *Monbu Daijinsho* (Minister of Education Award) and the second runner up receives the *Bunka Chokansho* (Chief of Culture Award). The second runner up award was formerly titled the Norin Daijinsho (Agricultural Minister's Award). The change reflects the transfer of jurisdiction over dog activities from the Agricultural to Cultural sector of Japanese government. The best of breed winner for each of the native breeds receives the *Saikosho* and best of opposite sex the *Jun Saikosho*. For each class additional Merit Awards are given based on the number and quality of dogs entered. At the national, 3 to 5 Merit Awards are usually given per class division. The awards are: *Waka Inusho* (includes *Waka Inu I* aged 7 to 12 months, *Waka Inu II* aged 7 to 18 months), *Sokensho* (18 months to 2½ years), and *Seikensho* (2½ years and over). Junior puppies do not participate at the national level so the additional awards of *Yochikensho* (under 4 months) and *Yokensho* (4 to 7 months) are only awarded at local and regional shows. The Nippo Prize (*Nihon Ken Honbusho*) is awarded to soken and seiken class winners at local and regional shows. The greater the number of entries the greater the number of Nippo prizes awarded. A large show of over 500 entries may give up to ten *Nippo Honbusho*. At the Nippo National *Nippo Honbusho* is only awarded to the Best of Breed winners. Other awards may be given by the regional or local clubs. *Toku Betsu Yokensho* is a special puppy Merit Award. *Nagano Chiijisho* is the governor's award given to the Best of Breed winner at the Nagano regional show. These special awards are not published in the Nippo magazine but trophies and certificates are given to the winners by the local clubs.

Prior to 1994, Nippo had no title equivalent to champion. In that year the title *Nihon Ken Saiyuryo* was introduced. Points are earned as follows: At the national show, *Saikosho* – 10 pts., *Jun Saikosho* – 8 pts., *Sokensho* or *Seikensho* – 5 pts., *Yuryo* – 2 pts. At a regional show, *Honbusho* – 4 pts., *Sokensho* or *Seikensho* – 3 pts., *Yuryo* – 1 pt. At a local show, *Honbusho* – 3 pts., *Sokensho* or *Seikensho* – 2 pts., *Yuryo* – 1 pt. The dog must gain 10 points at the national level and another ten points at the regional and local levels. The dog must have won these points under two different judges at the national, and at regional/local shows.

What does it take to become a Nippo judge? First you must be a chapter member with experience in breeding Japanese dogs for more than five years. You must be reliable and participate in club activities so that the chapter will feel inclined to nominate you to be a judge's assistant. There are around 400 judge's assistants. You must serve as an assistant for at least two years. If you do a good job you may be recommended to be a judge trainee. Only 30 people can be recommended at one time. You must work as a trainee for a minimum of five to six years. Finally, you become a junior judge and are allowed to judge at regional and local shows. Meanwhile you have attended the training academy every year and have passed various tests. It will be another five to six years before you may become a senior judge qualified to officiate at the national show and at foreign shows. If you are very good and very lucky it has only been 17 years since you first joined your local chapter.

U-UD, U-ACH Yankii's Tenshi UD and owner Carol Kendle go High in Trial with a score of 199.5 at a United Kennel Club Event. Tenshi became the first Shiba to earn the AKC's Utitlity Dog title.

Genetics for Breeders

THIS CHAPTER PRESENTS A BRIEF OVERVIEW of the fundamentals of genetics, then addresses two topics in detail: Coat color inheritance and inbreeding.

Like people, dogs are comprised of cells. Each cell in a dog has a nucleus that contains 39 pairs of chromosomes. Within each pair, one chromosome is inherited from the father and the other is inherited from the mother. Geneticists usually depict a chromosome as resembling a string of beads. Each bead on the string is a gene, made of DNA, that has a special location or *locus* on the chromosome string and is responsible for some aspect of the dog's appearance. Corresponding genes at the same locus in each of the chromosome pairs influence the same factor. Therefore, every factor that contributes to the appearance of the dog is influenced by a gene from the mother and a gene from the father (with the exception of sex-linked traits, which are not discussed here).

A gene at a particular locus may have several possible forms, only one of which appears on any given chromosome. These different gene forms are called *alleles*. For example, some coat color genes have as many as five known alleles that can occur at a particular locus. When the corresponding genes from each parent are the same allele, the two genes are called *homozygous*. If each parent contributes a different gene form the genes are *heterozygous*. In a pair of heterozygous alleles, one is often dominant and the other is recessive. The dominant gene often cloaks the gene inherited from the other parent. However, because the dominant gene does not always completely cover up the characteristics of the recessive gene (incomplete dominance), some dogs can show characteristics of both.

COAT COLOR INHERITANCE

The Shiba is considered a color breed in its country of origin. As such, only three colors are acceptable: a pure orange-red, bright as a flame; an elegant black with clean, crisp tan points; and a sesame reminiscent of autumn leaves brushed with a hint of soot—all with the white markings or *urajiro* that are the hallmark of the breed. Coat hair consists of a core or *medulla* that is surrounded by a cortex and a thin cuticle. Pigment granules called *melanin* are found in both the medulla and cortex. Melanin can be either brown/black (*eumelanin*) or yellow/red (*phaeomelanin*). Genes control the configuration of these pigment granules, and the configuration of the granules are what gives the coat its color.

Based on this explanation, color prediction should be easy. Unfortunately, studies of coat color inheritance in dogs have been limited to observed purebred breedings (none of which cover the Japanese native breeds) and some test cross-breedings. Not all studies were made in a controlled environment, and breeder reports cannot be considered completely reliable because individuals rarely describe color in the same way. Hence, the system of alleles we will describe can only be considered a good working hypothesis.

Geneticists studying the subject of coat color disagree on the finer points of the action of each allele and even on the existence of some alleles. Alleles are sometimes acted on by unknown modifying factors that cause a range of expression within each color. A possible explanation for these modifying factors is that a group of genes, no one of which would control a characteristic on its own, can act together as *polygenes* to control a particular characteristic or to modify the influence of a controlling gene. Plus and minus *rufus* polygenes are thought to cause a variation of depth of color in red/yellow dogs from rich red to cream, and *umbrous* polygenes may control the amount of black overlay in sables. In the Shiba breed, polygenes also appear to control the extension and reduction of the *urajiro* shadings and the tan points pattern in black and tans.

THE A (AGOUTI) ALLELE SERIES

A^s	black/brown
A^y	red/yellow (sable)
A^g	wolf gray (agouti)
a^{sa}	black/brown saddle on red/yellow
a^t	black/brown with red/yellow (tan) points

The A locus controls the expression of black/brown and red/yellow coat colors. Characteristics of this series are dogs that are dark at birth and gradually become lighter with age, coat color that is darker on the back shading to a lighter color on the underbelly, and individual hair shafts that are banded in color. We have listed the A alleles in order of dominance, with the strongest, A^s, listed first.

Two of the alleles in this series do not appear to exist in the Shiba gene pool. A^s is a solid black or brown dog (e.g., Curly Coated Retriever and Newfoundland). A^g, or agouti, is the wolf-gray color found in Norwegian Elkhounds, Keeshounds, and Alaskan Malamutes. The a^{sa} or saddle pattern allele found in German Shepherds probably does not exist in the Shiba either. Genetically, the few Shibas that exhibit a saddle pattern are most likely either very heavily marked red sables or black and tans in which the tan points pattern is extended to a large degree.

Red. A^y and a^t definitely occur in the Shiba. A^y is the classic red color that gives the Shiba its nickname of "Aka inu." A^y reds are born reddish brown with black hairs mixed in the coat, gradually turning red as they mature and the first guard hairs appear. A^y reds are red on the top and sides, shading to creamy white *urajiro* on the belly, neck, throat, cheeks, and underside of the tail (this shading is more extensive in the Shiba than in other A^y breeds. The extension or reduction of the shading

Sumeranishiki of Hadano Kawaguchiso owned by Harumi Suzuki. Multiple merit award winner at Nationals including Monbu Daijinsho at the 80th National.

is thought to be controlled by a set of *urajiro* polygenes). Each guard hair is banded in color, red at the tip and shading to white at the root. The puppy black mask that fades with maturity is also characteristic of A^y reds. In the A^yA^y Shiba (a Shiba that is homozygous A^y—an A^y allele inherited from each parent), the black hairs usually disappear completely in adults. Faults in the color red are dogs that are fawn or brown instead of a clear red, or dogs with too much or too little white shadings.

Black and Tan. The second allele easily observed in the Shiba is the a^t black-and-tan or *tan points* pattern. Black-and-red or red points would be a more accurate description in the case of the Shiba, but we will stick with the familiar name for this pattern. All black-and-tan Shibas are genetically a^ta^t, since a^t is a recessive allele, and black-and-tan color is not expressed if an A^y gene is present. These Shibas are primarily black with a red or gray undercoat. Tan points occur over the eyes, on the sides of the muzzle, on the feet and part way up the legs. In many other tan point breeds, tan is also found on the throat, belly, inside the ears, on the chest, around the anus, and the underside of the tail. In the Shiba breed, these last areas are usually white because of the Shiba *urajiro* in the same location. Mismarks occur when the tan points pattern is reduced or extended. The tan points pattern does not appear to be as stable in the Shiba as in other tan point breeds (such as the Doberman) and is probably influenced by modifying factors. An $a^t a^t$ Shiba may appear nearly solid black or, at the other end of the range, may appear as a red dog with a large solid black blanket. Less obvious mismarks are dogs with very little white or tan face coloring, muddy face coloring (black hairs mixed in the tan or white), and dogs with tan covering the bridge of the nose. Some black-and-tan Shibas have red hairs mixed with the black on the back of the skull. Occasionally white hairs will form an undesirable spectacle pattern around the eyes. It is also important to note that black-and-tan Shiba puppies will exhibit the same A series characteristic as red puppies in that the tan areas are dark at birth.

Takayu of Fukuzonoso owned by Shinobu Sato. Kinki regional show 1st place Waka Inusho.

Sable and Red Sesame. Shibas that inherit an A^y gene from one parent and an a^t gene from the other parent are the most complicated to detect and predict. Dogs that are genetically $A^y a^t$ can have any one of three color patterns: clear red, sable, or red sesame.

The first color, red, is the most commonly seen $A^y a^t$ variation in Japan. In these dogs, A^y is dominant to a^t and completely cloaks the tan point pattern. These dogs are indistinguishable from $A^y A^y$ reds. They may or may not have a ring of black hairs around the tail or a few black hairs on the back of the ears or under the chin that can only be seen on very close examination. One can only determine that these dogs are $A^y a^t$ if a parent or offspring is black and tan. These dogs are red in *phenotype* (meaning they look like $A^y A^y$ clear reds) but sable in *genotype* (meaning they are genetically $A^y a^t$).

Sable, or red with a sparse black overlay generally restricted to the back, is rarely seen in Japanese show dogs but is a fairly common $A^y a^t$ variation in the United States. The density of the black overlay in sables is thought to be controlled by umbrous polygenes. Most of these dogs are *incorrectly* registered as red sesame. Sable would be a more accurate term to use for identification purposes. The Japanese call these dogs "red with black inserts." In Japan, only an extremely sparse overlay of this kind is permissible. Due to lack of communication between Japanese and U.S. breeders in the early and mid-1980s, many dogs with heavy black overlay and dark muzzles were produced by breeding red to black and tan. The base color was often closer to a muddy fawn or brown than red.

The third color variation is the true red sesame or *akagoma*. The base color of these dogs is red with the characteristic Shiba *urajiro*. The red is overlaid evenly with a sprinkling of black throughout the red areas of the body. The key word here is *evenly*. Any concentration of black is considered improper. Often the overlay ends at the knees and hocks and in a definite widow's peak on the forehead, leaving the bridge of the nose and lower legs a clear red. Thus, this variation has a distinctive pattern that is very similar to the tan points pattern in that there are areas of clear red in the same areas where tan points appear in black and tans. This color is the most rare of the acceptable colors in both the United States and Japan. In true red sesames the dominant A^y gene appears to have incomplete dominance over the a^t gene because the black-and-tan pattern is not completely suppressed. In a correct red sesame the dog must not appear more than fifty percent black.

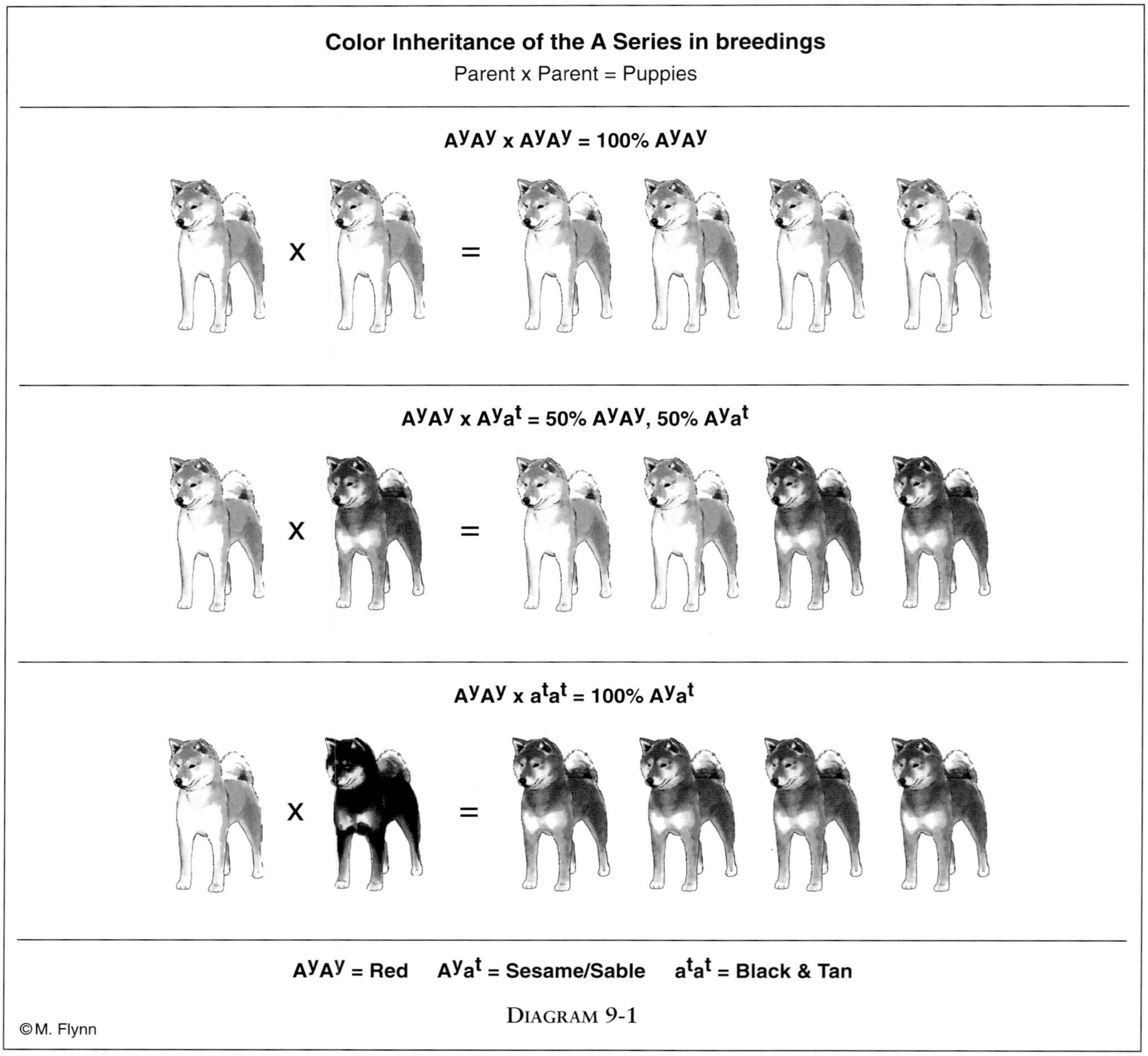

Color Inheritance of the A Series in breedings

Parent x Parent = Puppies

$A^yA^y \times A^yA^y = 100\% \ A^yA^y$

 X =

$A^yA^y \times A^ya^t = 50\% \ A^yA^y, \ 50\% \ A^ya^t$

 X  =

$A^yA^y \times a^ta^t = 100\% \ A^ya^t$

 X  =

A^yA^y = Red A^ya^t = Sesame/Sable a^ta^t = Black & Tan

DIAGRAM 9-1

© M. Flynn

Red sesames that are more than fifty percent black are usually called *kurogoma* or black sesame. This color is extremely rare in the Shiba and is not approved for Nippo shows. There is some doubt as to whether this color is genetically the same as the black sesame that occurs in the Japanese Shikoku breed. It is likely that the black sesame Shiba is a result of *plus* umbrous polygenes acting on the red sesame color. One Nippo judge lecturing in the United States said that he had never seen a black sesame Shiba and was not sure if the color existed in the breed. However, a very small number of

black sesame Shibas do exist in the United States, once again as a result of lack of color knowledge among early Shiba breeders.

The red base color in the A series is probably modified by rufus polygenes in all three combinations of alleles (A^yA^y, A^ya^t, and a^ta^t). Rich red is the preferred color, but red can be faded by *minus* rufus polygenes to a pale fawn. A^ya^t sables and sesames on rare occasions fade all the way to a white sesame color (a cream or pale fawn with a black overlay). In the same manner, the tan points on a black-and-tan Shiba can fade to the extent that the dog will be black and white. Extensive *urajiro* polygenes can also create black and white color in the Shiba by extending the white shading so it covers the tan points areas. These color combinations occur infrequently because the faded color is considered a fault in show dogs and breeders have selected against it. The possible expressions of the A series alleles are as follows:

A^{y}A^y

Possible Range:	fawn, red, brownish red
Ideal:	flame orange red is ideal, pale red to crimson acceptable

Mismarks:	fawn, extended or reduced white shadings (these mismarks apply to A^{y}a^t and a^{t}a^t as well)

A^{y}a^t

Possible Range:	shades of red, red sable, red sesame, black sesame
Ideal:	flame orange red, red sesame; sable with extremely light overlay acceptable
Mismarks:	heavily overlaid red sable, lingering puppy mask, black sesame

---

Color Inheritance of the A Series in breedings

Parent x Parent = Puppies

A^{y}a^t x A^{y}a^t = 25% A^{y}A^y, 50% A^{y}a^t, 25% a^{t}a^t

 X =

A^{y}a^t x a^{t}a^t = 50% A^{y}a^t, 50% a^{t}a^t

 X =

---

a^{t}a^t x a^{t}a^t = 100% a^{t}a^t

 X =   

DIAGRAM 9-2

$a^t a^t$

Possible Range:	red w/blk blanket, black and tan, near solid black
Ideal:	black and tan with rich tan points and clean white markings
Mismarks:	extended or reduced tan points, lingering puppy mask, white circles around the eyes

Hypothetical polygenes that possibly affect Shiba color:

Rufus	controls depth of red color
Umbrous	controls degree of black overlay
Urajiro	controls extension of white ventral shading
Tan Points	controls extension of tan points pattern
Irish	controls degree of white markings (socks, collar, etc.)

Color Inheritance of the A Series in breedings
Parents = Puppies
$A^y A^y$ x $A^y A^y$ = 100% $A^y A^y$
$A^y A^y$ x $A^y a^t$ = 50% $A^y A^y$, 50% $A^y a^t$
$A^y A^y$ x $a^t a^t$ = 100% $A^y a^t$
$A^y a^t$ x $A^y a^t$ = 25% $A^y A^y$, 50% $A^y a^t$, 25% $a^t a^t$
$A^y a^t$ x $a^t a^t$ = 50% $A^y a^t$, 50% $a^t a^t$
$a^t a^t$ x $a^t a^t$ = 100% $a^t a^t$

The percentages in this chart are a guide for the *average* outcome in a litter. An individual litter, with a small number of puppies, will not necessarily produce the expected ratio. For example, if you make an $A^y A^y$ x $A^y a^t$ cross, you might get 3 puppies that are all $A^y A^y$, but if you make several such crosses and get 20 or more puppies, the ratio will closely approach the predicted 50% $A^y A^y$, 50% $A^y a^t$. In any of the above crosses that predict 100% of a particular genotype, of course, that genotype is all you will get, unless a puppy in your litter carries an extremely rare point mutation. Keep in mind that the above percentages are merely for the *genotype*, and the *phenotype* (the color you see) may be different due to modifying factors or genes at other alleles.

THE C ALLELE SERIES

The next most important locus to Shiba breeders is that which controls the cream or stained white color. Shibas of this color range from cream with fawn or orange stains around the ears and back to pure white. Noses are nearly always black, but can be pink. This color is extremely undesirable in Nippo and JKC shows, and creams are usually given away as pets in Japan. A probable cause of this color is the c^{ch} or chinchilla gene, although there may be other alleles as well. The dominant C gene, when inherited from either parent (CC or Cc^{ch}) allows full expression of the pigment controlled by the A series (red or black). Homozygous c^{ch} ($c^{ch}c^{ch}$) dilutes reds and blacks to cream.

Note that the C series is separate from the A series. In other words, a Shiba has two alleles of the A series at one locus on its chromosomes and two alleles of the C series at a separate locus on its chromosomes. However, even though the loci are different, the genes at one locus can affect the expression of genes at another. For example, the homozygous cream genotype ($c^{ch}c^{ch}$) can mask the expression of the $A^s A^s$ genotype even though A^s is dominant to (masks) all the other alleles at its own locus. This is true even though the c^{ch} gene is recessive to C. This phenomenon is known as epistasis. The c^{ch} gene is epistatic to (covers up) A^s.

Another possible cause of the cream Shiba is minus rufus polygenes acting on the red color. However, two dogs that are richly colored reds or black and tans can produce creams, without producing the faded intermediary colors that would be likely if rufus polygenes were the primary cause of cream in the Shiba. In some breeds, it has been noted that while red x red matings sometimes produce creams, black-and-tan x black-and-tan matings rarely or never do. Geneticists have hypothesized that in those breeds there is an allele at the C locus that, when homozygous, is epistatic to A^y and hypostatic to a^t ("hypostatic" is the opposite of "epistatic" and means that the expression of the hypostatic gene is covered up by a gene at a different locus). Those who have advanced this theory call that allele c^{ch}, and posit another allele, c^e, which, when homozygous, is epistatic to both the A^y and a^t alleles. If this is correct, then it is likely that the Shiba gene pool contains the c^e allele, instead of the c^{ch} allele, since a black-and-tan x black-and-tan Shiba breeding can produce creams. However, in our charts we will simply use c^{ch} to indicate the C-series allele that produces cream color.

Possible expression of the C series:

CC — solid color red, sable, red sesame, or black and tan (as determined by the alleles at the A locus)

Cc^{ch} — solid color red, sable, red sesame, or black-and-tan carrier of the chinchilla gene

$c^{ch}c^{ch}$ — cream, stained white, or white regardless of the alleles present at the A locus

Color inheritance of the C series

CC x CC = 100% CC

CC x Cc^{ch} = 50% CC, 50% Cc^{ch}

CC x $c^{ch}c^{ch}$ = 100% Cc^{ch}

Cc^{ch} x Cc^{ch} = 25% CC, 50% Cc^{ch}, 25% $c^{ch}c^{ch}$

Cc^{ch} x $c^{ch}c^{ch}$ = 50% Cc^{ch}, 50% $c^{ch}c^{ch}$

$c^{ch}c^{ch}$ x $c^{ch}c^{ch}$ = 100% $c^{ch}c^{ch}$

THE S ALLELE SERIES

The S series of alleles is important to Shiba breeders because of the limitations in the Nippo and AKC Standards regarding white markings. The s^i or Irish allele is definitely present in the Shiba gene pool. Most Shibas are born with white toe tips or white chest and belly markings that fade into the *urajiro* by early adolescence. Occasionally white socks are seen and are acceptable as long as they do not reach past the hock or elbow. More extensive Irish markings are not desirable but are sometimes found: socks above the hock or elbow, white on the back of the neck, white collar around the neck, star, or nose stripe. The S (no white markings) and S^p (pinto) forms of this gene may also be present in small numbers in the gene pool.

OTHER ALLELIC SYSTEMS

Several other genes are thought to affect coat color in dogs but appear to have little or no variability in the Shiba. The alleles at the B locus determine whether dark pigmented areas such as the nose will be black or liver. Homozygous bb produces a chocolate coat color and liver nose in A^sA^s or A^tA^t dogs. It has no effect on red/yellow pigment. If the b allele existed in the Shiba we would see chocolate and tan in addition to black and tan.

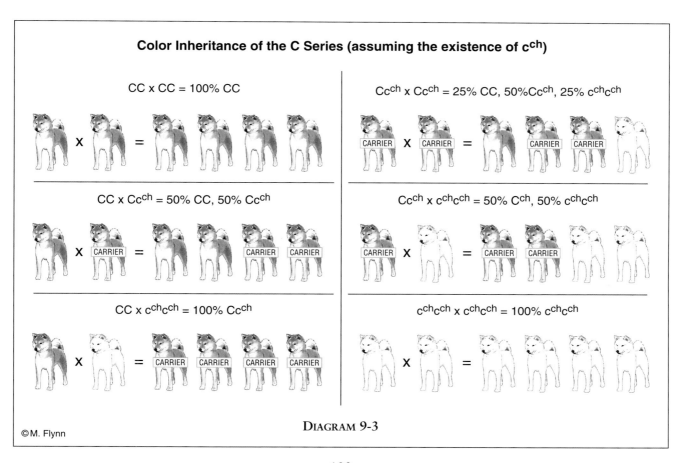

Color Inheritance of the C Series (assuming the existence of c^{ch})

CC x CC = 100% CC

Cc^{ch} x Cc^{ch} = 25% CC, 50% Cc^{ch}, 25% $c^{ch}c^{ch}$

CC x Cc^{ch} = 50% CC, 50% Cc^{ch}

Cc^{ch} x $c^{ch}c^{ch}$ = 50% Cc^{ch}, 50% $c^{ch}c^{ch}$

CC x $c^{ch}c^{ch}$ = 100% Cc^{ch}

$c^{ch}c^{ch}$ x $c^{ch}c^{ch}$ = 100% $c^{ch}c^{ch}$

©M. Flynn

DIAGRAM 9-3

Left: Maihime of Saijyoryuichiso owned by Y. S. Chuang of Taiwan. 87th Nippo National Seikensho. Shikoku Regional Nippo Kaichosho.

The D dilution gene determines whether black pigment will be black or blue and whether red pigment will become cream. Since we do not see any blue (dd) or lilac (bb and dd) Shibas and we do not see liver noses, it is unlikely that the d allele exists in the Shiba.

The E series is complex. The E allele allows black color to be black (that is, A^s or a^t at the A locus will be expressed), but in dogs with the recessive ee combination, all black is covered up by red or yellow (that is, the ee genotype is epistatic to A^y or a^t). If the e allele existed in the Shiba, a pair of black and tans (a^ta^t) who each carried one copy of the e allele (Ee) could produce a clear red (a^ta^t ee) puppy! We have heard rumors of red pups produced by black-and-tan parents, but no reliable examples from reputable breeders exist. It is also possible that a red pup could be produced from two black-and-tan parents by spontaneous mutation of an A^y allele to the a^t form, although this would be an exceedingly rare occurrence.

A more practical reason to dismiss the possibility of the e allele in the Shiba is the nature of the allele. The ee genotype produces a clear red with no black whatever. It does not explain the black hair found on Shiba puppies that become clear red adults.

Examples of ee reds include Golden Retrievers, Irish Setters, and yellow Labrador Retrievers. Thus, it is unlikely that the e allele occurs in the Shiba gene pool, and all Shibas are probably EE.

Some geneticists consider the black mask (E^m) to be part of the E series, while others consider it to be separate. This allele does not occur in the Shiba. The Shiba black mask is definitely a result of umbrous polygenes rather than E^m. Shiba puppies are often born with a black mask that fades at maturity. We have not seen evidence in the Shiba of the type of solid black mask that is visible in adult Great Danes or Pugs that is typical of E^m.

Another variation at the E locus is the brindling allele. The gene for brindle does not exist in the Shiba, although it does occur in the Japanese Kai and Akita breeds. Unless reliable evidence is produced to the contrary, breeders should assume that the Shiba carries only the dominant E allele in this series.

Likewise, variations at the G (graying), M (merle), and T (ticking) loci do not appear in the Shiba, as uniform color is the norm. Shibas can be considered homozygous for gg, mm, and tt.

THE W^H GENE

Another possible explanation of the cream color seen in the Shiba is the W^h gene. A relatively new theory about the cause of white in the German Shepherd suggests that the color is a simple recessive affecting both red and black color. W^h would

The cream color also called "stained white" due to the red tinge behind the ears is not preferred in the show ring. Cream puppies are often given away as pets by Japanese breeders. B. Zurawski.

be the colored form and w^h would be the white form. Cream appears to act as a simple recessive in the Shiba, but an epistatic gene at the C locus could produce the same effect. We have used the $c^{ch}c^{ch}$ gene combination to demonstrate the action of the cream color in our charts, but readers should be aware that the chinchilla allele is only one of several possible causes of cream color.

INBREEDING

Inbreeding and linebreeding are practices that are freely accepted by some dog breeders who believe that inbreeding practiced "properly" will lead to better dogs of more uniform type with no loss of health or vitality. Proper practice is said to involve breeding only the best to the best and rigid culling. It is said that inbreeding brings faults to the surface where they can be recognized and eliminated. However, while inbreeding can lead to an improvement in physical appearance and consistency of type, it cannot simultaneously lead to an increase in fitness, and indeed probably leads to an *inevitable* decrease in fitness. ("Fitness" is used to mean overall health, vigor, and survival ability). The following discussion is somewhat simplified (for example, it does not discuss hybrid vigor) but it covers the important points dog breeders should know.

When we talk about faults due to inbreeding, we are generally talking about recessive faults. Since one of the principles of inbreeding is to inbreed only on an outstanding animal, we would presumably never inbreed on an animal that showed a particular fault in conformation or health (i.e., had a dominant, expressed gene for that fault). Recessive genes for faults are not visible in the individual who is a "carrier" (has only one gene for the fault), and so we have no way of knowing if our outstanding animal carries a particular recessive or not when we begin inbreeding on it.

Genes come in pairs. Even if one gene is defective and does not produce the protein it is supposed to produce, the other gene usually produces enough to allow the animal to have a near normal level of the protein. For example, in humans, if only one gene in a gene pair produces the abnormal "sickle cell" hemoglobin, the person has sickle cell trait (rather than sickle cell disease), which has few if any bad health consequences. The reason is that the normal gene in the pair produces enough normal hemoglobin to allow the blood to transport oxygen properly.

The fact that genes come in pairs is one of the key mechanisms by which evolution takes place. Because of the protective effect of having two genes instead of one, random variations can take place, and the helpful variations can be saved without the defective variations meaning the animal will die. Thus, animals whose genes come in pairs have the best of both worlds—they can evolve without the inevitable "mistakes" being too detrimental. This is why all higher animals have genes that come in pairs.

Most random changes (mutations) in a gene pair are detrimental. The reason for this is that when you have a highly complex system, random changes are statistically much more likely to be in the direction of a less complex and therefore less functional system. For example, if you are typing a letter and you hit a few keys at random, it may produce a better word than you were going to use, but it is much more likely to produce nonsense.

An example of evolution is a wolf pack whose habitat is gradually getting colder and whose coats are gradually getting thicker. Assume that one gene pair controls the amount of undercoat that the wolves have. If that gene never changed, the wolves would have the same amount of undercoat all the time, and they would be unable to adapt to the changing temperatures.

But genes do change (by mistakes in replication), and after a while, a random change occurred in one gene that made a wolf's undercoat grow thicker. The wolf that had this mutation was better suited for the cold environment, and she produced more offspring than the other wolves. Half of her offspring carried the mutated gene, and soon the gene spread throughout the population, as the environment continued to grow colder. Meanwhile, most of the "bad" mutations that popped up in that gene pair (you could say these were designs that didn't work) did not harm the wolves that had them because they were hidden recessives. The protein they produced simply didn't work, but it didn't interfere with the protein produced by the good gene of the pair. When the "better" new gene came along, it did help the animal, and therefore the animal had a selective advantage.

There are two consequences of this general genetic scheme of gene pairs. One consequence is that animals are able to adapt to changed conditions. Another consequence is that populations accumulate some bad genes (the "failed experiments"). These bad genes are called "genetic load," and all higher animals have genetic load. However, in the wild, genetic load is not really harmful because the normal gene in the pair protects the animal. When an animal gets a bad gene at the same location from both parents neither gene in the animal's gene pair will produce the correct protein, and the animal will not have the benefit of that protein. If the protein is a protein that is crucial to the animal's life, like hemoglobin, the animal will die. If the protein is useful but not crucial, then the animal will survive but not be as healthy as it should be. In nature, it rarely happens that an animal inherits the same bad gene from both parents. The reason is that due to the random nature of mutation one animal generally has bad genes at different gene locations from another animal's bad genes. There are a huge number of genes in each animal, and only a few of them will be bad. Therefore the odds that an unrelated male and female have a bad gene at the same location are very small.

However, all this changes if the animals are related. Let's take the example of a father-daughter mating. The daughter has received half of her genes from her father, so half of her genes are identical to his. If the father is carrying twenty-four "bad" recessive genes (a typical number) as his genetic load, he will on average have passed twelve of these to his daughter. (Each parent gives each offspring one gene from each of that parent's gene pairs. The gene from the pair that the offspring gets is random, so it will be the nonfunctioning, bad gene 50% of the time and the functioning good gene the other 50%.) This means that the father and daughter will each have one nonfunctioning gene at twelve of the same gene-pair locations.

An offspring from a breeding of this father-daughter pair will, on average, receive a *pair* of nonfunctioning genes at *three* of the animal's gene locations. The result of this is that, because neither gene in the pair is functional, three proteins will not be made. The reason the offspring will have three locations with both bad genes is simple math—there is a 50% probability of a bad gene at each location in a particular gene pair. Multiplying .5 x .5 to find the probability that both genes in the pair will be bad equals .25. We then multiply 12 (gene pair locations with at least one bad gene) x .25 (probability that both genes will be bad) to find three (probable locations with both bad genes).

If one or more of these three proteins that are not made are crucial for survival, the offspring with the defect will not survive. The puppy may die in the uterus and be reabsorbed by the mother's body. It may be born and be a "fading puppy." If the absence of the protein is merely harmful, and not fatal, the animal may grow up and have a poor immune system, or a thyroid deficiency, or a bad temperament. Some of the offspring will not inherit two bad genes at any of their locations (remember, three locations with two bad genes at each is just the average), and some of the offspring who inherit a double dose of bad genes will have such subtle bad effects that they probably won't be noticed, but there will be a statistically significant increase in health defects in the inbred litter.

Now let's see what happens if the daughter is bred to an unrelated male. This male probably has the typical genetic load of the species, twenty-four bad genes—twelve from his mother and twelve from his father, each at a different gene pair. Neither the daughter nor this unrelated male is suffering any bad health effect from their bad genes because they also have a good gene in each pair. Just as in our first example, their puppies will each, on average, inherit a genetic load of approximately twelve bad genes from the sire and twelve bad genes from the dam. However, these bad genes will not likely have any bad effect. The reason is that the bad genes of their parents are probably all at different locations. Let's say each dog has 400,000 separate gene locations (a number chosen for illustrative purposes). The odds of the unrelated male and female having the same bad gene at one of only twenty-four out of 400,000 loci is quite low. Thus, these outcross puppies, unlike our inbred puppies, are likely to get at least one good gene in each of their genetic pairs.

The bad effects of inbreeding are the reason why virtually every genetically complex animal species has developed social mechanisms to ensure that populations will be outcrossing. We can see this in mammal social groups where the young are driven away from the pack upon reaching sexual maturity, and in fish like salmon that spawn in home rivers then travel far out to sea to breed, and in humans where there is an instinctive revulsion from incest.

Advocates of inbreeding do not generally deny that inbreeding increases the frequency of harmful genes, but they say that by proper selection you can start with an animal that has few deleterious genes, then use rigid culling of the offspring to get rid of the remaining harmful genes in the inbred stock. However, it is impossible to use this "weeding out" process to get inbred dogs that are as healthy as outcrossed dogs. One reason that is that most of the harmful genes that we have to worry about are completely invisible and undetectable in the carrier. This means we have no way of knowing if our foundation animal is clear of a particular trait, or if his offspring are.

Some people advocate test breeding as a way around this problem. Test breeding involves breeding an animal to animals known to be actually affected with a particular disease caused by recessive genes. On average, 50% of the puppies from such a breeding will be affected by the disease if the animal being tested is a carrier, and none will be affected (although all will be carriers) if the animal does not have the defective gene. Even assuming we know what we are testing for (which we usually don't), there are several problems with test breeding. First, there is the ethical question of whether it is right to knowingly produce puppies that are affected or are carriers of a genetic disease. Second, if a genetic disease is fatal before the puppy is born or soon afterwards, affected animals cannot be maintained for test breeding. However, the main objection to test breeding is that it is simply not practical, because there are so many possibilities that would have to be tested. Also, if a condition does not cause problems until later in life, it will not be detectable by test breeding in time to be of use in selecting breeding stock.

Even if tests were available that could detect one bad gene in a gene pair, so that we would have no need of test breeding, we still could not use inbreeding to "select out" harmful genes. It is mathematically impossible for an ethical breeder. An example will make this clear. Suppose we plan a brother-sister mating. The sire and dam of the brother and sister are not related to each other, are of very high quality, and have no visible faults in conformation or health. Let us assume that the brother and sister have each inherited only eight invisible, recessive faults each from their parents and we can identify these faults in a carrier. Let's assume further that the brother and sister have in common only three of these faults. Now, these conditions are not likely to be anywhere near this favorable in real life, but the results show that even if you start out with a situation much better than any you could obtain in real life, you will still have problems in inbreeding.

We will call the three gene locations where the brother and sister share defective genes A, B, and C. The defective alleles are a, b and c, so we have the relevant genetic complement of the brother and sister as Aa, Bb, and Cc. (Remember that if we were outcrossing, we would most likely have *no* gene pairs where both the sire and dam had defective genes.)

Now let's assume that we are going to try to get rid of these three defective genes, so that we will not have affected puppies keep cropping up in our line. We make the brother-sister mating and can diagram the breeding as follows:

Brother   Sister
Aa Bb Cc   x   Aa Bb Cc

What we are looking for is a puppy that is clear for all three traits; that is, a puppy who is AA BB CC. This puppy will not be a carrier of any of the defective genes. The odds of getting an AA BB CC puppy are figured mathematically by multiplying the odds of getting AA times the odds of getting BB, then multiplying that figure by the odds of getting CC. This will give you the odds of getting all three locations clear in one puppy. Since both parents are carriers, the odds of getting a puppy clear of the defective gene is 1 out of 4 for each of the three locations. That means we multiply 1/4 x 1/4 x 1/4 = 1/64.

Thus, only one out of sixty-four puppies will be AA BB CC (clear for all three traits)! The other sixty-three puppies will be carriers for one or more of the harmful traits, and many of the puppies will not just be carriers, but will be affected by one or more of the diseases, since they will get a defective gene from each parent. If we had outcrossed (bred to an unrelated animal), that animal would be unlikely to carry a, b, or c, and we would have one out of eight puppies completely clear (AA, BB, CC), instead of only one out of sixty-four. We would also have a lower incidence of carriers, and *no* puppies affected by disease.

When we think about a real world situation where a full brother and sister are likely to share more than three harmful recessives, where we cannot test for or even identify carriers of most of the harmful recessives, and where harmful recessives may not even show up until the animal is two or three years or older, we can see that it is impossible in practical terms to breed out all recessive faults by inbreeding to "bring them to the surface." The conclusion to be drawn is that the best we can do with genetic defects is to keep them hidden by outcrossing. This is a perfectly acceptable solution, and it is the solution Nature herself uses. A second conclusion is that selection can be used to improve only a very few characteristics at one time, unless we are able to produce vast numbers of animals to select from, which dog breeders cannot do and don't want to do.

It is true that sometimes inbred animals are healthy and sound. But what we don't often see are the littermates that died. In addition, the inbred animal may have problems we cannot see, such as being a difficult breeder, or sterile, or having a temperament problem, or dying in middle age.

Dog breeders who plan to use linebreeding or inbreeding in spite of the health consequences should know how to calculate the degree of inbreeding. The "inbreeding coefficient" (IC) is the standard measurement of the degree of inbreeding. Today there are computer programs available that will figure the inbreeding coefficient for you once you have typed in your dogs' pedigrees.

Sometimes people will think a dog is extremely inbred when in fact the IC shows it is not inbred at all or only inbred to a very small extent. For example, a dog may have a particular ancestor that appears five times in a five generation pedigree of its sire. However, unless that dog has the same ancestor appearing on the mother's side as well, the IC is zero. If a particular dog appears five times in the fifth generation on the sire's side of a pedigree, and three times in the fifth generation on the dam's side of the pedigree, for a total of eight times, many people would think the offspring would be extremely inbred. In fact, a puppy from such a breeding will have an IC of only about 3%, which is less than half the IC of a puppy from a mating of first cousins! The reason for this is that the IC decreases rapidly as the number of generations back to the common ancestor increases. A dog in the fifth generation of a pedigree has only a minute effect on the degree of inbreeding compared to dogs closer up.

As another example, many people think of grandfather-granddaughter or aunt-nephew breedings as linebreedings. In fact, for both these types of breedings the IC is 12.5% — a rather high number. So, the degree of inbreeding needs a little knowledge to determine, and some people who think they are inbreeding are really not doing so to any great extent, while others are doing more than they realize.

The inbreeding coefficient for some typical inbreedings is as follows:

father/daughter	25%
mother/son	25%
full brother/sister	25%
half brother/half sister	12.5%
grandfather/granddaughter	12.5%
double first cousins	12.5%
uncle/niece	12.5%
first cousins	6.2%
first cousins once removed	3.1%
second cousins	1.6%

When you are tempted to inbreed on an outstanding animal, you owe it to the puppies you will produce to educate yourself about genetics and know the downside of inbreeding. Your knowledge can make the difference between a healthy litter and one that brings heartbreak to the unfortunate owners of inbred dogs.

A long-coated Shiba makes an adorable pet for someone who enjoys grooming. "Parker" is owned by Stanleigh Karki.
E. Behrens.

The Breed Gallery

INTRODUCTION TO
THE BREED GALLERY

THIS BREED GALLERY IS DESIGNED to help new and old Shiba fanciers with pedigree studies. Most of the Shibas selected for the Breed Gallery are Japanese imports. Using your pedigree from your Shiba's breeder and the pedigrees in the Breed Gallery, we hope you will be able to trace your Shiba back to its Japanese roots and get a better idea of the type of your Shiba's ancestors.

In addition to Japanese imports, we have also included several American-bred Shibas that have won specialties held by the Shiba Club of America, Beikoku Shibainu Aikokai, National Shiba Club of America or the Shiba Ken Club. One thing you will notice right away is that we have not included any American breed club titles in the Breed Gallery. The reason for this is that all three American rare breed clubs granted titles prior to AKC recognition, and we felt it would be too confusing to use all the different titles, as well as take up a great deal of space. So as you are reading, remember that many of the dogs listed have titles from one or more American breed clubs.

When we collected the pedigrees for this gallery we discovered that many of the Japanese dogs' names were translated three or four different ways. Nippo translations generally string all of the characters of the dog's name and its kennel name together to form two long words. The Japan Kennel Club translations break up the characters to form individual words in an attempt to make the name more understandable in English. JKC also inserts the English "of" between the dog's name and kennel name. The "of" is not really a part of the name of the Japanese dog. "So" is used to spell the word ending for kennel in Nippo translations.

JKC spells the same character "sow." "Kensha" is still another word meaning kennel. Some of the translations that were completed by individuals leave the character "go" at the end of the dog's name. This character has no real English equivalent and is used only when writing the name of a dog in Japan. It is seldom used when speaking the dog's name. Both Nippo and JKC omit "go" from translations.

One of the chief difficulties for translators is that a Japanese character (kanji) can have either a Japanese or Chinese pronunciation. Although most characters were properly converted to English letters (romaji), occasionally mistakes were made. For example, the dam of the popular Japanese stud Jouji of Fussaen appears as Yukime of Fussaen in some pedigrees and Sachime of Fussaen in others. The name Jou (also Joukichi or Jouji) is also translated at Jyo or simply Jo in some AKC pedigrees. The Japanese stud Tamanishiki of Fujinomiya Kensha has also been listed as Tamanishiki-go Fujinomiyakensha,Tamanishiki of Fujimiya Kensha, or Tama Niskiki Fujimiya Inu Sha. Tamanishiki's son Sumeranishiki of Hadano Kawaguchiso was incorrectly translated as Knoishiki at some point (the character can be pronounced either as Sumera or Ko) and appears that way in many AKC pedigrees. We received a photo of Sumeranishiki for this book from his owner in Japan and corrected the name in all of the pedigrees that appear in this breed gallery.

We have tried to be as consistent as possible in listing the names that appear in these pedigrees so that readers may trace the relationship of these dogs to each other and to their Japanese ancestors. In many, but not all, cases, we were able to contact the owners of the dogs in Japan directly for the correct translation.

1

Call Name: Aka
DOB: 01-02-73
Color: Red
Sex: Male
Breeder:
Kohji Ikeda
Owner:
Kaiji Katsumoto

Meiho of Shimamura
Tenshou of Toumon
Ayame of Ayaseichikawaso
Sire: Tengou of Aikenso
Korotake of Ayaseichikawaso
Sawahime of Oume Utsukiso
Senhime of Koganeiso
Nidai Akajishi of Sagami Ikeda Kensha
Meiho of Shimamura
Tenshou of Toumon
Ayame of Ayaseichikawaso
Dam: Akajishi of Mukenso
Senryu of Touenso
Akaiahime of Koganeiso
Kokonoe of Touenso

Noteworthy Facts: Import. First import of which a record exists of registered progeny.

2

Call Name: Kojika
DOB: 10-01-76
Color: Red
Sex: Female
Breeder:
Shigeharu Mitamura
Owner:
Julia Cadwell

Beniyuki of Sakuraso
Matsumaru of Shinshu Nakajima
Akafusame of Mita Kensha
Sire: Matsumaru of Chojuso
Matsumaru of Shinshu Nakajima
Kuri of Kawagoeso
Akaishime of Sankoso
Shina no Ichihime of Shinshu Mitamuraso
Beniyuki of Sakuraso
Matsumaru of Shinshu Nakajima
Akafusame of Mita Kensha
Dam: Ichifujihime of Shinshu Mitamuraso
Matsumaru of Shinshu Nakajima
Ichimarume of Shinshu Mitamuraso
Fujiryokuhime of Eijuso

Noteworthy Facts: Imported in 1978. Had a litter with "Rusty" on Thanksgiving Day in 1979.

3

Call Name: Rusty
DOB: unknown
Color: Red
Sex: Male
Breeder: unknown
Owner:
Julia Cadwell

Rusty
(Pedigree Unknown)

Noteworthy Facts: Found running loose and was later certified and registered by JKC as a purebred Shiba. Pedigree unknown but probably born 08-29-77, sired by Maya of Ogigauraso and out of Fuji of Saitama Ogiso in California.

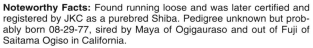

4

Call Name: Hanako
DOB: 07-11-79
Color: Red
Sex: Female
Breeder: Kotobuki
Sasayama
Owner:
Jean Uchida

Hidejishi of Sonanso
Hideyuki of Seikaso
Higurai Sakura of Toyohashi Miyamotoso
Sire: Rikiishi of Toyohashi Hozanso
Ryokuko of Minowaso
Senhime of Nidai Baneiso
Chisato of Dairinso
Rikihome of Yoshizen Kotobukiso
Nobushi no Takeshi of Yamabiko
Tokai no Takeshi of Toyohashi Beneiso
Fujihime of Nichijinso
Dam: Hozanme of Toyohashi Hozanso
Toyomitsu of Toyohashi Tanabeso
Toyohime of Seikaso
Hozan Himesakura of Toyohashi Hozonso

Noteworthy Facts: Import.

5

Call Name: Philly
DOB: 11-24-79
Color: Red
Sex: Female
Breeder:
Takehiko
Takebayashi
Owner:
Yuko and Gino
Salvadori

Tenko of Jonenso
Shina no Kobushin of Morita Jikkendobutsu Hanshokusho
Kimaruhime of Niigata Masagoso
Sire: Tenzan of Shinshu Yudaiso
Nobushi no Take of Yamabiko
Takehime of Nidaimannenso
Taihobenihime of Nidaimannenso
Koyukihime of Shinshu Yudaiso
Tenko of Jonenso
Hayabusa Inayama Shibainukai
Tsubakihime of Ezaki Kensha
Dam: Michiyohime of Ezaki Kensha
Tamamitsu of Inoguchi
Tamaruhime of Ezaki Kensha
Momoichihime of Ezaki Kensha

Noteworthy Facts: Import.

6

Call Name: Ryu
DOB: 01-02-80
Color: Red
Sex: Male
Breeder:
Masao Ikuta
Owner:
Jean Uchida

Katsuranishiki of Enshu Ichirikiso
Tamanishiki of Fujinomiya Kensha
Beniichime of Enshu Sogaso
Sire: Koto No Tamamidori of Kotoso
Koto no Mitsusuke of Kotoso
Koto No Tamahime of Kotoso
Sengyokume of Kotoso
Soto No Gyokuryu of Sotoso
Dai Ni Nakaryu of Hiroshima
Ryutoso
Eiryu of Kumamoto Usubaso
Shinjuhime of Nagasakiso
Dam: Ryushohime of Sotoso
Kirin Ni Sei of Shinshu Kirinso
Shohime of Shibakenkai
Benitomi of Shibakenkai

Noteworthy Facts: Import.

7

Call Name: Chibi
DOB: 01-02-80
Color: Black and
Tan
Sex: Female
Breeder:
Kohji Ikeda
Owner:
Kaiji Katsumoto

Tsuyutaka of Sagami Murasakiso
Kurojishi of Sagami Murasakiso
Tsuyufuji of Sagami Murasakiso
Sire: Kuroichi of Rozanso
Taketoyo of Hokoso
Toyomihime of Shimosa Mukenso
Matsume of Harase Garten
Kuromatsume of Sagami Ikeda Kensha
Ichisuke of Inoguchi
Yasuke of Fussaen
Kotomohime of Akitaso
Dam: Kuri of Hanemura Takamizu
Yasuke of Fussaen
Chibi of Fussaen
Kurata No Yukihime of Ano Kurataso

Noteworthy Facts: Import.

8

Call Name: Termite
DOB: 08-11-80
Color: Red
Sex: Female
Breeder:
Mitsuhiko Fukuda
Owner:
Frank and Merry
Atkinson

Matsumaru of Shinshu Nakajima
Fujimaru of Fujinomiya Kensha
Beniichime of Enshu Sogaso
Sire: Fuji No Tomotake of Dairy Farm
Tenjo of Mita Kensha
Matsutomo of Dairy Farm
Kunichika of Dairy Farm
Benitakehime of Dairy Farm
Komayu of Asahinaso
Yumaru of Nishihata Mameso
Benihaname of Kaoruso
Dam: Watase no Yuhime of Dairy Farm
Matsu of Shinshu Tsubameso
Takamatsuhime of Dairy Farm
Marihime of Dairy Farm

Noteworthy Facts: Import. 1981 SCA National Specialty BOS. Mexican Champion.

9

Call Name: Bell
DOB: 11-20-80
Color: Red
Sex: Male
Breeder:
Kaiji Katsumoto
Owner:
Kaiji Katsumoto

Tenshou of Toumon
Tengou of Aikenso
Sawahime of Oume Utsukiso
Sire: Nidai Akajishi of Sagami Ikeda Kensha
Tenshou of Toumon
Akajishi of Mukenso
Akaiahime of Koganeiso
Shishi of Kenwaso
Kurojishi of Sagami Murasakiso
Kuroichi of Rozanso
Toyomihime of Shimosa Mukenso
Dam: Kuromatsume of Sagami Ikeda Kensha
Yaesuke of Fussaen
Kuri of Hanemura Takamizu
Chibi of Fussaen

Noteworthy Facts: Import.

10

Call Name: Kaze
DOB: 12-29-80
Color: Black and
Tan
Sex: Male
Breeder:
Tadao Suzuki
Owner: Frank and
Merry Atkinson

Tsuyutaka of Sagami Murasakiso
Kurojishi of Sagami Murasakiso
Tsuyufuji of Sagami Murasakiso
Sire: Kuroichi of Rozanso
Taketoyo of Hokoso
Toyomihime of Shimosa Mukenso
Matsume of Harase Garten
Kuroyuki of Nanko Suzuki Kensha
Kurojishi of Sagami Murasakiso
Kuroichi of Rozanso
Toyomihime of Shimosa Mukenso
Dam: Kurobenihime of Sagami Ikeda Kensha
Minomaru of Hakone Tsuda
Yukihime of Sagami Ikeda Kensha
Miyohime of Sagami Ikeda Kensha

Noteworthy Facts: Import. 1981 and 1982 SCA National Specialty BOB. 1983 SCA National Specialty BOS. 1984 World Champion, Champion of the Americas, Int'l. Champion, CACIB, Mexican Champion.

11

Call Name: Kaizo
DOB: 02-12-81
Color: Red
Sex: Male
Breeder: Sadao Ito
Owner:
Sheryl Langan

Katsuramaru of Kawagoeso
Shinran of Fujinomiya Kawaguchi Kensha
Azusahime of Fujinomiya Kawaguchi Kensha
Sire: Tofuuhikari of Yukawa Kita Kensha
Mishima no Aka of Fussaen
Maruhime of Mishimajuku Akadamaso
Benimarume of Mishima Suigo
Teruarashi of Fuji Itoso
Beniyu of Tachibanaso
Benimaru of Shizuoka Otsuka
Benimaruhime of Shizuoka Tsuchiya
Dam: Fujibeni of Kazumiso
Tenko of Joneneso
Benimitsu of Fujieda Otsuka
Nadaka Beniharu of Fujiedaso

Noteworthy Facts: Import.

12

Call Name: Shana
DOB: 07-08-81
Color: Red
Sex: Female
Breeder:
Kazuhiro Tsuchiya
Owner:
Julia Cadwell

Tenko of Joneneso
Mitsumaru of Shinshu Mitamuraso
Ichimarume of Shinshu Mitamuraso
Sire: Shinko of Ichikawa Aoki
Ichisuke of Inoguchi
Komari of Inoguchi
Senmi of Inoguchi
Tsubaki of Chiba Shiraneso
Tenryu of Shinshu Takeiso
Mitsuryu of Bizen Tsurumakiso
Mitsuhime of Bizen Kotobukiso
Dam: Tsukitamahime of Kurashiki Fukumoriso
Tenryu of Shinshu Takeiso
Tenhime of Kurashiki Fukumoriso
Fumuhime of Kurashiki Fukumoriso

Noteworthy Facts: Import.

13

Call Name: Keidai
DOB: 08-02-81
Color: Black and Tan
Sex: Male
Breeder: Ako Aoki
Owner: Julia Cadwell

Noteworthy Facts: Import.

```
                                              Taketoyo of Hokoso
                          Banetsu no Azuma of Banetsu Azumaso
                                              Tochisanhime of Mito Takai
            Sire: Tokiwa no Benisuke of Kasukabe Tokiwaso
                                              Mitsutaro of Mie Kozanso
                          Hoshihime of Seisho Kensha
                                              Benimitsuhime of Seisho Kensha
            Tetsumaru of Ichikawa Aoki
                                              Taketoyo of Hokoso
                          Banetsu no Azuma of Banetsu Azumaso
                                              Tochisanhime of Mito Takai
            Dam: Fukubenihime of Ichikawa Aoki
                                              Fukuo of Fussaen
                          Koro of Ouchi
                                              Korobenihime of Chiba Yoshinagashi
```

14

Call Name: Yoshi
DOB: 08-08-81
Color: Red
Sex: Female
Breeder: Tsuyoshi Kumazawa
Owner: Mary Malone

Noteworthy Facts: Import.

```
                                              Katsuranishiki of Enshu Ichiriki
                          Tamanishiki of Fujinomiya Kensha
                                              Beniichime of Enshu Sogaso
            Sire: Tamashiro of Hadano Nagoroso
                                              Kiyoichi of Mie Kozanso
                          Osumi no Maihime of Hadano Nagoroso
                                              Tama no Benihisahime of Tama Koshizukaso
            Haruka of Hadano Nagoroso
                                              Hidemaru of Enshu Kaiunso
                          Wakajishi of Enshu Tatsumiso
                                              Benikahime of Enshu Tatsumiso
            Dam: Kurokocho of Habikino
                                              Bijomaru of Misonoso
                          Koharu of Misonoso
                                              Benitsubaki of Misonoso
```

15

Call Name: Chippies
DOB: 08-15-81
Color: Red
Sex: Female
Breeder: Jean Uchida
Owner: Joan Young

Noteworthy Facts: 1989 NSCA National Specialty BOS from Veteran's Class.

```
                                              Tamanishiki of Fujinomiya Kensha
                          Koto no Tamamidori of Kotoso
                                              Koto no Tamahime of Kotoso
            Sire: Soto no Gyokuryu of Sotoso
                                              Eiryu of Kumamoto Usubaso
                          Ryushohime of Sotoso
                                              Shohime of Shibakenkai
            Graham Uchida's Mischief Maker
                                              Hideyuki of Seikaso
                          Rikiishi of Toyohashi Hozanso
                                              Senhime of Nidai Baneiso
            Dam: Rikihome of Yoshizen Kotobukiso
                                              Tokai no Takeshi of Toyohashi Beneiso
                          Hozanme of Toyohashi Hozanso
                                              Toyohime of Seikaso
```

16

Call Name: Senshi
DOB: 08-24-81
Color: Red
Sex: Male
Breeder: Yoshi Takaezu
Owner: Julia Cadwell

Noteworthy Facts: Import.

```
                                              Tenryuichi of Shinshu Tenryuso
                          Tamaryuji of Kansai Nikken
                                              Shinshu Midorihime of Shinshu Mitamuraso
            Sire: Ginjishi of Ibuki no Tsukasaso
                                              Tamaryuji of Kansai Nikken
                          Ibuki no Kiku of Ibuki no Tsukasaso
                                              Benitakame of Ibuki no Tsukasaso
            Ginzakura of Chiba Yoshizenso
                                              Tenko of Jonenso
                          Yamabiko of Ryokuchu Kensha
                                              Yukiya of Ryokuchu Kensha
            Dam: Sakura of Kamifusa Shiroyamaso
                                              Minomaru of Fujinomiya Kensha
                          Kamifusa no Sakura of Kamifusa Shiroyamaso
                                              Mibu no Tetsume of Dairy Farm
```

17

Call Name: Mama
DOB: 09-02-81
Color: Red
Sex: Female
Breeder: Akio Sato
Owner:
Jane Vanderpool

Katsuranishiki of Enshu Ichiriki
Tamanishiki of Fujinomiya Kensha
Beniichime of Enshu Sogaso
Sire: Koro no Matsunishiki of Aunso
Kozan no Zuiho of Daini Kozanso
Korome of Aunso
Koromaruhime of Shinshu Shiomineso
Seitenhime of Aunso
Tenryu of Shinshu Takeiso
Tenko of Shikoku Kofujiso
Akatatsume of Sugawaso
Dam: Teniohihime of Nishitake Kensha
Beniaka of Senboso
Satome of Echigo Nakagoso
Nagamatsuhime of Echigo Nakagoso

Noteworthy Facts: Import. 1983 SCA National Specialty BOB.

18

Call Name: Yuki
DOB: 01-20-82
Color: Red Sesame
Sex: Male
Breeder:
Kohji Ikeda
Owner:
Kaiji Katsumoto

Tsuyutaka of Sagami Murasakiso
Kurojishi of Sagami Murasakiso
Tsuyufuji of Sagami Murasakiso
Sire: Kuroichi of Rozanso
Taketoyo of Hokoso
Toyomihime of Shimosa Yumeinuso
Matsume of Harase Garden
Fujio of Sagami Ikeda Kensha
Jyaku of Inoguchi
Nakaba of Fussaen
Koyohime of Ome Shimizuso
Dam: Sachihime of Bushu Shogunso
Fukuryu of Akishima Fukudaso
Yorihime of Bikoen
Sachihime of Akishima Fukudaso

Noteworthy Facts: Import. 1986 BSA Specialty BOB.

19

Call Name: Sam
DOB: 01-27-82
Color: Black and Tan
Sex: Male
Breeder:
C. S. Van Allen
Owner: Fred Duane

Kurojishi of Sagami Murasakiso
Kuroichi of Rozanso
Toyomihime of Shimosa Mukenso
Sire: Kuroyuki of Nanko Suzukiso
Kuroichi of Rozanso
Kurobenihime of Sagami Ikeda Kensha
Yukihime of Sagami Ikeda Kensha
Mokusei Takeshi of Mokuseiso
Kurojishi of Sagami Murasakiso
Kuroichi of Rozanso
Toyomihime of Shimosa Mukenso
Dam: Kayame of Chigasaki Moroboshi
Kuroichi of Rozanso
Kurohime of Nanko Suzuki Kensha
Kurotamahime of Sagami Ikeda Kensha

Noteworthy Facts: First NSCA Specialty BOB. (Of four specialties held by NSCA in 1984, this was the first.)

20

Call Name: Penny
DOB: 05-14-82
Color: Red
Sex: Female
Breeder:
Toshio Sotokawa
Owner: Fred Duane

Mizakura of Okuichiso
Fujizakura of Wake Sunamiso
Fujiyakkohime of Ichimatsuso
Sire: Hisazakura of Joshu Toyooka Kensha
Yukiizumi of Joshu Ringiso
Toyohime of Joshu Toyooka Kensha
Takemime of Tago Kensha
Yukimehime of Yukiguniso
Beninaka of Kawagoeso
Benitaro of Harutakeso
Asakahime of Kasukabe Itsumiso
Dam: Beniichihime of Harutakeso
Koro of Suyamaso
Harusenhime of Harutakeso
Harume of Harutakeso

Noteworthy Facts: Import.

21

Call Name: Kabuki
DOB: 05-16-82
Color: Black and Tan
Sex: Female
Breeder: Toshimasa Yasumaru
Owner: Nancy Baugus

Hakuba no Gen of Rokakuso
Azumi no Hana of Shinshu Azuminoso
Shina no Ichibenihime of Shinshu Azuminoso
Sire: Hanichi of Genseiso
Takamaru of Mita Kensha
Chikahime of Mita Kensha
Nana of Mita Kensha
Kuronana of Hayakoso
Hanaichi of Ginseiso
Momoichi of Ginseiso
Hanahime of Ginseiso
Dam: Nanibana no Harume of Shibainu Satsukikai
Azumi no Hana of Shinshu Azuminoso
Kuro no Hana of Wake Sunamiso
Maruhime of Wake Sunamiso

Noteworthy Facts: Import.

22

Call Name: Cinnamon
DOB: 05-25-82
Color: Red
Sex: Female
Breeder: Kenji Hayasaka
Owner: Mary Malone

Oki no Tamakazura of Iwaki Okiso
Umemaru of Koriyama Hashimotoso
Chihayahime of Bankokuso
Sire: Sakura no Kiyotaka of Akanuma Sakuraso
Namibana Nishiki of Shibaken Ikuseikai
Hitachi no Beni of Hitachi Hakuyoso
Kiyohime of Hiyofukuso
Haya no Kiyomi of Akanuma Hayasakaso
Inamaru of Ezaki Kensha
Kumonoue no Hamamaru of Iwaki Kumonoueso
Kotoyakko of Yamatoro Kensha
Dam: Beniaihime of Akanuma Sakuraso
Nadaka Benitaka of Fujimine Kensha
Nadaka Beniai of Ashikaga Komiyaso
Aiko of Ashikaga Komiyaso

Noteworthy Facts: Import.

23

Call Name: Issei
DOB: 05-25-82
Color: Red
Sex: Female
Breeder: Kenji Hayasaka
Owner: Julia Cadwell

Oki no Tamakazura of Iwaki Okiso
Umemaru of Koriyama Hashimotoso
Chihayahime of Bankokuso
Sire: Sakura no Kiyotaka of Akanuma Sakuraso
Namibana Nishiki of Shibaken Ikuseikai
Hitachi no Beni of Hitachi Hakuyoso
Kiyohime of Hiyofukuso
Haya no Kiyohime of Akanuma Hayasakaso
Inamaru of Ezaki Kensha
Kumonoue no Hamamaru of Iwaki Kumonoueso
Kotoyakko of Yamatoro Kensha
Dam: Beniaihime of Akanuma Sakuraso
Nadaka Benitaka of Fujimine Kensha
Nadaka Beniai of Ashikaga Komiyaso
Aiko of Ashikaga Komiyaso

Noteworthy Facts: Import.

24

Call Name: Chazy
DOB: 05-27-82
Color: Red
Sex: Female
Breeder: Yasuo Ineda
Owner: Fred Duane

Tenko of Jonenso
Mitsumaru of Shinshu Mitamuraso
Ichimaru of Shinshu Mitamuraso
Sire: Shinko of Ichikawa Aoki
Ichisuke of Inoguchi
Komari of Inoguchi
Chimi of Inoguchi
Ichibeni of Ineda Meikenso
Yukihide of Kyowaso
Tatsujishi of Harimaso
Nakamarume Harimaso
Dam: Akafuji of Ineda Meikenso
Komakiyo of Toyohashi Asaokaso
Komamihime of Garyukutsu
Tokuhime of Garyukutsu

Noteworthy Facts: Import.

25

Call Name: Amber
DOB: 05-31-82
Color: Red
Sex: Female
Breeder:
Yasu Masa Kamino
Owner:
Ed and Tiare Arndt

Noteworthy Facts: Import.

```
                              Tenko of Shikoku Kofujiso
                 Shidemine of Mifujiso
                              Tenryuyuhime of Shikoku Kofujiso
        Sire: Zuko of Shichi Fukuso
                              Katsumaru of Tsunugaso
                 Katsuhime of Kinkozanso
                              Kikumaru of Shichi Fukuso
Haru Sakura of Kagawa Shichihoso
                              Wakanishiki of Fujinomiya Kensha
                 Suzuwaka of Shichi Fukuso
                              Suzuhime of Sanuki Suiyoso
        Dam: Fukuyoshiichime of Kagawa Shichihoso
                              Terunishiki of Takuma Fukuokaso
                 Terumatusme of Shichi Fukuso
                              Matsuichime of Shichi Fukuso
```

26

Call Name: Shu
DOB: 10-20-82
Color: Red
Sex: Male
Breeder:
Frank Sakayeda
Owner:
Sheryl Langan

Noteworthy Facts: Import.

```
                              Katsuranishiki of Enshu Ichiriki
                 Tamanashiki of Fujinomiya Kensha
                              Beniichime of Enshu Sogaso
        Sire: Hidenishiki of Fujinomiya Kensha
                              Takaichimaru of Aunso
                 Takame of Yamanashi Minamiso
                              Hideko of Yamanashi Minamiso
Tsuru of Satoriso
                              Tamanishiki of Fujinomiya Kensha
                 Koro no Matsunishiki of Aunso
                              Korome of Aunso
        Dam: Seitenhime of Aunso
                              Tenko of Shikoku Kofujiso
                 Tenichihime of Nishitaki Kensha
                              Satome of Echigo Nakagoso
```

27

Call Name: Sassy
DOB: 11-09-82
Color: Black and
Tan
Sex: Female
Breeder:
Not Available
Owner:
Bob and ulie
Jennings

Noteworthy Facts: Import.

```
                              Fujimaru of Fujinomiya Kensha
                 Fuji no Tomotake of Dairy Farm
                              Matsuchika of Dairy Farm
        Sire: Sowa no Takeichi of Dairy Farm
                              Kokuryu of Imabariso
                 Kiyotatsumi of Dairy Farm
                              Kiyofusahime of Dairy Farm
Tega no Namiyo of Dainana Kashiwayamaso
                              Kurojishi of Sagami Murasakiso
                 Kuroichi of Rozanso
                              Toyomihime of Shimosa Yumeinuso
        Dam: Haruhime of Musashi Noboritoso
                              Tasuke of Tyogiriso
                 Tamatsuru of Noborito Nakaneso
                              Yuzuruhime of Shimosa Marunaka Kensha
```

28

Call Name: Tomo
DOB: 11-25-82
Color: Red
Sex: Male
Breeder:
Minoru Shirai
Owner:
Mary Malone

```
                              Azumi no Hana of Shinshu Azuminoso
                 Mitaki no Hana of Mie Meihoso
                              Hikarimarume of Kachoso
        Sire: Hanamaru of Meiwaso
                              Taiho of Tsuyama Kataoka Kensha
                 Shohome of Kichibiso
                              Akamarume of Kichibiso
Gangu no Gen of Sanuki Ganguso
                              Tenryu of Shinshu Takeiso
                 Tenko of Shikoku Kofujiso
                              Akatatsume of Mikawaso
        Dam: Tenkome of Sanuki Ganguso
                              Naka of Garyuso
                 Nakaori of Shibukawa Koto Kensha
                              Orihime of Muko Hikariso
```

Noteworthy Facts: Import. BOB in the 1987 and 1988 Kennel Review Tournament of Champions.

29

Call name: Mitsu
DOB: 10-13-83
Color: Red
Sex: Female
Breeder:
Teruhisa Azuma
Owner:
Ed and Tiare Arndt

Katsuranishiki of Enshu Ichiriki
Tamanishiki of Fujinomiya Kensha
Beniichime of Enshu Sogaso
Sire: Tama no Katsuramaru of Aunso
Mitsutenryu
Tennoyuhime of Nishitaki Kensha
Satome
Mitsutamahime Awaazumaso
Kuro
Hidenishiki of Sanuki Shirouchiso
Nishikihidehime
Dam: Komanishikihime of Sashusetoso
Harukoma
Komamarume of Sanuki Shirouchiso
Matsumarume

Noteworthy Facts: Import.

30

Call Name: Sai
DOB: 02-02-84
Color: Red
Sex: Female
Breeder:
Kiichi Sato
Owner:
Kaiji Katsumoto

Yaesuke of Fussaen
Jouji of Fussaen
Sachime of Fussaen
Sire: Juokichi of Yamanashi Fujikenso
Tatsumaru of Akishima Fukutaso
Tatsumihime of Yamanashi Ono
Beniyakko of Amano Kensha
Aya of Fussaen
Kyushu no Kurotaka of Kyushu Eto Kensha
Kyushu no Kurobeni of Kyushu Eto Kensha
Kurokiku of Bungoichinomiya Kensha
Dam: Sachibenime of Fussaen
Oh of Fussaen
Sachime of Fussaen
Tomi of Fussaen

Noteworthy Facts: Import. 1987 BSA Specialty BOB.

31

Call Name: Joe Joe
DOB: 02-10-84
Color: Red
Sex: Male
Breeder:
Nobumitsu Uchida
Owner:
Julia Cadwell

Mitsumaru of Shinshu Mitamuraso
Jaku of Inoguchi
Kiyomi of Inoguchi
Sire: Tetsunobu of Saisho Kensha
Soichi of Tokyo Tamagawaso
Senmi of Hakuryuso
Mucho of Tokyo Tsutsumiso
Horyumaru of Saisho Kensha
Yaesuke of Fussaen
Daisuke of Toyogiriso
Matsuhime of Markie
Dam: Yumihime of Toyogiriso
Konishiki of Takami Kensha
Chihohime of Futagaryo Kezuka
Sakon Matsuhime of Izumiso

Noteworthy Facts: Import.

32

Call Name: Kuro
DOB: 04-25-84
Color: Black and Tan
Sex: Female
Breeder:
Akira Kanamoto
Owner:
Sheryl Langan

Shinshuichi of Shinshu Mitamuraso
Shinshu Tatsumaru of Ina Mitsumineso
Mitsutamahime of Ina Mitsumineso
Sire: Sakushu Tatsumaru of Mitsuwa Kensha
Mitsumaru of Aichi Inaba
Fukuhime of Aichi Inaba
Kofumihime of Izawaso
Kuroichime of Awa Kinseiso
Shinshu Tatsumaru of Ina Mitsumineso
Sakushu Tatsumaru of Mitsuwa Kensha
Fukuhime of Aichi Inaba
Dam: Sakushu Natsume of Awa Kinseiso
Hideichi of Aunso
Yuko of Awa Kinseiso
Azumi no Kurohana of Ginseiso

Noteworthy Facts: Import.

33

Call Name: Kenny
DOB: 05-01-84
Color: Red
Sex: Male
Breeder:
Frank Sakayeda
Owner: Fred Duane

Shinran of Fujinomiya Kawaguchi Kensha
Tofuhikari of Yukawa Kita Kensha
Maruhime of Mishimajuku Akadamaso
Sire: Teruarashi of Fuji Itoso
Benimaru of Shizuoka Otsuka
Fujibeni of Kazumiso
Benimitsu of Fujieda Otsuka
Kintaro of Satoriso
Tamanishiki of Fujinomiya Kensha
Hidenishiki of Fujinomiya Kensha
Takame of Yamanashi Minamiso
Dam: Hana of Satoriso
Koro no Matsunishiki of Aunso
Seitenhime of Aunso
Tenichihime of Nishitaki Kensha

Noteworthy Facts: Early east coast sire.

34

Call Name:
Mortisha
DOB: 05-05-84
Color: Black and
Tan
Sex: Female
Breeder:
Michiaki Mochizuki
Owner: Fred Duane

Tamamitsu of Inoguchi
Hidemitsu of Mino Katayama
Beniumemi of Hitotsuyamaso
Sire: Hidemaru of Eppuso
Daiichi of Suzuki Kensha
Koshihime of Eppuso
Tetsuhime of Mitsui Kensha
Sa no Kuroyuri of Konan Mochizuki
Mita no Matsuo of Shinshu Nakajima
Kikumaru of Mita Kensha
Nakakurohime of Mita Kensha
Dam: Koshu Kurogikume of Shikoraku Kadamaso
Gen of Shinano Misuzuso
Kinta Michihime of Kintaso
Omi no Michihime of Sakunoso

Noteworthy Facts: Import.

35

Call Name: Natasu
DOB: 07-15-84
Color: Red
Sex: Female
Breeder:
Kazuo Kuwahara
Owner:
Janice Cowen

Kurata no Hachiko of Ano Kurataso
Kurata no Haruichi of Ano Kurataso
Kurata no Momome of Ano Kurataso
Sire: Yuki no Shinichi of Saitama Shiawaseso
Takaichi of Shizunami Kensha
Takafusame of Kawagoeso
Akafusame of Chojuso
Yukihime of Gardenaso
Tengou of Aikenso
Nidai Akajishi of Sagami Ikeda Kensha
Akajishi of Mukenso
Dam: Shishihime of Kenwaso
Kuroichi of Rozanso
Kuromatsume of Sagami Ikeda Kensha
Kuri of Hanemura Takamizu

Noteworthy Facts: 1987 Kennel Review Tournament of Champions
BOS.

36

Call Name: Aki
DOB: 02-01-85
Color: Red
Sex: Female
Breeder:
Y. Mizusawa
Owner: Yuko and
Gino Salvadori

Senko of Araki Kensha
Tenko of Jonenso
Tamahime of Yorokobiso
Sire: Mitsutoyo of Mita Kensha
Shachi of Kamiyaso
Senkofusahime of Mita Kensha
Kiyohime of Mita Kensha
Aki of Mizusawa
Nana of Mita Kensha
Benikuni of Mita Kensha
Akarikihime of Mita Kensha
Dam: Kikuzukime of Echigo Yukiguniso
Tenko of Jonenso
Tenkinme of Mita Kensha
Konihime of Mita Kensha

Noteworthy Facts: Import.

37

Call Name: Chibi
DOB: 04-02-85
Color: Red
Sex: Male
Breeder:
Kaoru Koike
Owner: Chris Ross

Tamanishiki of Fujinomiya Kensha
Sumeranishiki of Hadano Kawaguchiso
Mizunashi no Keizanme of Hadano
Kawaguchiso
Sire: Kiminishiki of Tamakazeso
Tatsumaki of Misonoso
Kimi of Tamakazeso
Benihide of Furuyazoso
Ch. Shinshu Chibisuke of Shinshu Ueda Tenguso ROM
Senko of Araki Kensha
Tenko of Jonenso
Tamahime of Yorokobiso
Dam: Tenichihime of Shinshu Ueda Tenguso
Mita no Matsuoh of Mita Kensha
Mitatenhime of Mita Kensha
Mitsufusahime of Mita Kensha

Noteworthy Facts: Import.

38

Call Name: Foxey
DOB: 07-28-85
Color: Red
Sex: Female
Breeder:
Kuniaki Nagafuji
Owner:
Sheryl Langan

Mine no Tenpyo of Okutani
Kaiazuma of Akaharuso
Hosahime of Shinshu Takeiso
Sire: Yatsu no Kuromaru of Kai Ryusenso
Tamamitsu of Serikawa
Hide no Komamidorihime of Ishiwa Oguraso
Hide no Chiyomidorihime of Akaharuso
Kirihime of Dohgakuderaso
Kounishiki of Hadano Kawaguchiso
Tamaaki of Fujinomiya Kensha
Takame of Yamanashi Minamiso
Dam: Himenishiki of Dohgakuderaso
Katsuranishiki of Enshu Ichiriki
Kinshuhime of Shimizu Kobushiso
Shuhohime of Shimizu Kobushiso

Noteworthy Facts: Import.

39

Call Name: Happy
DOB: 08-06-85
Color: Red
Sex: Male
Breeder:
Okamotose
Owner:
Debbie Meador

Daishin
Daimatsu of Kyototerao
Fujime
Sire: Kiyomatsu of Kitatanakaso
Kiyoichinami
Taiho no Kiyohime of Takatsuki Toyotaso
Chiminimarume
Daichi of Toyonaka Okomotoso
Inaichi
Yodo no Mitsukoma of Yodo Gawa Hayashiso
Kimika
Dam: Hanakoma of Osaka Kire
Rikiichikoma
Mitsuhime of Osaka Kire
Ega no Senohime

Noteworthy Facts: 1989 NSCA National Specialty BOB.

40

Call Name: Dreamer
DOB: 09-15-85
Color: Red Sesame
Sex: Male
Breeder:
Mary Malone
Owner:
Mary Malone

Mitaki no Hana of Mie Maeihoso
Hanamaru of Meiwaso
Shohome of Kichibiso
Sire: Gangu no Gen of Sanuki Ganguso
Tenko of Shikoku Kofujiso
Tenkome of Sanuki Ganguso
Nakaori of Shibukawa Koto Kensha
Minimeadow Dreamer
Tamanishiki of Fujinomiya Kensha
Tamashiro of Hadano Nagoroso
Osumi no Maihime of Hadano Nagoroso
Dam: Haruka of Hadano Nagoroso
Wakajishi of Enshu Tatsumiso
Kurokocho of Habikino
Koharu of Misonoso

Noteworthy Facts: 1986 NSCA #1 Shiba.

41

Call Name: Beni
DOB: 10-15-85
Color: Red
Sex: Male
Breeder:
Kaiji Katsumoto
Owner:
Ed and Tiare Arndt

Tengo of Aikenso
Nidai Akajishi of Sagami Ikeda Kensha
Akajishi of Mukenso
Sire: Shishi of Kenwaso
Kuroichi of Rozanso
Kuromatsume of Sagami Ikeda Kensha
Kuri of Hanemura Takamizu
Beniwashi Kenwaso
Jouji of Fussaen
Joukichi of Yamanashi Fujikenso
Tatsumihime of Yamanshi Ono
Dam: Aya of Fussaen
Kyushu no Korobeni of Kyushu Eto Kensha
Sachibenime of Fussaen
Sachime of Fussaen

Noteworthy Facts: 1987 BSA Specialty Best Male.

42

Call Name: Airwolf
DOB: 11-22-85
Color: Red
Sex: Male
Breeder:
Joan Young
Owner:
Sue Barnett and
Joan Young

Kuroyuki of Nanko Suzuki Kensha
Kurotake of Kenwaso
Kuromatsume of Sagami Ikeda Kensha
Sire: Fire Fox of Minimeadow
Sakura no Kiyotaka of Akanuma Sakuraso
Haya no Kiyomi of Akanuma Hayasakaso
Beniaihime of Akanuma Sakuraso
Kinouk Airwolf
Koto no Tamamidori of Kotoso
Soto no Gyokuryu of Sotoso
Ryushohime of Sotoso
Dam: Graham Uchida's Mischief Maker
Rikiishi of Toyohashi Hozanso
Rikihome of Yoshizen Kotobukiso
Hozanme of Toyohashi Hozanso

Noteworthy Facts: 1987 NSCA National Specialty BOB. 1989 SKC National Specialty BOS and Stud Dog.

43

Call Name: Foxy
DOB: 04-01-86
Color: Red Sesame
Sex: Male
Breeder:
Suki Mahar
Owner: Tim and
Gretchen Haskett

Sakura Nishiki of Murakami Gagyuu
Sakura no Takayuu of Yoshifukuso
Izumi no Takahime of Kohriyama Izumiso
Sire: Takayu of Shimotsuke Nantaiso
Shiomine of Shimotsuke Nantaiso
Shimotsuke Yuhime of Shimotsuke Nantaiso
Yoyohime of Utsunomiya Gotoh
Yukan of Aoyama Mahar
Yoshikiyo of Yamabiko
Yoshiyuki of Kiyokuniso
Fukumi of Kiyokuniso
Dam: Fujihime of Kiyokuniso
Tomikaze of Kiyokuniso
Benifujime of Kiyokuniso
Masahime of Kiyokuniso

Noteworthy Facts: 1987 and 1988 SKC Showdog of the Year. First SKC Champion. 1988 SKC National Specialty Stud Dog.

44

Call Name: Fuji
DOB: 04-10-86
Color: Red
Sex: Male
Breeder:
Hiroyuki Kaida
Owner:
Steve Satake

Sakushugen of Tsuyama Kunimotoso
Kitakyu no Genta of Fukuoka Ishikawa
Genkai no Hime of Fukuoka Emoto
Sire: Sanshiro of Horieso
Senjuhomare of Fudogataki Kensha
Horie no Suzu of Horieso
Suzumari of Hojoso
Fujizakura of Hikari Kaidaso
Shukoh of Shonai Izumiso
Shukohmaru of Izumiso
Kumi of Izumiso
Dam: Kurohana of Suohshimasueso
Shoryu of Ohitasankou
Momoichihime of Iwakuni Doujiso
Ayuhime of Iwakuni Doujiso

Noteworthy Facts: Import.

45

Call Name: Chibi
DOB: 04-15-86
Color: Red Sesame
Sex: Male
Breeder:
Shogo Oikawa
Owner:
Richard Tomita

Sakushugen of Tsuyama Kunimotoso
Habiki no Gen of Habikinoso
Miyukime of Izumiso
Sire: Koshu no Gen of Echigo Suwaso
Ichiryumaru of Kamiyaso
Senhime of Suruga Oishi Kensha
Mineko of Yaizu Ishihara
Ch. Katsuranishiki of Oikawa House
Fuji no Takamaru of Amano Kensha
Fuji no Wakataka of Amano Kensha
Yatsuhime of Omata Kensha
Dam: Musashi no Beniyukime of Oikawa House
Koshu no Gen of Echigo Suwaso
Hanamine of Oikawa House
Minehime of Showa Makoto Kensha

Noteworthy Facts: Import. 1989 Super Match BIM over entry of 1500. 1990 Kennel Review Tournament of Ch. Rare Breed Dog of the Year.

46

Call Name: Walla
DOB: 06-30-86
Color: Red
Sex: Female
Breeder: Regina
Hagberg
Owner: Tim and
Gretchen Haskett

Hanamaru of Meiwaso
Gangu no Gen of Sanuki Ganguso
Tenkome of Sanuki Ganguso
Sire: Minimeadow Samurai First
Tamashiro of Hadano Nagoroso
Haruka of Hadano Nagoroso
Kurokocho of Habikino
Dunroven Kogata
Kuroyuki of Nanko Suzuki Kensha
Kurotake of Kenwaso
Kuromatsume of Sagami Ikeda Kensha
Dam: Minimeadow Bonsi
Sakura no Kiyotaka of Akanuma Sakuraso
Haya no Kiyomi of Akanuma Hayasakaso
Beniahime of Akanuma Sakuraso

Noteworthy Facts: 1987 and 1988 SKC #2 Bitch. 1988 SKC National Specialty Brood Bitch.

47

Call Name: Jou
DOB: 04-02-87
Color: Red
Sex: Male
Breeder:
Kaiji Katsumoto
Owner:
John Mizuno

Kitakyu no Genta of Fukuo Kaishikawa
Sanshiro of Horieso
Horie no Suzu of Horieso
Sire: Fujizakara of Hikari Kaidaso
Shukohmaru of Izumiso
Kurohana of Suohshimasueso
Momoichihime of Doujiso
Jou Kenwaso
Jouji of Fussaen
Joukichi of Yamanashi Fujikenso
Tatsumihime of Yamanashi Ono
Dam: Aya of Fussaen
Kyushu no Kurobeni of Kyushu Eto Kensha
Sachibenime of Fussaen
Sachime of Fussaen

Noteworthy Facts: 1989 BSA Specialty BOB.

48

Call Name: Uni
DOB: 04-02-87
Color: Red
Sex: Female
Breeder:
Kaiji Katsumoto
Owner: Bruce and
Jeri Braviroff

Kitakyu no Genta of Fukuokaishikawa
Sanshiro of Horieso
Horie no Suzu of Horieso
Sire: Fujizakara of Hikari Kaidaso
Shukohmaru of Izumiso
Kurohana of Suohshimasueso
Momoichihime of Iwakuni Doujiso
Fukuhime Kenwaso
Jouji of Fussaen
Joukichi of Yamanashi Fujikenso
Tatsumihime of Yamanashi Ono
Dam: Aya of Fussaen
Kyushu no Kurobeni of Kyushu Eto Kensha
Sachibenime of Fussaen
Sachime of Fussaen

Noteworthy Facts: 1990 BSA Specialty BOB. 1990 SKC National Specialty BOS.

49

Call Name: Shogun
DOB: 05-05-87
Color: Red Sesame
Sex: Male
Breeder:
Hiroyuki Kaida
Owner: Doug and
Evelyn Behrens

Takiryu of Shinshu Takeiso
Seto no Takimaru of Hachioso
Kyushu no Takahime of Kyushu Koikeso
Sire: Mitsuryu of Bingo Nakayamso
Sakushu Momomaru of Marikuriso
Mitsuhanahime Matsunaga Omura Kensha
Mitsuhime of Matsunaga Ono Kensha
Tetsuryu of Hikari Kaidaso ROM
Kuro of Sasagawaen
Kuromitsu of Ibuki Nanguso
Koyo Benisakurahime of Koyodo
Dam: Kurotakahime of Hikari Kaidaso
Shukomaru of Izumiso
Beniyukihime of Hikari Kaidaso
Kikuhime

Noteworthy Facts: Import.

50

Call Name: Ryu
DOB: 05-18-87
Color: Red
Sex: Male
Breeder:
Keiji Yamazaki
Owner:
Donald Robinder

Yaesuke of Fussaen
Jouji of Fussaen
Sachime of Fussaen
Sire: Tenichiryu of Ryokushinso
Fujiryu of Sukematsuso
Hama no Onna of Hamamidoriso
Kokahime of Omori Notaniso
Ryutaro of Yamazakiso Kensha
Gyokuju of Hadano Nagoroso
Kotabuki of Naka Araiso
Azuma no Beniyuki of Higashi Tokorozawaso
Dam: Chika of Yamazakiso Kensha
Minefuji of Tobu Nakajimaso
Azumagiku of Iino Fujinoso
Benizakura of Kawagoeso

Noteworthy Facts: Import.

51

Call Name: BEEF
DOB: 06-02-87
Color: Red
Sex: Male
Breeder:
Fred Lanting
Owner:
Fred Lanting

Suwakai of Shinshu Takeiso
Shinshu Ichimiya of Minowa Masumi Kensha
Ran of Minowa Masumi Kensha
Sire: Komaryu of Ina Seifuso
Matsufusa of Kanbaraso
Benifusame of Ganwaso
Benimarume of Nagano Jinjo Kensha
BEEF of Willow Wood
Matsukawa no Sasuke of Matsukawa Kensha
Shishimaru of Matsukawa Kensha
Matsuhime of Matsukawa Kensha
Dam: Fujigikuhime of Ina Seifuso
Tetsuyu of Haruchika Kensha
Kikubeni of Haruchika Kensha
Hiroakame of Ina Beniya

Noteworthy Facts: Import. 1991 SCA National Specialty BOB. Mexican, Bahamian, States Kennel Club Champion, CACIB.

52

Call Name: Vixen
DOB: 07-10-87
Color: Red
Sex: Female
Breeder:
Kuri Kasue
Owner:
Bob Russell

Koumaru Tamakuriso
Taikazan Iagaguriso
Sakushu Komachi Tamakuriso
Sire: Konishiki of Suoukumagaya
Youryu Ooita Sankoso
Kuzuname of Yamaguchi Kawamura Kensha
Nishiki no Hanahime Tamakuriso
Ch. Midorihime of Igaguriso CD
Genjiro Hatsuse Kensha
Kougen of Izueiryuso
Tamaryume Hadano Kawaguchiso
Dam: Anjinkouhime of Miura Anjinso
Genta Okamotoso
Kazusakinuhime of Akugawaso
Seto Uchikinuhime Kobayashiso

Noteworthy Facts: Import.

53

Call Name: Toy
DOB: 07-25-87
Color: Black and Tan
Sex: Male
Breeder: Kiyoko Fukuda
Owner: Francis Attridge

Genkoh of Kurashiki Tsuchiyaso
Tama no Fuji of Fujinomiya Inoue Kensha
Tamakomachi of Fujinomiya Inoue Kensha
Sire: Akaginishiki of Gunma Fukuda
Musashi no Goroh of Musashino Bishuso
Musashi no Tetsuhime of Musashino Bishuso
Musashi no Yuri of Musashino Bishuso
Fukurinmaru of Gunma Fukuda Kensha
Tama no Fuji of Fujinomiya Inoue Kensha
Fujigen of Gunma Katsumiso
Habuka no Hime of Tochigi Yutakaso
Dam: Miohime of Gunma Fukuda
Yoshiryuu of Tsuyama Kawaguchiso
Misuzuhime of Gunma Katsumiso
Tonehime of Gunma Fukuda

Noteworthy Facts: Import.

54

Call Name: Kuma
DOB: 08-08-87
Color: Red
Sex: Female
Breeder: Suki Mahar
Owner: Bill and June Gilmore

Yoshikiyo of Yamabiko
Yoshiyuki of Kiyokuniso
Fukumi of Kiyokuniso
Sire: Yoshimaru of Kiyokuniso
Azumamaru of Ichikawa Aoki
Azumagiku of Kiyokuniso
Nobuyukime of Kiyokuniso
Kuma Mitsu of Aoyama Mahar
Sakuranishiki of Murakami Gagyuu
JKC Ch. Taketora of Yodaso
Takahime of Suzuki Kensha
Dam: Kinki of Aoyama Mahar
Fukusuke of Morowa Shirakoso
Mizuhohime of Nishikoyamaso
Izumi no Tsuruzakurahime of Koriyama Azumiso

Noteworthy Facts: 1988 SKC National Specialty BOS.

55

Call Name: Summer
DOB: 08-17-87
Color: Red
Sex: Female
Breeder: Kaoru Koike
Owner: Chris Ross

Kotetsu of Kohtokuso
Shina no Kotetsu of Shinshu Ueda Tenguso
Tenpohime of Shinshu Uedatenguso
Sire: Rokumonsen Kotetsu of Shinshu Ueda Tenguso
Mita no Matsuoh of Mita Kensha
Mitatenhime of Mita Kensha
Mitsufusahime of Mita Kensha
Tsumugi no Konatsu Rokumonsen Tsumugiso
Beniaka of Kawagoeso
Suzuaka of Echigo Nakazatoso
Benisuzu of Joetsu Yanagisawaso
Dam: Sakuhime of Shinshu Jonenso
Kazutaka of Mita Kensha
Tadahime of Mita Kensha
Nishikime Mita Kensha

Noteworthy Facts: Import.

56

Call Name: Ryu
DOB: 08-20-87
Color: Red
Sex: Male
Breeder: Norio Watanabe
Owner: Kaiji Katsumoto

Yusaku of Kunitachikitajimaso
Kichisaku of Sagami Shueiso
Yumihime of Fussaen
Sire: Kogen of Ryokushinso
Hisakado of Hadano Nagoroso
Osumi no Hisame of Hadano Nagoroso
Tamakocho of Hadano Nagoroso
Nobumitsu of Komiyawatanabeso
Jouji of Fussaen
Yaesuke of Hadano Nagoroso
Osumi no Tamahime of Hadano Nagoroso
Dam: Suzuichime of Hamamidoriso
Tetsuryu of Izumiso
Takayakkow of Izumiso
Katsurayakkow of Enshu Hamamatsuni Kensha

Noteworthy Facts: Import. 1988 BSA Specialty BOB.

57

Call Name: Chaz
DOB: 09-12-87
Color: Red
Sex: Male
Breeder:
Janice Cowen
Owner: Kathleen
Brown-Truax and
Bruce Truax

Fujio of Sagami Ikeda Kensha
Fujimaru of Ogon Taiyoso
Benitakehime of Dairy Farm
Sire: Fujitaka of Maranata
Shishi of Kenwaso
Ogon no Takahime of Ogon Taiyoso
Tetsutakame of Saisho Kensha
Akira of Cowen Third
Matsu of Satoriso
Gento's Grizzly Bear
Kuronana of Hayakoso
Dam: Tomoko of Cowen Third
Yuki no Shinichi of Saitama Shiawaseso
Yukihime of Gardenaso
Shishihime of Kenwaso

Noteworthy Facts: 1988 NSCA #1 Shiba. 1989 SKC #2 Dog.

58

Call Name: Munch
DOB: 09-13-87
Color: Red Sesame
Sex: Female
Breeder:
Kono Shinishi
Owner: Bob Russell

Jouji Fussaen
Yuji of Yamanashi Andoso
Tenichihime Shinshu Takeiso
Sire: Kuniyu Hakukenso
Kurohomare Hiroshima Fujiso
Beniko of Hakukenso
Benikoharu Kawaokaso
Ch. Miyukihime of Iwakuniso
Koushun Renbo Yamamoto
Koumaru of Igaguriso
Tamami Suna Sudareso
Dam: Haruyamame of Iwakuni Takedaso
Kotetsu Kohtokuso
Haruhime of Hiroshima Kuhiso
Keiko Kyuryu Soofuso

Noteworthy Facts: Import.

59

Call Name: Aka
DOB: 10-14-87
Color: Red Sesame
Sex: Male
Breeder: Ryoko
Mosley
Owner: Jane Chal-
fant

Koto no Tamamidori of Kotoso
Soto no Gyokuryu of Sotoso
Ryushohime of Sotoso
Sire: Graham Uchida's Satoshi no Benzaiten
Tetsumaru of Ichikawa Aoki
Uchida's Akiko
Haya no Kiyohime of Akanuma Hayasakaso
Taka Justa Bold N Brassy
Shinano Homare of Shinshu Kinjuso
Tetsushiro of Kyoto Ryogaso
Komari of Kyoto Nakagawaso
Dam: Suzuhime of Suzukuniso
Shippo Midori of Fudogataki Kensha
Kikukohime of Bigo Fuji Kensha
Kikuhime of Bigo Fuji Kensha

Noteworthy Facts: 1988 NSCA National Specialty BOB. 1989
Kennel Review Tournament of Champions BOB and Rare Breed Dog
of the Year.

60

Call Name: Su
DOB: 10-18-87
Color: Red
Sex: Female
Breeder:
Nitaro Inamura
Owner: Kathleen
Brown-Truax
and Bruce Truax

Suwadai of Shinshuu Takeiso
Matsukawa no Sasuke of Matsukawa Kensha
Matsukawa no Futahime of Matsukawa
Kensha
Sire: Shishimaru of Matsukawa Kensha
Matsukawa no Iwamaru of Matsukawa
Kensha
Matsuhime of Matsukawa Kensha
Kikuichime of Takatoritaniso
Royal Blood Benihana
Ryuujiroh of Fudougataki Kensha
Akagiryuu of Kiryuu Iwashita
Tamami of Gunma Tamura
Dam: Tamahime of Johshuu Murakiso
Kikuichimaru of Tomoyoshiso
Tomoka of Komagataso
Hanako of Kijohso

Noteworthy Facts: Import.

61

Call Name: Kuro
DOB: 12-15-87
Color: Black and Tan
Sex: Female
Breeder: Takeshi Miyazawa
Owner: Ryoko Mosley

```
                                    Ryu of Hitotsuyamaso
                  Tenryumaru of Hitotsuyamaso
                                    Sachiko of Hitotsuyamaso
     Sire: Kokuryumaru of Hitotsuyamaso
                                    Kiyoichi of Mie Kozanso
                  Kiyohime of Hitotsuyamaso
                                    Kurokosuzu of Jinmeiji Kensha
Koroyuki of Hitosuyamaso
                                    Ryu of Hitotsuyamaso
                  Tenryumaru of Hitotsuyamaso
                                    Sachiko of Hitotsuyamaso
     Dam: Takihime of Hitotsuyamaso
                                    Nakakoma of Toyohama Susaso
                  Marihime of Toyohama Susaso
                                    Kuroyakko of Toyohama Susaso
```

Noteworthy Facts: Import.

62

Call Name: Bonny
DOB: 02-14-88
Color: Red
Sex: Female
Breeder: Francis Attridge
Owner: Francis Attridge

```
                                    Kuroyuki of Nanko Suzuki Kensha
                  Kurotake of Kenwaso
                                    Kuromatsume of Sagami Ikeda Kensha
     Sire: Minimeadow Kid Valentine
                                    Sakura no Kiyotaka of Akanuma Sakuraso
                  Haya no Kiyomi of Akanuma Hayasakaso
                                    Beniaihime of Akanuma Sakuraso
O'Date's Shots of Honey
                                    Soto no Gyokuryu of Sotoso
                  Windrift's Beni Taiyo
                                    Rikihome of Yoshizen Kotobukiso
     Dam: Windrift's Tenshi of O'Date
                                    Gangu no Gen of Sanuki Ganguso
                  Minimeadow's Belladonna
                                    Haruka of Hadano Nagoroso
```

Noteworthy Facts: 1989 Kennel Review Tournament of Champions BOS.

63

Call Name: Riki
DOB: 02-14-88
Color: Red
Sex: Male
Breeder: Miyoji Matsushita
Owner: Vivian Miller and Yuko Salvadori

```
                                    Yaesuke of Fussaen
                  Jouji of Fussaen
                                    Sachime of Fussaen
     Sire: Beniryu of Yamanashi Andoso
                                    Tenryuichi of Shinshu Takeiso
                  Tenichihime of Shinshu Takeiso
                                    Kiyoichime of Shinshu Takeiso
Tamariki of Banrakuso
                                    Daikoku of Mita Kensha
                  Kuroaki of Mita Kensha
                                    Meihohime of Mita Kensha
     Dam: Tamafukuhime of Banrakuso
                                    Mitsutoyo of Mita Kensha
                  Aki-go Mizusawa
                                    Kikuzukime of Echigo Yukiguniso
```

Noteworthy Facts: Import.

64

Call Name: Tama
DOB: 02-14-88
Color: Red
Sex: Female
Breeder: Miyoji Matsushita
Owner: Vivian Miller and Yuko Salvadori

```
                                    Yaesuke of Fussaen
                  Jouji of Fussaen
                                    Sachime of Fussaen
     Sire: Beniryu of Yamanashi Andoso
                                    Tenryuichi of Shinshu Takeiso
                  Tenichihime of Shinshu Takeiso
                                    Kiyoichime of Shinshu Takeiso
Tamabeni of Banrakuso
                                    Daikoku of Mita Kensha
                  Kuroaki of Mita Kensha
                                    Meihohime of Mita Kensha
     Dam: Tamafukuhime of Banrakuso
                                    Mitsutoyo of Mita Kensha
                  Aki-go Mizusawa
                                    Kikuzukime of Echigo Yukiguniso
```

Noteworthy Facts: Import.

65

Call Name: Taki
DOB: 03-16-88
Color: Black and Tan
Sex: Male
Breeder: Tim and Gretchen Haskett
Owner: Tim and Gretchen Haskett

Sakura no Takayuu of Yoshifukuso
Takayu of Shimotsuke Nantaiso
Shimotsuke Yuhime of Shimotsuke Nantaiso
Sire: Yukan of Aoyama Mahar
Yoshiyuki of Kiyokuniso
Fujihime of Kiyokuniso
Benifujime of Kiyokuniso
Takishiido of Foxfire CD
Gangu no Gen of Sanuki Ganguso
Minimeadow Samurai I
Haruka of Hadano Nagoroso
Dam: Dunroven Kogata
Kurotake of Kenwaso
Minimeadow Bonsi
Haya no Kiyomi of Akanuma Hayasakaso

Noteworthy Facts: 1989 SKC National Specialty BOW. 1989 SKC #1 Dog. 1990 SKC National Specialty BIS Obedience and Stud Dog. First SKC Companion Dog.

66

Call Name: Ei
DOB: 04-24-88
Color: Red
Sex: Male
Breeder: Yasushi Shimazaki
Owner: Donald Robinder

Masakado of Chikugo Okawaso
Yoshikado of Hakkoso
Suruga Komachi of Yaizu Ishihara
Sire: Kadotsukasa of Oshima Yasudaso
Yoshikado of Hakkoso
Kurokocho of Oshima Yasudaso
Benichiyo of Atami Izumiso
Ei of Yasushi Kensha
Yoshimidori of Echigo Suwaso
Fusamidori of Echigo Suwaso
Meiho Kurofusame of Daiwaso
Dam: Fusayoshime of Yasushi Kensha
Kiyofusa of Hadano Nagoroso
Osumi no Fusame of Hadano Nagoroso
Erihime of Chukoso

Noteworthy Facts: Import.

67

Call Name: Teagan
DOB: 08-04-88
Color: Red Sesame
Sex: Female
Breeder: Kathleen Brown-Truax and Bruce Truax
Owner: Kathleen Brown-Truax and Bruce Truax

Kuroyuki of Nanko Suzuki Kensha
Kuronami of Maranata
Tega no Namiyo of Dainana Kashiwayamaso
Sire: Kuro no Onami of Maranata
Shishi of Kenwaso
Ogon no Taka Hime of Ogon Taiyoso
Tetsutakame of Saisho Kensha
Foxtrot Sizzling Sin-Sation
Gento's Grizzly Bear
Shin of Cowen Third
Yukihime of Gardenaso
Dam: Foxtrot Some Spellbinder
Tetsumaru of Ichikawa Aoki
Benzaiten Im Impressive
Graham Uchida's Yume no Benzaiten

Noteworthy Facts: 1989 SKC National Specialty BOB. 1989 SKC Showdog of the Year.

68

Call Name: Ryu
DOB: 08-04-88
Color: Red
Sex: Male
Breeder: Michihisa Mochizuki
Owner: Ryoko Mosley

Homareshishi of Enshu Kaiunso
Shurin of Enshu Kaiunso
Kozue of Enshu Kaiunso
Sire: Takekoma of Enshu Kaiunso
Homareshishi of Enshu Kaiunso
Benitsubaki of Enshu Kaiunso
Beniichime of Enshu Kaiunso
Takemaru of Chita Mochizukiso
Shina no Homare of Shinshu Kinjuso
Tetsujo of Kyoto Ryogaso
Komari of Kyoto Nakagawaso
Dam: Fukihime of Suzukuniso
Shippo Midori of Fudogataki Kensha
Kikukohime of Bingo Fuji Kensha
Kikuhime of Bingo Fuji Kensha

Noteworthy Facts: Import.

69

Call Name: Miya
DOB: 08-12-88
Color: Red
Sex: Female
Breeder:
Kiyoshi Fukada
Owner:
Carolyn Kaufmann

Hidemidori of Noto Ishidoso
Suzuwaka of Hongo Ishidoso
Misuzuhime of Nakatokuso
Sire: Asahifuji of Kyokujitsuan
Seto no Takimaru of Hachiohso
Akiohme of Kyokujitsuan
Yutetsume of Kyokujutsuan
Katsura no Miyahime of Izumi no Motoso ROM
Hojiro of Hiroshima Daicho Katayamaso
Jiromaru of Fushimaso
Akizakura of Fukui Ozawaso
Dam: Akikazehime of Izumi no Hotoso
Takafuji of Miyagi Tomofujiso
Mitsufusame of Izumi no Motoso
Kogyokume of Izumi no Motoso

Noteworthy Facts: Import. Mexican Champion. 1992 BSA Specialty BOS.

70

Call Name: Genji
DOB: 08-27-88
Color: Red Sesame
Sex: Male
Breeder:
Richard Tomita
Owner:
Leslie Engen

Habiki no Gen of Habikinoso
Koshu no Gen of Echigo Suwaso
Senhime of Suruga Oishi Kensha
Sire: Ch. Katsuranishiki of Oikawa House
Fuji no Wakataka of Amano Kensha
Musashi no Beniyukime of Oikawa House
Hanamine of Oikawa House
Ch. Jacquet Baron
Yoshihana of Oshima Yasudaso
Kurohana of Kunimutsuso
Fujihime of Sannoko
Dam: Kuromarihime of Kunimutsuso
Kagetora of Bizen Koyoso
Rikahime of Hokuso Takayamaso
Maruhime of Yamanashi Andoso

Noteworthy Facts: 1991 NSCA National Specialty BOB.

71

Call Name: Willow
DOB: 09-12-88
Color: Red Sesame
Sex: Female
Breeder:
Mikado Shibada
Owner:
Laura Perkinson

Yaesuke of Fussaen
Jouji of Fussaen
Sachime of Fussaen
Sire: Joukichi of Yamanashi Fujikenso
Tatsumaru of Akishima Fukutaso
Tatsumihime of Yamanashi Ono
Beniyakko of Amano Kensha
Ch. Homaretennome of Gishifujiso
Jouji of Fussaen
Beniryu of Yamanashi Andoso
Tenichihime of Shinshu Takeiso
Dam: Takeda no Yukihime of Ishiiso
Shinshu Ematsumaru of Shinshu Kinjuso
Akamihime of Yukiyamaso
Hagihime of Yukiyamaso

Noteworthy Facts: Import. 1991 SKC National Specialty BOS. 1992 NSCA National Specialty BOS.

72

Call Name: C.J.
DOB: 10-07-88
Color: Red
Sex: Male
Breeder: Kathleen
Brown-Truax and
Bruce Truax
Owner: Pam Brown

Fujimaru of Ogon Taiyoso
Fujitaka of Maranata
Ogon no Takahime of Ogon Taiyoso
Sire: Akira of Cowen Third
Gento's Grizzly Bear
Tomoko of Cowen Third
Yukihime of Gardenaso
Ch. Foxtrot Chip of Chaz
Tokiwa no Benisuke Kasukabe Tokiwaso
Tetsumaru of Ichikawa Aoki
Fukubenihime of Ichikawa
Dam: Benzaiten I'm Impressive
Graham Uchida's Tsubasa
Graham Uchida's Yume no Benzaiten
Tamashibahime of Sotoso

Noteworthy Facts: 1990 SKC National Specialty BOB.

73

Call Name: Maru
DOB: 11-10-88
Color: Black and Tan
Sex: Male
Breeder: Yonemi Kawada
Owner: Laura Payton, Frank Sakayeda

Sakushugen of Tsuyama Kunimotoso
Kotobuki no Gen of Suganoso
Seto no Yuhime of Suganoso
Sire: Kotobuki no Eisaku
Nakamaru of Morowa Shirakoso
Maki of Nishigamiso
Shiba Rumi of Doteizanso
Ch. Kotobuki no Kuroichi of Tosa Otaniso
Tetsukoma of Sansui Kensha
Komaichi of Takatokuso
Kikumarume of Takatokuso
Dam: Ichiome of Izumi no Motoso
Mitsumaru of Guji Toriiso
Kogyokume of Izumi no Motoso
Ogyokuka of Izumi no Motoso

Noteworthy Facts: Import.

74

Call Name: Sumo
DOB: 12-12-88
Color: Red
Sex: Male
Breeder: Bruce and Jeri Braviroff
Owner: Bruce and Jeri Braviroff

Kichisaku of Sagami Sueiso
Kogen of Ryokushinso
Osumi no Hisame of Hadano Nagoroso
Sire: Nobumitsu of Komiyawatanabeso
Yaesuke of Hadano Nagoroso
Suzuichime of Hamamidoriso
Takayakko of Izumiso
Ch. Fukuryu Beikokusekiryuso ROM
Sanshiro of Horieso
Fujizakura of Hikari Kaidaso
Kurohana of Shuoh Shimazueso
Dam: Fukuhime Kenwaso
Joukichi of Yamanashi Fujikenso
Aya of Fussaen
Sachibenime of Fussaen

Noteworthy Facts: 1991 BSA Specialty Best Male. 1992 BSA Specialty BOB. 1992 SCA National Specialty BOB.

75

Call Name: Kaz
DOB: 01-17-89
Color: Red
Sex: Male
Breeder: Mitsuhiko Fukuda
Owner: Fred Duane

Takeichi of Shinshu Takeiso
Tenryuichi of Shinshu Takeiso
Tenhime of Shinshu Takeiso
Sire: Koromaru of Shinshu Takeiso
Tenryuichi of Shinshu Takeiso
Korohime of Shinshu Takeiso
Tanimarume of Shinshu Takeiso
Yuki no Ishi of Dairy Farm
Keishomaru of Shinshu Momoseso
Tatsuwakamaru of Daigenyaso
Hosako of Shinshu Takeiso
Dam: Nakatakehime of Dairy Farm
Jota of Yamanashi Andoso
Suzutakemi of Dairy Farm
Takasuzumi of Dairy Farm

Noteworthy Facts: Import.

76

Call Name: Mariko
DOB: 03-18-89
Color: Red
Sex: Female
Breeder: Richard Tomita
Owner: Leslie Engen

Jouji of Fussaen
Tenichiryu of Ryokushinso
Hama no Onna of Hamamidoriso
Sire: Ryutaro of Yamazakiso Kensha
Kotobuki of Naka Araiso
Chika of Yamazakiso Kensha
Azumagiku of Iino Fujinoso
Ch. Jacquet Thu Ru Hime
Hikima no Gen Hikimanoso
Koshu no Gen of Echigo Suwaso
Senhime of Suruga Oishi Kensha
Dam: Minamoto no Hanagiku of Oikawa House
Fuji no Wakataka of Amano Kensha
Musashi no Hana of Musashi Nakanishiso
Fuji no Haruna of Kitaroku Kensha

Noteworthy Facts: 1990 NSCA National Specialty BOB.

77

Call Name: Momo
DOB: 05-04-89
Color: Red
Sex: Female
Breeder:
Michihisa
Mochizuki
Owner:
Leslie M. Sorensen

Homarejishi of Enshu Kaiunso
Gyokurin of Enshu Kaiunso
Kozue of Enshu Kaiunso
Sire: Takekoma of Enshu Kaiunso
Homarejishi of Enshu Kaiunso
Benitsubaki of Enshu Kaiunso
Beniichime of Enshu Kaiunso
Ch. Taketomi of Chita Mochizukiso
Shina no Homare of Shinshu Kinjuso
Tetsushiro of Kyoto Ryogaso
Komari of Kyoto Nakagawaso
Dam: Tokihime of Suzukuniso
Shippo Midori of Fudogataki Kensha
Kikukohime of Bingo Fuji Kensha
Kikuhime of Bingo Fuji Kensha

Noteworthy Facts: Import. First AKC Champion of Record.

78

Call Name: Tigger
DOB: 11-17-89
Color: Red Sesame
Sex: Female
Breeder:
Kimberly Ottenbrite
Owner:
Linn and Bill
Greene

Soto no Gyokuryu of Sotoso
Graham Uchida's Satoshi no Benzaiten
Uchida's Akiko
Sire: Taka Justa Bold N Brassy
Tetsushiro of Kyoto Ryogaso
Suzuhime of Suzukuniso
Kikukohime of Bigo Fuji Kensha
Lietash Whirling Dervish
Beniozan of Kimuta Trails
Trebell's Kuroi Jiisu of CRT
Kuroyuri of Ogon Taiyoso
Dam: Langan's Brushwood Tasmanian Devil
Sakushuu Tatsumaru of Mitsuwa Kensha
Kuroichime of Awa Kinseiso
Sakushuu Natsume of Awa Kinseiso

Noteworthy Facts: 1990 SKC Showdog of the Year.

79

Call Name: Seiko
DOB: 01-13-90
Color: Red Sesame
Sex: Female
Breeder:
Dorothy Warren
Owner:
Dorothy Warren

Fusakichi of Shirotaso
Hokkai no Ryu of Haramichiso
Kurome of Kunimutsuso
Sire: Hokkai no Kotetsu
Takanishiki of Shimamura
Canada Komachi Otakaso
Fujihime of Shimamura
Ch. Ranchlake's Tamarisk Samsara ROM
Fusakichi of Shirotaso
Hokkai no Ryu of Haramichiso
Kurome of Kunimutsuso
Dam: Canada Kogiku
Takanishiki of Shimamura
Canada Komachi Otakaso
Fujihime of Shimamura

Noteworthy Facts: Mexican Champion, National Shiba Club of
America ROM.

80

Call Name: Toki
DOB: 04-07-90
Color: Red
Sex: Male
Breeder: Mitsuhisa
Kawakami
Owner: Frank
Sakayeda, Alice
Sakayeda, Carol
Parker, Camille
Wong

Genjiro of Hatsuse Kensha
Ryujiro of Fudogataki Kensha
Kurotamajyo of Fudogataki Kensha
Sire: Hamajiro of Toyohama Unryuso
Hikari of Shikoku Kofujiso
Hikarinishikijyo of Mitsutoyo Sakuraso
Ch. Toyojiro of Nidai Maneiso ROM
Takehachimaru of Nadai Maneiso
Genjyomaru of Nidai Maneiso
Toyohanajyo of Nidai Maneiso
Dam: Haruhidejo of Nidaimaneiso
Tojikano Genta of Daini Moromotoso
Himemomoko of Tetsuzanso
Himemisuzu of Tetsuzanso

Noteworthy Facts: Import. 1993 NSCA National Specialty BOB, #1
Shiba AKC 1993 and 1994. Japan Kennel Club, Mexican, International
Champion.

81

Call Name: R.C.
DOB: 06-15-90
Color: Red Sesame
Sex: Male
Breeder: June and
Bill Gilmore
Owner: Kathleen
Brown-Truax
and Bruce Truax

Seto no Takimaru of Hachioso
Mitsuryu of Bingo Nakayamso
Mitsuhanahime Matsunaga Omura Kensha
Sire: Tetsuryu of Hikari Kaidaso
Kuromitsu of Ibuki Nanguso
Kurotakahime of Hikari Kaidaso
Beniyukihime of Hikari Kaidaso
Hansha Remote Control ROM
Yoshiyuki of Kiyokuniso
Yoshimaru of Kiyokuniso
Azumagiku of Kiyokuniso
Dam: Kuma Mitsu of Aoyama Mahar
JKC Ch. Taketora of Yodaso
Kinki of Aoyama Mahar
Mizuhohime of Nishikoyamaso

Noteworthy Facts: National Shiba Club of America ROM.

82

Call Name: Cricket
DOB: 06-30-90
Color: Red
Sex: Female
Breeder:
Miyoko Shibata
Owner:
Laura Perkinson

Yaesuke of Fussaen
Jouji of Fussaen
Sachihime of Fussaen
Sire: Beniryu of Yamanashi Andoso
Tenryuichi of Shinshu Takeiso
Tenichihime of Shinshu Takeiso
Kiyoichime of Shinshu Takeiso
Ch. Kiyoichime of Gishifujiso
Jouji of Fussaen
Joukichi of Yamanashi Fujikenso
Tatsumihime of Yamanashi Ono
Dam: Benikiyoichime of Gishifujiso
Beniryu of Yamanashi Andoso
Takeda no Yukihime of Ishiiso
Akamihime of Yukiyamaso

Noteworthy Facts: Import.

83

Call Name: Smiley
DOB: 07-14-90
Color: Red
Sex: Male
Breeder:
Matsuo Yoshioka
Owner: Fred Duane

Yoshikado of Hakkoso
Kadotsukasa of Oshima Yasudaso
Kuro Kocho of Oshima Yasudaso
Sire: Otomi no Kadoichi
Yoshi no Suke of Yasushi Kensha
Kotomi of Risokyo
Imahime of Bushu Jinbaso
Suzuhomare of Yoshimatsu Kensha
Takayoshi of Tokyo Mizutani
Yoshimaru of Fujinomiya Kensha
Tamanahime of Fujinomiya Nakano
Dam: Yurihime of Yoshimatsu Kensha
Tamaarashi of Joshu Takenakaso
Sayuri of Yoshmatsu Kensha
Hogyokuhime of Yoshimatsu Kensha

Noteworthy Facts: Import.

84

Call Name:
Plum Blossom
DOB: 07-28-90
Color: Red
Sex: Female
Breeder:
Kaoru Koike
Owner: Chris Ross
and Jacey Holden

Shina no Kotetsu of Shinshu Ueda Tenguso
Rokumonsen Kotetsu of Shinshu Ueda Tenguso
Mitatenhime of Mita Kensha
Sire: Tokijiro of Rokumonsen Tsumugiso
Suzuaka of Echigo Nakatoso
Sakuhime of Shinshu Jonenso
Tadahime of Mita Kensha
Ch. Shinshu Benime Rokumonsen Tsumugiso
Matsugoro of Mita Kensha
Kazutaka of Mita Kensha
Mita no Marunaka of Mita Kensha
Dam: Benimitsume of Mita Kensha
Kuroaki of Mita Kensha
Kurokichime of Mita Kensha
Mitsubenifusa of Mita Kensha

Noteworthy Facts: Import.

85

Call Name: Max
DOB: 08-31-90
Color: Red
Sex: Male
Breeder:
Joan Young
Owner:
Debbie Meador

Daimatsu
Kiyomatsu of Kitatanakaso
Taiho no Kiyohime
Sire: Daichi of Toyonaka Okomotoso
Yodo no Mitsukoma
Hanakoma of Osakakire
Mitsuhime
Ch. Kinouk's Road-Warrior Tanasea
Fire Fox of Minimeadow
Kinouk's Hell on Wheels
Graham Uchida's Mischief Maker
Dam: Kinouk's Ray of Sunshine
Soto no Gyokuryu of Sotoso
Porshe of Kinouk
Uchida's Akiko

Noteworthy Facts: 1992 NSCA National Specialty BOB.

86

Call Name: Casey
DOB: 11-11-90
Color: Red
Sex: Male
Breeder:
Mikado Shibad
Owner:
June Gilmore

Jouji of Fussaen
Joukishi of Yamanashi Fujikenso
Tatsumihime of Yamanashi Ono
Sire: Tochi no Shogun of Gishifujiso
Beniryu of Yamanashi Andoso
Takeda no Yukihime of Ishiiso
Akamihime of Yukiyamaso
Shoguniemitsu of Gishifujiso
Moji of Ohshimayasudaso
Fujitsukasa of Shirotaso
Joukichihime of Shirotaso
Dam: Benirinme of Gishifujiso
Tetsu of Iwaso
Takeda no Maihime of Shirotaso
Tsukasa no Maihime of Shirotaso

Noteworthy Facts: Import. 1995 BSA Specialty BOS.

87

Call Name: Cassidy
DOB: 05-24-91
Color: Red
Sex: Male
Breeder:
Carolyn Kaufmann
Owner:
Carolyn Kaufmann

Kogen of Ryokushinso
Nobumitsu Komiyawatanabeso
Suzuichime of Hamamidoriso
Sire: Ch. Fukuryu of Beikokusekiryuso
Fujizakura of Hikari Kaidaso
Fukuhime Kenwaso
Aya of Fussaen
Ch. Windcastle's Free Spirit
Suzuwaka of Hongo Ishidoso
Asahifuji of Kyokujitsuan
Akiohme of Kyokujitsuan
Dam: Katsura no Miyahime of Izumi no Motoso
Jiromaru of Fushimaso
Akikazehime of Izumi no Hotoso
Mitsufusame of Izumi no Motoso

Noteworthy Facts: 1993 BSA BOB. Canadian, Mexican, International Champion.

88

Call Name: Otsu
DOB: 07-08-91
Color: Red
Sex: Female
Breeder:
Hideo Chyunai
Owner: Bill Bobrow,
Carol Parker,
Frank Sakayeda

Ryujiro of Fudogataki Kensha
Hamajiro of Toyohama Unryuso
Hikarinishikijo of Mitsutoyo Sakuraso
Sire: Ch. Toyojiro of Nidai Maneiso
Genjyomaru of Nidai Maneiso
Haruhidejo of Nidai Maneiso
Himemomoko of Tetsuzanso
Mihanahime of Kosei Shirogikuso
Genjoro of Hatsuse Kensha
Togashino Genta of Daini Morimotoso
Benihana Kiyojo of Toyohashi Morimotoso
Dam: Hanakiyojo of Nidai Maneiso
Kiyonishiki of Toyohashi Maneiso
Hanahime of Toyohashi Maneiso
Hana Yatkko of Toyohashi Maneiso

Noteworthy Facts: Import.

89

Call Name: Kenny
DOB: 08-03-91
Color: Red
Sex: Female
Breeder:
Miyako Morimine
Owner:
Timothy Haskett

Sakushugen of Tsuyama Kunimotoso
Tensugen of Bichu Eikanso
Kokuyume of Tsukiyataniso
Sire: Tetsuka no Gen of Sanuki Mizumotoso
Kotobuki no Eisaku of Hichiso
Suzukahime of Takamatsu Morita
Osumi no Mika of Hadano Nagoroso
Ch. Heki no Ken of Daini Hekihoso
Shinobu of Daishizen
Shoko of Daishizen
Maiko of Bichu Nakamuraso
Dam: Daruma no Kohime of Iwakuni Darumaso
Kyushu no Jakunishiki of Kyushu Eto Kensha
Kyushu no Jakuhime of Kyushu Eto Kensha
Kyushu no Kurohime of Kyushu Eto Kensha

Noteworthy Facts: Import.

90

Call Name: Calli
DOB: 08-25-91
Color: Red
Sex: Female
Breeder: Harumi
Suzuki
Owner:
Laura Perkinson

Sumeranishiki of Hadano Kawaguchiso
Katsura of Fujinomiya Kensha
Kijyo of Yamanashi Minamiso
Sire: Ryu of Fujinomiya Kensha
Katsura of Fujinomiya Kensha
Ai of Fujinomiya Kensha
Yoshimi of Aoki Taira
Ch. Sarihime of Fujinomiya Kensha
Hachiosuke of Tadano Nagoroso
Hachio of Ryokushinso
Osumi no Kotobukijyo of Hadano Nagoroso
Dam: Benikohime of Fujinomiya Kensha
Fukumaru of Shirotaso
Kimi of Fujinomiya Kensha
Kijyo of Yamanashi Minamiso

Noteworthy Facts: Import.

91

Call Name: Jiro
DOB: 08-28-91
Color: Red
Sex: Male
Breeder:
Mitsuhiko Fukuda
Owner:
Yuko Salvadori

Kichi of Yasameso
Daikichi of Yasameso
Asahi of Shirokoshi Kensha
Sire: Kai Dai of Daini Sekishunso
Kai Jiro of Sekishunso
Genichihime of Daini Sekishunso
Maho of Daini Sekishunso
Ch. Eikichi of Dairy Farm
Tenryuichi of Shinshu Takeiso
Koromaru of Shinshu Takeiso
Korohime of Shinshu Takeiso
Dam: Tenchomi of Dairy Farm
Mitsuhana of Toyohashi Kasugaso
Nagahanami of Dairy Farm
Fuji no Nagahime of Dairy Farm

Noteworthy Facts: Import.

92

Call Name: Suzy
DOB: 10-12-91
Color: Red
Sex: Female
Breeder:
Morihito Ono
Owner:
Timothy Haskett

Tetsugen of Bichu Eikanso
Tetsuka no Gen of Sanuki Mizumotoso
Suzukahime of Takamatsu Morita
Sire: Rikimaru of Sanuki Mizumotoso
Kyushu no Tetsuyuki of Kyushu Eto Kensha
Momohime of Matsubaraso
Akane of Kanmuri Itsumineso
Ch. Azusakikuhime of Matsunaga Ono Kensha
Tetsugen of Bichu Eikanso
Hamaou of Fudogataki Kensha
Matsuurame of Fudogataki Kensha
Dam: Azusaichihime of Sanuki Mizumotoso
Tetsugen of Bichu Eikanso
Azusa of Sanuki Mizumotoso
Aki of Shimomatsu Harukaso

Noteworthy Facts: Import.

93

Call Name: Kimo
DOB: 11-05-91
Color: Black and Tan
Sex: Female
Breeder: Yuichi Tomimoto
Owner: Carol Parker, Camille Wong, Frank Sakayeda

Noteworthy Facts: Import.

```
                          Harukoma of Kohtokuso
               Toratetsu of Kohtokuso
                          Chiharu of Kohtokuso
      Sire: Kurotetsu of Izumiso
                          Tenryu of Shinshu Takeiso
               Tenryu Noborihime of Izumiso
                          Kurokomajyo of Shinshu Tenryuso
      Ch. Kurohana of Ryukyu Wruma
                          Hamajiro of Toyohama Unryuso
               Kuninishiki of Kosei Shiragikuso
                          Kunihime of Hamakita Nanzanso
      Dam: Nishikihana of Ryukyu Wruma
                          Fujinishiki of Tetsuzanso
               Senhime of Ryukyu Wruma
                          Hamahime of Nidai Maneiso
```

94

Call Name: Guru
DOB: 12-19-91
Color: Red
Sex: Male
Breeder: Mitsuhisa Kawakami
Owner: Laura Payton, Frank Sakayeda

Noteworthy Facts: Import.

```
                          Tamanishiki of Fujinomiya Kensha
               Sumeranishiki of Hadano Kawaguchiso
                          Mizunashi no Keizanme of Hadano
                          Kawaguchiso
      Sire: Koji of Serikawa
                          Harukomaryu of Nidai Maneiso
               Matsuhaname of Serikawa
                          Mitsuhanahime of Serikawa
      Ch. Koryu of Nidai Maneiso
                          Ryujiro of Fudogataki Kensha
               Hamajiro of Toyohama Unryuso
                          Hikarinishikijo of Mitsutoyo Sakuraso
      Dam: Toyobenihime of Nidai Maneiso
                          Genjyomaru of Nidai Maneiso
               Haruhideme of Nidai Maneiso
                          Himemomoko of Tetsuzanso
```

95

Call Name: Kiku
DOB: 05-09-92
Color: Red
Sex: Female
Breeder: Mitsuhisa Kawakami
Owner: Bill Bobrow, Carol Parker, Camille Wong, Frank Sakayeda

Noteworthy Facts: Import. 1995 NSCA National Specialty High In Trial.

```
                          Tamanishiki of Fujinomiya Kensha
               Sumeranishiki of Hadano Kawaguchiso
                          Mizunashi no Keizanme of Hadano
                          Kawaguchiso
      Sire: Koji of Serikawa
                          Harukomaryu of Nikai Maneiso
               Matsuhaname of Serikawa
                          Mitsuhanahime of Serikawa
      Ch. Matsukiyome of Nidai Maneiso CGC CD
                          Tokano Genta of Daini Mroimotoso
               JKC Ch. Ryugenmaru of Nidai Maneiso
                          Hamakocho of Nikoso
      Dam: Hidekocho of Nidai Maneiso
                          Hamajiro of Toyohama Unryuso
               Hamakobeni of Nidai Maneiso
                          Toyotomi Maki of Nidai Maneiso
```

96

Call Name: Sachi
DOB: 05-09-92
Color: Red
Sex: Female
Breeder: Mitze Reid
Owner: Sam and Maggie Torres

Noteworthy Facts: 1994 BSA Specialty BOB.

```
                          Kitakyu no Genta of Fukuoka Ishikawa
               Sanshiro of Horieso
                          Horie no Suzu of Horieso
      Sire: Fujizakura of Hikari Kaidaso
                          Shukohmaru of Izumiso
               Kurohana of Suohshimasueso
                          Momoichihime of Iwakuni Doujiso
      Ch. Sachihime of Paladin
                          Komanishiki of Biryuso
               Fukujiro of Shonanyasuda
                          Mimihime of Shonanyasuda
      Dam: Akane Kashumitsuuchiso
                          Nobumitsu of Komiyawatanabeso
               Aki of Kashumitsuuchiso
                          Benizakura of Beikokusoenso
```

97

Call Name: Phoenix
DOB: 09-27-92
Color: Red
Sex: Male
Breeder:
Harumi Suzuki
Owner:
Laura Perkinson

Katsura of Fujinomiya Kensha
Ryu of Fujinomiya Kensha
Ai of Fujinomiya Kensha
Sire: Hiryu of Fujinomiya Kensha
Yoshimaru of Yaizu Mariokaso
Yoshitsuma Himeichi of Kosozan
Machikohime of Akinoyamaso
Ch. Hideryu of Fujinomiya Kensha
Sumeranishiki of Hadano Kawaguchiso
Tamafusa of Fujinomiya Kensha
Takame of Yamanashi Minamiso
Dam: Ryubi of Enshu Tokuyama
Fukuhime of Izu Nagaoka Watanabeso
Aihime of Fujinomiya Kensha
Tsukihime of Fujinomiya Kensha

Noteworthy Facts: Import.

98

Call Name: Cabot
DOB: 01-22-93
Color: Red Sesame
Sex: Male
Breeder: Mitsuhisa
Kawakami
Owner:
Laura Payton,
Frank Sakayeda

Kyonishiki of Kawakumaso
Ryo of Fujinomiya Kensha
Tatsumi of Enshu Tokuyama
Sire: Hakken of Iwatoyoso
Kensho of Fujinomiya Kensha
Takafusame of Iwatoyoso
Koyuki of Kawakumaso
Ch. Kotobuki no Gen of Nidai Maneiso
Seto no Daisuke of Hachioso
Kotobuki no Tetsu of Tohoso
Seijume of Tohoso
Dam: Kotobuki no Beni of Izumiso
Kotaro of Jinnanbi Kensha
Takanohime of Sanuki Mizumotoso
Meitohime of Meito Horaiso

Noteworthy Facts: Import.

99

Call Name: Stimpy
DOB: 02-25-93
Color: Red
Sex: Male
Breeder:
Mitsuhisa
Kawakami
Owner:
Lillian Kletter,
Frank Sakayeda

Tamanishiki of Fujinomiya Kensha
Sumeranishiki of Hadano Kawaguchiso
Mizunashi no Keizanme of Hadano
Kawaguchiso
Sire: Koji of Serikawa
Harukomaryu of Nikai Maneiso
Matsuhaname of Serikawa
Mitsuhanahime of Serikawa
Ch. Kotoyomaru of Nidai Maneiso
Tokano Genta of Daini Mroimotoso
JKC Ch. Ryugenmaru of Nidai Maneiso
Hamakocho of Nikoso
Dam: Hidehaname of Nidai Maneiso
Hamajiro of Toyohama Unryuso
Hamakobeni of Nidai Maneiso
Toyotomi Maki of Nidai Maneiso

Noteworthy Facts: Import.

100

Call Name: Guy
DOB: 03-27-93
Color: Red
Sex: Male
Breeder:
Leslie Ann Engen
Owner:
Carol Parker,
Camille Wong,
Frank Sakayeda,
Laura Payton

Ryujiro of Fudogataki Kensha
Hamajiro of Toyohama Unryuso
Hikarinishikijyo of Mitsutoyo Sakuraso
Sire: Ch. Toyojiro of Nidai Maneiso
Genjyomaru of Nidai Maneiso
Haruhidejo of Nidai Maneiso
Himemomoko of Tetsuzanso
Ch. San Jo Wise Guy
Ch. Katsuranishiki of Oikawa House
Ch. Jacquet's Baron
Kuromarihime of Kunimutsuso
Dam: Ch. San Jo's Tickled Pink
Ryutaro of Yamazakiso Kensha
Ch. Jacquet Thu Ru Hime
Minamoto no Hanagiku of Oikawa House

Noteworthy Facts: 1995 and 1996 Shiba Club of Greater New York
Specialty BOB. 1995 Westminster BOB. 1995 #1 Shiba All Breed Sys-

101

Call Name: Hapi
DOB: 04-10-93
Color: Red
Sex: Female
Breeder:
Yuichi Tomimoto
Owner:
Sharon Lundberg,
Alice Sakayeda,
Tammy Crome

Toka no Genta of Daini Morimotoso
  Ryugen of Nidai Maneiso
    Hamakocho of Nikoso
Sire: JKC Ch. Yujiro of Toyohashi Morimotoso
    Hamajiro of Toyohama Unryuso
  Chachahaname of Toyohashi Morimotoso
    Benihaname of Toyohashi Kawanaso
Hamayumi of Gold Typhoon
    Hananishiki of Toyohashi Morimotoso
  Fujinishiki of Tetsuzanso
    Kawana no Beniyakko of Toyohashi Kawanaso
Dam: Chiaki of Ryukyu Uruma
    Kurotetsu of Izumiso
  Ayasehime of Ryukyu Uruma
    Yukiji of Yoshiyukiso

Noteworthy Facts: Import.

102

Call Name: Bo
DOB: 04-28-93
Color: Red
Sex: Male
Breeder:
Laura Perkinson
Owner:
Gloria Ketcher,
Laura Perkinson

    Ch. Jacquet's Baron
  Elliott of Taichung
    Ch. Homaretennome of Gishifujiso
Sire: Ch. Taichung Tempted By A Lady
    Beniryu of Yamanashi Andoso
  Ch. Kiyoichime of Gishifujiso
    Benikiyoichime of Gishifujiso
Ch. Taichung Bold Concept At OPR
    Katsura of Fujinomiya Kensha
  Ryu of Fujinomiya Kensha
    Ai of Fujinomiya Kensha
Dam: Ch. Sarihime of Fujinomiya Kensha
    Hachio of Ryokushinso
  Benikohime of Fujinomiya Kensha
    Kimi of Fujinomiya Kensha

Noteworthy Facts: 1994 NSCA National Specialty BOS. 1995
NSCA National Specialty BOB.

103

Call Name: Tommy
DOB: 07-16-93
Color: Red
Sex: Male
Breeder:
Fred Duane
Owner: Fred Duane

    Kadotsukasa of Oshima Yasudaso
  Otomi no Kadoichi
    Kotomi of Risokyo
Sire: Suzuhomare of Yoshimatsu Kensha
    Yoshimaru of Fujinomiya Kensha
  Yurihime of Yoshimatsu Kensha
    Sayuri of Yoshmatsu Kensha
Ch. Frerose Otomi
    Koshu no Gen of Echigo Suwaso
  Ch. Katsuranishiki of Oikawa House
    Musashi no Beniyukime of Oikawa House
Dam: Frerose Punkin Pie
    Kintaro of Satoriso
  Frerose Giselle of Frerose
    Sa no Kuroyuri of Konan Mochizuki

Noteworthy Facts: 1995 #1 Shiba Breed System. 1996 Westminster
BOB.

104

Call Name: Taka
DOB: 09-10-93
Color: Red
Sex: Male
Breeder: Mitsuhisa
Kawakami
Owner:
Laura Payton,
Frank Sakayeda

    Jouji of Fussaen
  Takeharu of Nishitaka Kensha
    Emi of Shonan Yasuda
Sire: Ecchu Takehachiro of Ecchu Maneiso
    Hidetaka of Toyohashi Masatakaso
  Hidehana of Nidai Maneiso
    Hanahime of Toyohashi Maneiso
Ch. Kiyotakamaru of Nidai Maneiso
    Sumeranishiki of Hadano Kawaguchiso
  Koji of Serikawa
    Matsuhaname of Serikawa
Dam: Shungikume of Nidai Maneiso
    Hamajiro of Toyohama Unryuso
  Toyohime of Nidai Maneiso
    Haruhideme of Nidai Maneiso

Noteworthy Facts: Import.

105

Call Name: Cutter
DOB: 11-20-93
Color: Red
Sex: Male
Breeder:
Yuichi Tomimoto
Owner:
Leslie Ann Engen,
Frank Sakayeda

```
                                    Genjiro of Hatsuse Kensha
                   Toka no Genta of Daini Morimotoso
                                    Benihana Kiyome of Toyohashi Morimotoso
Sire: Ryugenmaru of Nidai Maneiso
                                    Hamajiro of Toyohama Unryuso
                   Hamakocho of Nikoso
                                    Kitase no Kana of Nikoso
```

Ch. Genta of Gold Typhoon

```
                                    Toratetsu of Kohtokuso
                   Kurotetsu of Izumiso
                                    Tenryu Noborihime of Izumiso
Dam: Hamahime of Ryukyu Uruma
                                    Kurotetsu of Izumiso
                   Hamahime of Nidai Maneiso
                                    Kiyomaruhime of Toyohashi Maneiso
```

Noteworthy Facts: Import.

106

Call Name: Hana
DOB: 08-18-94
Color: Red
Sex: Female
Breeder: Mitsuhisa
Kawakami
Owner:
Laura Payton,
Frank Sakayeda

```
                                    Kyonishiki of Kawakumaso
                   Ryo of Fujinomiya Kensha
                                    Tatsumi of Enshu Tokuyama
Sire: Hakken of Iwatoyoso
                                    Kensho of Fujinomiya Kensha
                   Takafusame of Iwatoyoso
                                    Koyuki of Kawakumaso
```

Ch. Sachiharume of Nidai Maneiso

```
                                    Jouji of Fussaen
                   Takehachimaru of Nidai Maneiso
                                    Harukobeni of Nidai Maneiso
Dam: Sachikobeni of Nidai Maneiso
                                    Hamajiro of Toyohama Unryuso
                   Benihaname of Nidai Maneiso
                                    Fujihime of Toyohashi Maneiso
```

Noteworthy Facts: Import.

Glossary of Traditional Japanese Shiba Names

AS WE MENTIONED IN OUR INTRODUCTION to the Breed Gallery, Japanese names do not always have literal translations to English. Don't try to use just any combination of words to name your Shiba if you are not familiar with the Japanese language. If you combine words at random, they might have a totally different meaning than what you would expect, or they might not make sense. It is best to consult a Japanese native for names or use combinations that you have already seen in pedigrees. The Japanese language has many complicated rules for combining words, and numerous meanings are possible for most of the syllables. You are not likely to create a correct combination by accident!

Something you should know is that "no" usually means "of" in Japanese. If you would like to call your dog "Red of America," you would actually say "America of Red" or "Beikoku no Aka" (listing the place name first). Because a Japanese dog is usually referred to without the kennel name, some Japanese breeders insert the place name in both the dog's name and the kennel name to make sure everyone knows where the dog came from. Thus, "Red's" full name could be "Beikoku no Aka of Beikokusow" or "Beikoku no Aka of Beikoku Kensha" instead of simply "Aka of Beikokusow." To name this dog Nippo style, you would write "Aka Beikokuso" and omit the English "of."

Some Japanese names can perplex English-speaking readers unless they know the connotations behind the words. The following is a partial list:

Fuji — Mt. Fuji; symbol of Japan and Japanese spirit; also wisteria.

Fuku — wealth; fortune, riches, good luck, happiness.

Fusa — tassel; a silk tassel, tufted. This name refers to the furry coat of a Shiba.

Ishi — stone; strong character, steadfast.

Koma — horse, charger in battle dress.

Matsu — pine tree; traditional Japanese symbol meaning long life.

Midori — green; fresh, new. Also Midori no Kurokami — raven black hair.

Mitsu — depending on the *kanji* (character) used can mean honey, shine, succeed, or progress fully.

Naka — middle; center, meaning quality from balance, not extreme. Name of famous Shiba.

Nishiki — brocade; gold silk imperial banner. The capture of a brocade war banner from an enemy would make for an especially triumphant return home. Something beautiful and precious earned with great effort or high cost.

Sakura — cherry blossom; traditional Japanese symbol. Extremely beautiful but fleeting.

Tama — crystal ball; perfection.

Tsuru — crane; elegance; symbol of long life.

Yatsu — eight; a lucky number.

The names listed in this glossary are root words. Although gender-specific endings are nearly always attached to female Shiba names, root words can be used without suffixes if the root is obviously feminine. The following examples show how suffixes can be used to specify gender:

me — woman
hime — princess
maru — boy
taro — boy (less common)
suke — man (less common)
yakko — male servant or woman (less common)

Akaishime (Aka ishi me) — red stone woman
Akikazehime (Aki kaze hime) — autumn wind princess
Kurotakamaru (Kuro taka maru) — black hawk boy
Momotaro (Momo taro) — peach boy
Chibisuke (Chibi suke) — small man

GLOSSARY

Aiko — love child
Aka — red
Akafuji — red Mt. Fuji
Akafusa — red tassel
Akaishi — red stone
Akajishi — red lion
Akane — crimson; color of sunrise and sunset
Akemi — bright; beautiful
Aki — autumn; bright (in combination with another word)
Akikaze — autumn wind
Akiko — bright child
Akimitsu — autumn shine
Akira — bright or glitter; common boy's name
Akizakura — autumn cherry blossom
Asa — morning
Asahifuji — Mt. Fuji in the morning light
Asako — morning child
Aya — damask
Ayako — brocade child
Ayame — iris
Azumagiku — eastern Japan chrysanthemum
Azusa — catalpa; common girl's name
Beni — bright red
Beniaka — red
Benifuji — red Mt. Fuji
Benifusa — red tassel
Benigiku — red chrysanthemum
Benihana — flower used for making red dye
Beniharu — red spring
Benihide — red excellent
Beniichi — red no. 1
Benika — red fragrance
Benimitsu — red honey
Beninaka — red middle
Beniryu — red dragon
Benisuzu — red bell
Benitaka — red hawk
Benitaro — red boy
Benitomi — red fortune

Benitsubaki — red camellia
Beniumemi — red plum sightseeing
Beniyakko — red woman
Beniyuki — red snow
Benizakura — red cherry blossom
Benkei — historical hero's name
Chako — brown child
Chibi — small
Chigusa — wildflower
Chiharu — thousand spring
Chikako — close child; common girl's name
Chisato — thousand village
Chiyo — thousand era
Chiyoko — thousand era child
Chiyomidori — thousand era (ever)green
Daichi — to stand firm on the earth
Daiichi — no. 1
Daikoku — Shinto god of wealth
Daimatsu — big pine tree
Ei — excellent, prosper
Eiko — excellent child
Eiryu — excellent dragon
Emi — favored beautiful; smile
Emiko — favored beautiful child
Etsu — joy
Etsuko — joyful girl
Etsuyo — joyful era
Fuji — Mt. Fuji; wisteria
Fujiarashi — Mt. Fuji storm
Fujibeni — Mt. Fuji red
Fujigiku — Mt. Fuji chrysanthemum
Fujiko — Mt. Fuji child; wisteria girl
Fujiryu — Mt. Fuji dragon
Fujiyakko — Mt. Fuji servant; wisteria woman
Fujizakura — Mt. Fuji cherry blossom
Fukubeni — wealth red
Fukuko — good fortune child
Fukuyo — good fortune era
Fukuyoshiichi — wealth riches good no. 1
Fusa — tassel
Fusako — tassel child
Fusamidori — green tassel
Fusayoshi — tassel good
Fuyu — winter
Fuyuko — winter child
Gen — source
Ginjishi — silver lion
Gyoku — jewel or crystal ball
Gyokuryu — jewel dragon
Hagi — bush clover
Hama — beach, seashore

Hamako — beach girl
Hamaoh — beach king
Hanafusa — flower tassel
Hanako — flower child
Hanakoma — flower horse
Hanamine — flower summit
Hanayo — flower era
Haru — spring
Haruichi — spring no. 1
Haruka — spring fragrance
Haruko — spring child
Harukoma — spring horse
Harumi — spring beautiful
Harumitsu — spring shine
Harusen — spring thousand
Haruyo — spring era
Hide — excellent
Hideaki — excellent bright
Hidehisa — excellent long time
Hideko — excellent child
Hideko — sun appears child
Hidematsu — excellent pine tree
Hidemidori — excellent green
Hidemitsu — excellent to progress fully
Hidenishiki — excellent brocade
Hidetama — excellent crystal ball
Hideyo — excellent era
Hideyuki — excellent snow
Hikari — sparkle
Hisa — long time
Hisako — long time girl
Hisazakura — long time cherryblossom
Hogyoku — jewel, treasure
Homaretenno — honor heavenly
Hoshi — star
Ichi — no. 1 or market
Ichifuji — no. 1 Mt. Fuji
Ichiko — no. 1 child
Ichimiyahime — no. 1 imperial princess
Ichiryu — no. 1 dragon
Inu — dog
Ishi — stone
Ishiyo — stone era
Iso — stone beach
Isoko — beach child
Iwa — rock
Izumi — fountain
Ji-inu — native dog
Jiro — second son
Junko — pure child
Kagetora — shadow tiger

Kanekichi — gold fortunate
Katsu — victory
Katsuichi — victory no. 1
Katsuko — victory child
Katsuyoshi — victory good
Katsura — Katsura tree
Katsuranishiki — Katsura tree brocade
Keiko — scenery girl
Keisho — beautiful scenery
Ki — spirit
Kiichi — joy no. 1
Kiku — chrysanthemum
Kikubeni — red chrysanthemum
Kikuichi — chrysanthemum no. 1
Kikuko — chrysanthemum child
Kikumi — chrysanthemum beautiful
Kikuzuki — chrysanthemum moon
Kimi — noble
Kimiko — noble child
Kinshu — autumn with beautiful leaves
Kinu — silk
Kinuko — silk child
Kiri — mist
Kiyo — pure
Kiyofusa — pure tassel
Kiyoka — pure fragrance
Kiyoichi — pure no. 1
Kiyoko — pure child
Kiyomatsu — pure pine tree
Kiyomi — pure beautiful
Kiyotatsu — pure dragon
Kogyoku — jewel
Koharu — small spring (warm day)
Kokuryu — black dragon
Komaichi — horse no. 1; horse market
Komakiyo — horse pure
Komamidori — horse green
Komanishiki — horse brocade
Komari — small ball
Komaryu — horse dragon
Konishiki — small brocade
Koro — popular name for a dog
Korobeni — red dog
Kotetsu — steel
Koto — Japanese harp
Kotobeni — harp red
Kotobuki — good wishes
Kotohana — harp flower
Kotoyakko — harp woman
Koume — small plum
Koyuki — small snow

Kuri — chestnut
Kuroaki — black autumn
Kurobeni — black red
Kurogiku — black chrysanthemum
Kurohana — black flower
Kuroichi — black no. 1
Kurojishi — black lion
Kurokocho — black butterfly
Kuromari — black ball
Kuromatsu — black pine tree
Kuromitsu — black shine
Kuronami — black wave
Kurotaka — black hawk
Kurotake — black bamboo
Kuroyuki — black snow
Kuroyuri — black lily
Mai — dancing
Maki — evergreen bush
Makoto — sincere
Mamoru — guard
Mari — yarn ball
Mariko — yarn ball child
Masa — Paulownia tree
Masakado — historical hero
Masako — sincere girl
Matsu — pine tree
Matsufusa — pine tree tassel
Matsuichi — pine tree no. 1
Matsuko — pine tree child
Matsuoh — pine tree king
Matsutomo — pine tree companion
Megumi — blessing, grace
Meiho — famous treasure
Michi — road
Michiko — road girl
Mieko — common girl's name
Mihoko — beautiful keep child
Mika — modern girl's name
Mine — summit
Minefuji — summit Mt. Fuji
Mineko — summit girl child
Mino — straw raincoat
Minoryu — straw raincoat dragon
Mio — waterway
Misa — faithful
Misako — faithful girl
Misuzu — beautiful bell
Mitaki no Hana — waterfall flower
Mitsu — full; shine; honey
Mitsuaki — shine fall
Mitsufusa — full tassel

Mitsuhana — full flower
Mitsuharu — shine spring
Mitsuko — shine child
Mitsukoma — shine horse
Mitsuryu — full dragon
Mitsutama — shine crystal ball
Mitsutaro — full boy
Mitsutenryu — full heavenly dragon
Miyahime — imperial princess
Miyo — beautiful era
Miyuki — beautiful snow
Mizakura — beautiful cherry blossoms
Mizuho — fresh ears of rice
Momo — peach
Momoichi — peach no. 1
Momoko — peach child
Nagamatsu — long pine tree
Naganobu — historical hero
Naka — middle
Nakakoma — middle horse
Nakakuro — middle black
Nakaori — middle opportunity
Nakaryu — middle dragon
Nakatake — middle bamboo
Namibananishiki — wave flower brocade
Nana — number seven
Natsu — summer
Natsuko — summer child
Nishikihide — brocade excellent
Nobuaki — believe bright
Nobuichi — believe no. 1
Nobumitsu — believe full
Nobuyoshi — believe good
Nobuyuki — believe snow
Oh — king
Ohshio — high tide
Ori — opportunity
Ran — orchid
Riki — power
Rikiichikoma — power no. 1 horse
Rikiishi — power stone
Rikizakura — power cherry blossom
Ryujiro — dragon second boy
Ryutaro — dragon boy
Sachi — blessing, luck, happy
Sachibeni — happy red
Sachiko — happy child
Saku — town in Nagano Prefecture
Sakura — cherry blossom
Sakuranishiki — cherry blossom brocade
Sakuraharu — cherry blossom spring

Sato — hometown
Sawa — small valley
Sayuri — small lily
Seiten — clear sky
Sengyoku — thousand jewel
Senhime — historical hero (F)
Senjuhomare — thousand honor
Senkofusahime — thousand tassel princess
Shiba — brushwood
Shinichi — true no. 1
Shinju — pearl
Shinko — new child
Shinobu — endure
Shishi — lion
Sho — victory
Shoji — screen door with paper
Shoryu — victory dragon
Shuho — autumn treasure
Shuko — autumn light
Shuriki — autumn power
Sumera — emperor
Sumeranishiki — emperor brocade
Suzu — small bell
Suzuaka — small bell red
Suzuichi — small bell no. 1
Suzumari — small bell ball
Suzumi — small bell beautiful
Suzutakemi — small bell bamboo beautiful
Suzuwaka — small bell young
Tada — honest
Tadaaki — honest cheerful
Tadahisa — honest long time
Tadanobu — honest believe
Tadashi — honest
Taiho — famous Sumo wrestler
Taka — hawk; noble; dutiful; high
Takafuji — hawk Mt. Fuji
Takafusa — hawk tassel
Takaichi — hawk no. 1
Takamatsu — hawk pine tree
Takasuzumi — hawk small bell beautiful
Takayakko — hawk servant
Takayoshi — hawk good
Takayu — hawk manly
Take — bamboo
Takeichi — bamboo no. 1
Takemine — bamboo summit
Takeshi — bamboo warrior
Taketoyo — good health abundant
Taki — waterfall
Takiryu — waterfall dragon

Tamaaki — crystal ball autumn
Tama — crystal ball
Tamachiyo — crystal ball thousand era
Tamafuku — crystal ball wealth
Tamakazura — crystal ball vine
Tamakocho — crystal ball butterfly
Tamami — crystal ball beautiful
Tamamidori — crystal ball green
Tamamitsu — crystal ball full
Tamanishiki — crystal ball brocade
Tamaryu — crystal ball
Tamashiro — crystal ball white
Tamatsuru — crystal ball crane
Tatsu — dragon
Tatsugoro — dragon fifth son
Tatsujishi — dragon lion
Tatsumaki — tornado
Tatsumi — dragon beautiful
Tatsuwaka — dragon young
Ten — heavenly
Tenichi — heavenly no. 1
Tenichiryu — heavenly no. 1 dragon
Tenko — heavenly light
Tenkoriki — heavenly light power
Tenryu — heavenly dragon
Tenryukiyofusa — heavenly dragon pure tassel
Tenryuichi — heavenly dragon no. 1
Tenshin — heavenly heart
Tenzan — heavenly mountain
Teru — sunshine
Teruarashi — sunshine storm
Terumatsu — sunshine pine tree
Terunishiki — sunshine brocade
Teruyoshi — sunshine good
Tetsu — iron
Tetsugen — iron source
Tetsuka no Gen — iron fragrance source
Tetsunobu — iron believe
Tetsuryu — iron dragon
Tetsutaka — iron hawk
Tetsuyu — iron manly
Tetsuyuki — iron snow
Toku — virtue
Tokuhikari — virtue sparkle
Tokuichi — virtue no. 1
Tomi — wealth
Tomikaze — wealth wind
Tomotake — companion bamboo
Tora — tiger
Toshi — age
Toyo — abundant

Toyoaki — abundant bright
Toyoharu — abundant spring
Toyomi — abundant beautiful
Toyomitsu — abundant full
Tsubaki — camellia
Tsukitama — moon crystal ball
Tsuru — crane
Tsuruichi — crane no. 1
Tsuruzakura — crane cherry blossom
Tsuyufuji — dewdrop Mt. Fuji
Tsuyutaka — dewdrop hawk
Ume — small Japanese apricot
Wakajishi — young lion
Wakataka — young hawk
Wakatake — young bamboo
Yae — double flowering
Yamabiko — echo

Yatsu — eight
Yoshi — good; courageous; happy; splendid
Yoshiaki — happy sparkle
Yoshiharu — happy spring
Yoshihide — good excel
Yoshikiyo — good pure
Yoshimidori — good green
Yoshiryu — good dragon
Yoshiyuki — good snow
Yu — excellent
Yuki — snow
Yukihide — snow excellent
Yukiizumi — snow fountain
Yukimi — snow beautiful
Yukishiro — snow white
Yumi — bow
Yuri — lily

BIS/AKC/JKC/INT Ch. Tomi No Chaka Go Ryuukyuu Uruma. All-time top-winning Japan Kennel Club Shiba. Chaka was shown for several months in the USA. She was awarded multiple Group Firsts, BOB at a NSCA Regional Specialty, and First Award of Merit at the 2002 NSCA National Specialty. Bred by Yuichi Tomimoto and owned in the United States by Engen, Lanterman, and Sakayeda.

Bibliography

BOOKS:

Ayala, F., and J. Kiger. *Modern Genetics*. 2nd Edition. Menlo Park, CA: Benjamin/Cummings, 1984.

Darwin, C. *The Variation of Plants and Animals Under Domestication*. London, 1868.

Ehrlich, P., and A. Ehrlich. *Extinction*. New York: Ballantine Books, 1981.

Ehrlich, P., Holm, R. and D. Parnell. *The Process of Evolution*. 2nd Edition, New York: McGraw Hill, 1974.

Ishikawa, G. *Shiba Dog*. Tokyo: Seibundo Shinkosha, 1984.

Ishikawa, G. and H. Watanabe. *Taidan: Shiba Ken No Kaikata*. Tokyo: Seibundo Shinkosha, 1976.

Little, C. *The Inheritance of Coat Color in Dogs*. New York: Howell Book House, 1979.

Mettler, L. and T. Gregg. *Population Genetics and Evolution*. Englewood Cliffs, New Jersey: Prentice Hall, 1969.

Robinson, Roy. *Genetics For Dog Breeders*. Oxford: Pergamon Press, 1990.

Watanabe, H. *Nihon Ken Hyakka*. Tokyo: Seibundo Shinkosha, 1974.

Willis, Malcolm B. *Genetics of the Dog*. New York: Howell Book House, 1989.

Wright, S. *Evolution and the Genetics of Populations* (4 volumes), Chicago: The University of Chicago Press, 1977.

ARTICLES:

Higuchi, Takio. "The Coat Color of the Shiba - Focus on Sesame." *Nihon Ken* No. 3 (1991).

Motoyama, H. "Interview." *Aiken No Tomo* (Nov. 1984).

Note: Some of the material in this book has appeared previously in *The Shiba Journal* (1987-1995) in slightly different format.

A Canadian winter doesn't stop this Shiba from enjoying the great outdoors with his owner. L. DeMecha.

Other Sources of Information

FOR MORE INFORMATION ON THE SHIBA, we suggest that you consult the clubs and websites listed below:

American Kennel Club (Headquarters)
260 Madison Avenue
New York, NY 10016
212-696-8200
www.akc.org

American Kennel Club (Operations Center)
5580 Centerview Drive
Raleigh, NC 27606-3390
919-233-9767

National Shiba Club of America
www.shibas.org
(Club newsletter is the Shiba-E-News, contact the AKC for the address of the current club secretary)

Beikoku Shibainu Aikokai (BSA)
2842 Elmlawn Dr.
Anaheim, CA 92804

Colonial Shiba Club (Shiba Classic)
P.O. Box 353
Braddock Heights, MD 21714

Nihon Ken Hozonkai
Surugadai Sanraizu Bldg. 1F
2-11-1, Kanda Surugadai
Chiyoda-ku, Tokyo 101-0062 JAPAN
www.nihonken-hozonkai.or.jp

Japan Kennel Club
1-5 Kanda, Suda-cho
Chiyoda-ku, Tokyo 101 JAPAN
www.jkc.or.jp

GENETIC SCREENING:

Canine Eye Registration Foundation (CERF)
Purdue University
CERF/Lynn Hall
625 Harrison Street
Lafayette, IN 47907-2026
765-494-8179
www.vet.purdue.edu/~yshen/cerf.html

Orthopedic Foundation For Animals (OFA)
2300 E. Nifong Boulevard
Columbia, MO 65201-3856
573-442-0418
www.offa.org

PennHIP
3900 Delancey Street
Philadelphia, PA 10104-6010
www.vet.upenn.edu/researchcenters/pennhip

GENERAL REFERENCE MATERIAL:

Nihon Ken. Nihon Ken Hozonkai, 1935-1995.

Shiba-E-News. National Shiba Club of America, 1987-1995.

Shiba Journal. The Shiba Ken Club, 1987-1990.

Shiba Journal. Cynosure Publications, Inc., 1991-1995.

Shiba Showcase. Mary Jo Cato and Maureen Lacey Reed, 1986.

NATIONAL SHIBA CLUB OF AMERICA REGISTER OF MERIT

(An ROM sire must have fathered eight AKC championship offspring, while a dam must have produced four. The owner or breeder of the Shiba must apply to the club Awards Chairperson in order for the dog to be recognized, and the applicant must be a club member.)

1994	SIRES	Hansha Remote Control	Tetsuryu of Hikarikaidaso
	DAMS	Ch. Homaretennome of Gishi Fujisow	Ch. Kiyoichime Gishifujiso
		TMS Foxtrot Femme Fatale	Foxtrot Ebony Envy
		Jacquet Kikyohime	

1995	SIRES	Ch. Toyojiro of Nadaimanei Sow	Suzuhomare of Yoshimatsu Kensha
		Ch. Kinouk's Road-Warrior Tanasea	Top Gun of Satorisow
		Fukurinmaru of Gunma Fukuda Kensha	
	DAMS	Ch. Frerose's Punkin Pie	Ch. Ranchlake Tamarisk Samsara
		Ch. San Jo's Tickled Pink	Ch. Sea Breeze Miss Behavin
		Ch. Frerose Ariel Red Wing	

1996	SIRES	Ch. Hideryu of Fujinomiya Kensha	
	DAMS	Ch. Kurohana Of Ryukyu Wruma	Kantu's Can Do It Too Ya
		Ch. Yaezakura Hime	Taichung San Jo Sparkle Plenty
		Ch. Kurohime of Kosei Shiragiku Sow	Kinoukis Fast Forward
		Ch. Mikahime Ibitakano	Ch. O'Date's Shots of Honey
		Ch. O'Date's Red Riding Hood, CD	Shibas Nest of O'Date Ginki
		Mokelumne Simply Scarlet	Ch. Blue Mountain Scarlet Lace

1997	SIRES	Ch. Hansha Shin Yu of Shandell	Ch. Independence of Taichung
		Ch. Reno Sakura Jackpot	
	DAMS	Ch. Blue Mountain Black Gold	Shandell Blue Mountain Summer
		Tsumuginokonatsu Rokumonsentsumugiso	Ch. Reno Sakura Mokelumnes Sunny

1998	SIRES	Ch. Kori Bushi of Kitsunebiso	Ch. Windcastle's Rising Sun
		Ch. Koryu Of Nidai Maneiso	Ch. Kiyitakamaru Go Nidai Maneiso
		Ch. Sunojo's Toshiba Go	
	DAMS	Ch. Storm Kloud's Cuz Sonya So	Ch. Seishonagon of Satorisow
		Ch. Sea Breeze Fancy Footwork	Fansu's Without A Care
		Am/Can Ch. Hanako Of Hokuso Takayamasow	Am/Can Ch. Sakura No Kiyomihime Of Akanuma

1999	SIRES	Ch. Kogen Of Nidai Maneiso	Am/Can/Mex/Int'l Ch. Windcastle's Free Spirit
		Ch. Fanfair's Zento of Wynhaven	
	DAMS	Ch. Ishiyama Line Of Fire	Ch. Storm Kloud's Chance O' Bark Riv'R
		Ch. San Jo's Western Edition	Ch. Foxtrot High Lites

| 2000 | DAMS | Ch. Hi-Jinx Midnight Kiss | Satori's Southampton Kiyoshi |

| 2001 | SIRES | Ch. K-B Southern Gentleman | |
| | DAMS | Ch. Southampton Hotaru Hime | Ch. C And L's Wild Cherry |

2002	SIRES	Ch. Hi-Jinx Pimiento	Ch. Kuniyoshi Go Shikaisow
	DAMS	Ch. Kure No Hikari Kitsunebiso	Ch. Justa Scarlet Harlot
		Hokutono Kiki	Ch. Sachiharume Go Nidai Baneisow
		Ch. Fanfair's Kiwi of Nikima, CD	

About the Authors

GRETCHEN HASKETT (below left) has owned, shown and bred Shibas since 1987 under the kennel name Foxfire Shibas/Kitsunebiso. Kitsunebiso dogs have earned both conformation and obedience titles. Ms. Haskett was a charter member of the Shiba Ken Club and the Fox Valley Shiba Fanciers (northern Illinois) and served as board member, point chairman, newsletter editor and standard committee chairman for the Shiba Ken Club. As a member of the National Shiba Club of America she was elected Vice-President and served as standard committee chairman, judge's education chairman, and as a member of the illustrated standard committee. As the publisher and managing editor of *The Shiba Journal* from 1988 to 1996, she received multiple awards from the Dog Writer's Association of America for writing and editing. Ms. Haskett traveled to Japan in 1991 as a guest of Japanese Shiba breeders to view the Nihon Ken Hozonkai National Show and interview judges and breeders. Ms. Haskett is a former flute teacher and computer technical manager. She is currently employed as a church music director in Lake Forest, Illinois. She lives with her husband, two children, and four gracefully aging Shibas.

SUSAN HOUSER (right) is an attorney practicing in Washington, D.C., who has owned and shown Akitas and Shibas since 1982. She was the founder of *The Shiba Journal* and the co-founder of the Shiba Ken Club. Drawing on the knowledge she gained while earning her B.S. degree in biology and working as a medical technologist (A.S.C.P.), she has written several articles on genetics, health, and inbreeding for Akita and Shiba breed magazines. She also translated the bulk of the Japanese source material used in the chapter on the "ideal Shiba."

Therapy dogs visit a senior center in England. M. Clews.

Breed Gallery Index

The dogs found in the breed gallery are listed by order of birth.

Shinshu Chibisuke of Shinshu Ueda Tenguso ROM (37)
Shishi of Kenwaso (9)
Shoguniemitsu of Gishifujiso (86)
Soto No Gyokuryu of Sotoso (6)
Suzuhomare of Yoshimatsu Kensha (83)
Taichung Bold Concept At OPR (102)
Taka Justa Bold N Brassy (59)
Takemaru of Chita Mochizukiso (68)
Taketomi of Chita Mochizukiso (77)
Takishiido of Foxfire CD (65)
Tamabeni of Banrakuso (64)
Tamariki of Banrakuso (63)
Tega no Namiyo of Dainana Kashiwayamaso (27)

Teruarashi of Fuji Itoso (11)
Tetsumaru of Ichikawa Aoki (13)
Tetsuryu of Hikari Kaidaso ROM (49)
Toyojiro of Nidai Maneiso ROM (80)
Tsubaki of Chiba Shiraneso (12)
Tsumugi no Konatsu Rokumonsen Tsumugiso (55)
Tsuru of Satoriso (26)
Windcastle's Free Spirit (87)
Yukan of Aoyama Mahar (43)
Yuki no Ishi of Dairy Farm (75)
Yukihime of Gardenaso (35)
Yukimehime of Yukiguniso (20)

2003 Westminster Kennel Club BOB Ch. Fanfair Sno-Storm Ringside Rebel, bred by Laura Payton and Haylee Preece and owned by Mary and Deanna Rotkowski, Dr. Robert V. Hutchison and Laura Payton. A perennial favorite, Rebel won Awards of Merit at NSCA National Specialties in 1999, 2000, and 2002. He also garnered Awards of Merit at three NSCA Regional Specialties in 2000 and 2002. © Tom Di Giacomo.

Index

Group-winning Ch. Kure No Hikari Kitsunebiso ROM was bred by Gretchen Haskett and owned by Yori Green. © Ross.